NO DIRECTION HOME

THE DRIFTER CHRONICLES; VOLUME ONE

WORDS & ILLUSTRATIONS BY GREG CAYEA

CHAPTER ZERO

FUCKED

We drove Northeast from the Atlanta airport and were now somewhere in the barren Appalachian Mountains. I sat in the front seat of a red pickup truck, crammed in between two scary hick private investigators with a gun rack and rifle mounted to the rear window. Country music twanged morosely on the truck radio. No one said a word. Nothing in sight except for an approaching archaic-looking board with splattered red paint that read FRESH PEACHES → ONE MILE AHEAD. The small population of each rural town diminished as we headed further and further into the middle of nowhere. A sign read: "CUMMING, Population 3,433", then another sign: "DAWSONVILLE, Population 3,233", then another: "AURARIA, Population 2,383" and finally: "DAHLONEGA Est. 1833 Site of First Major U.S. Gold Rush. Pop. 1,263.

We drove past a General Store with a cruddy porch. Old men from the cast of Deliverance sat outside on wooden chairs, wearing dirty white tee shirts covered in coffee stains and red clay, spitting tobacco juice, peering into our truck as if they'd never seen one… And when I say they were from the cast of Deliverance, I don't mean that metaphorically. I found out later this is where they shot the film. I watched from my window as they (and I) faded from existence. The truck kept moving until we were completely out of town. The backwoods swallowed the sides of the road and darkness swept the sky. My fate awaited. For the first time since middle school I felt terrified.

Then came a jerky turn onto an even more desolate street that read: "Camp Wahsega Road". There was nothing. My thoughts were inaudible. My speech went missing. Every bump on the road stirred my anxiety. No point in crying for help, there was no help and I knew it.

A startling sharp right shot us onto a small pathway. Without warning we were trucking up a huge mountain. Randy, the monstrous man with a fat face and tight ponytail, shut off the radio. I spotted a small cabin in front of us.

What the FUCK was that?

My eyes followed the cabin until my head could turn no more.

Shit.

Where am I? Don't think about it. Just keep cool. I took deep breaths, trying to remain calm. I could see something in the distance. We drove closer. It was some kind of brick building. We got closer and closer and closer and then

STOP

There were three dormitories.

I saw this group of malnourished kids walking slowly and methodically toward me in a straight line, holding pick-axes, shovels and rakes. A large man in military uniform ordered the group to halt. In silence, and with complete obedience, everyone stopped as if their lives depended on it. Their eyes drifted in my direction. I could see it in their souls. It wasn't pretty.

"You're fucked."

That's what they were telling me.

GET OUT!

But how? How do I get out? I'm paralyzed with fear. Where the hell am I? How'd I fucking get here? Where is Long Island?? But their heads made no such movement. There was horror in their eyes. Something felt really off. I needed to wake up from this nightmare.

The two private investigators yanked me unceremoniously out of the truck and took me into a barracks-like building then left me alone in a small room with a grizzled Vietnam war vet and a large burly mountain man with a flush red face and rug-like beard.

"Put yankee-boy-doodle in the bathroom and strip him", the older man ordered.

"Yes Colonel."

I was taken into a bathroom.

The door closed behind us.

"Take your clothes off and throw them in the corner."

Uhhhh--

"SHUT YOUR MOUTH! I DON'T NEED TO REPEAT MYSELF!

Everything's cool.

Remain calm.

"Trousers too"

"My pants?"

"WHAT THE HELL IS YOUR MALFUNCTION? ARE YOU DEAF? SHOULD I TALK LOUDER? HAS YOUR RIGHT EAR GONE BAD ALREADY? MAYBE YOU NEED A HEARING AID, WOULD THAT HELP?! I CAN FIX IT SO YOU'LL NEED ONE, SHOULD I?!!"

My heart was pounding.

"TAKE EM OFF!"

"Get… naked—?"

"—YOU THINK I LIKE DOING THIS?! TAKE YOUR GODDAMN BRIEFS OFF BEFORE I YANK EM OFF YOUR YANKEE ASS!"

Off they went.

"PUT YOUR HANDS BEHIND YOUR HEAD AND BEND YOUR KNEES!"

Fear dripped down my neck.

"TURN AROUND AND JUMP LIKE A FROG!"

Pause.

He took three steps forward, clenched his jaw, looked me straight in my eyes and

JUMP!!!!!!!! **LIKE A GODDAMN FROG!!!!!!!!**

I was naked, jumping like a frog for the amusement of two redneck inbreds, thousands of miles from my nice three-story home with elevator in Roslyn, New York. I was fifteen years-old.

How the FUCK did I get here?

PART I

HOW IT ALL STARTED

CHAPTER 1

LEGENDARY LOSER

It was the first day of middle school. The hallway crowded with hostile sixth graders, half from East Hills Elementary School, and the rest from Harbor Hill Elementary School. The two schools had always remained divided until today. For the first time, we were combined to attend the same junior high, and the separation between the two schools was similar to rivalry.

There could be no other day as significant as today. Today would determine who was cool, and who was a loser for the rest of our lives. Whatever happened in elementary school didn't matter. The canvas was completely blank as the girls explored the new landscape of boys while the boys carefully selected which crew best defined their character.

I stood alone.

It seemed as though all the other lockers were full of excitement, with pictures, photos, drawings and love notes, but that wasn't true, it was the first day of school and all the other lockers were completely empty. But still, my locker looked pale green without a shred of personality, probably unlike all the other kids' lockers, which I imaged might be vibrant and breathtaking in a few weeks or so. I had the most boring locker in the world in my mind, and nothing could change it.

I had no friends.

From afar, I could see Brooke Avery surrounded by the click of boys that were handsome enough to have the honor of being seen with her in public. I dreamt of one day saying hi to her, or maybe getting lucky enough to sit next to her in class, any class. I often busied myself with unlikely thoughts such as these.

The bell rang, it was an odd sounding bell, more like a beep, and the kids scattered from out the hallways to their homeroom, another unfamiliar word.

Homeroom. What's that even mean? I wasn't used to multiple classes. As far as I knew school to be, you showed up to one class and stayed till a normal sounding bell rang then went home on a bus. Anyhow, I looked at my class schedule printed on some yellow index card but had no idea where to find the room I was supposed to be in. Everyone rushed right by me like I was infected with some weird cold or disease no one wanted to catch by fear of rubbing against me. The hallway was nearly empty by the time I found my seat in homeroom.

Jake Stern sat next to me with a look of disgust as if he were the unluckiest kid in the world to have to sit next to me. It didn't occur to me disgust was just Jake's normal look. Jake was this kinda ugly husky kid with broad shoulders, which is just a nice way to say he was pretty fat. I had never seen him before that day. Then came these weird sniffs. He kept sniffing, sniffing around his desk, searching for some kinda smell that was coming from some hidden hole or whatever. I saw it from the corner of my eye, cause I mean, I didn't wanna just look at him, stir up attention, but it was makin me nervous for some reason. I was always a bit nervous. Maybe that's where the tics came from? It always seemed like the bricks of the building might come crumbling down around me but only land on my head and save everyone else.

Then he turned to look at me, I didn't know why, and he shouted, even though I was like two feet away from him, he yelled straight at my face, "What's that smell!?" He said that in front of everyone, even Olivia, Brooke Avery's best friend.

Brooke and Olivia were the goal of school. Just get to them and existence would somehow make sense. I hadn't ever seen girls like that before. They musta kept em hidden at Harbor Hill Elementary, but now this kid, Jake, this kid I never even met before is sayin I stunk, threatening my existence.

He turned to me and took a large breath, like he wanted to make sure the scent was me, even though he already said it was me. Then he gave another, more affirmative "Yo, you STINK!" My face went cold as I delicately looked around the room to see who heard him.

Everyone.

Kids that hadn't yet said one word to me or even seen me before for that matter, in that moment, they all looked at me with a look of sorrow, a pitiful look, but quickly busied themselves with meaningless drawings and fake conversation to hide the awkwardness after a moment or two.

Then the beep-sounding bell rang.

They all scurried out and I was left alone as I smelled my armpits tryina figure out what he was talkin about, but I didn't smell a thing. I looked at my index card schedule thingy to see what class was next. Great, another class to find. Why can't the classes just be easy to find? Like right next to each other? What's the point of a maze? I hoped to God that no one from my homeroom would recognize me in the next period so I put on my jacket to hide the tee shirt I was wearing to disguise myself and block the odor, which I wasn't even sure was there.

But it was too late.

I was branded as "the kid that stunk" from that day forward.

Every morning Jake came to homeroom and tried to reinvent his insults using different words and rearranging his sentences with what little vocabulary he had. A week later there wasn't a soul in school willing to risk their social status associating with me. One bully turned into two when Jake invited his best friend, Dave, to join in on the fun of making my life a blistering hell. Dave was this kid with blonde hair that you'd just walk right by without noticing even if he was the only kid on the face of the Earth, so I guess I was an easy target for him. Jake and Dave musta had these long, drawn out brainstorm sessions thinking of every humiliating remark they could possibly scrounge up, cause they never stopped. Not once. All day, every day. I had no choice other than to accept my social standing as worthless, worse than worthless at that, so I hid from everybody as best I could.

Three months into the tortuous hell middle school had become, Alex, an even bigger loser than myself by comparison, jumped on the "Greg's a loser" bandwagon, I guess hoping to become a little less of a loser than I was. Anything was better than me apparently, so he gave it his best shot when he asked me "Are you wearing eyeliner?" That's how my long, jet-black eyelashes came into play. Little by little I broke down to a nervous wreck, afraid of every next step. Showers had stopped, family life filled with silence, and my grades slowly tanked. Everyday became worse than the last. I was sluggish and depressed.

I stared at myself in the mirror every day after school and told my mom everything was fine. I stared at myself even harder, trying to see what everyone else saw. To me I was just a normal kid. My eyelashes were a bit long I guess, and dark. My skin was kind of pale, I suppose. I put on extra deodorant then smelled my armpits and they smelled fine. I was so confused. If I could just see what the others saw, maybe I could fix it.

The next day I woke up and put on my best outfit, a black tee shirt that was kinda too big and hung off my shoulders and these skater jeans

I thought were cool cause the kids at the train tracks wore them. The kids by the train tracks were always cool cause they were skateboarders and skateboarders were cool and everyone always looked at them do tricks and stuff. Maybe I should buy a skateboard?

To match my oversized black tee shirt I put on some Vans sneakers that my mom bought for me cause I also thought they were cool, cause the kids at the train tracks wore em. I showered extra hard and brushed my teeth firmly, all over, and put loads of deodorant on. I walked into homeroom quickly and took my seat that day so that no one would notice my entrance, but was unsuccessful. Jake walked right up to me and stared at my outfit.

"What's up faggot? Now you're a poser too?" and he punched me in the chest so hard it knocked my binder outa my hands and the wind right outa my lungs. Even worse, the three rings from my binder came undone and the papers went loose and fell all over the floor, but not before the air glided them as far away from me as possible so that I had to go around and collect them from underneath everyone's feet and shit. I wanted to punch him, but I did nothing back. I didn't want to smell bad *and* get beat up, so I just wandered around the room and picked up all the papers and sat down in my seat pretending like it didn't hurt, like nothing had happened… but it did, I could barely breathe and now I was a bigger loser than I was ten minutes ago.

It was a glorious day when I discovered that these two kids actually knew my name, Robby Deltorro and Jon Greenley. Robby was this Italian kid that was a skater-lookin punk, a loser too, but big enough so that no one ever said anything wrong to him, but he also had no friends, except Jon. Jon *really* had no friends, except Robby. Jon wore these *huge* jeans and weird choker necklaces and I think the only reason he was spared humiliation was cause his older brother left a good type of legacy. I was in the process of leaving *my* younger brother a legendary loser legacy.

Anyway, Robby and Jon made fun of me more than Jake or any of the other bullies that aimed all their adolescent frustration in my direction, but at *some* point of every day, they would say *something* nice to me, *and,* they knew my name! They even let me hang with them after school from time to time. It couldn't get any better in my eyes. For the first time I was a part of a crew. That was what mattered to me.

I had to secure my spot.

Music was a huge part of our boring discussions. They wanted me to like the music they liked, and so I did. I would run home and try my hardest to memorize Robby's favorite bands. I wanted to fit in so bad. I thought that this would be the key to his respect, so I made it my life and started studying bands I had no interest in at all. I learned the lead singer's names, how many band members were in each group, and at least three album titles. I never enjoyed The Toasters, but they were Robby's favorite ska band, so I memorized the lyrics to every song. Ska music was so stupid to me, I just hated it. It was this dumb typa reggae rock soundin music with trombones and shit. But whatever, I had to pretend the saxophone was incredible and the trumpet really brought the chorus together. I'll never forget the look on Robby's face when I made the *big* leap of drawing The Toaster's logo on my math binder…

"Name one song by them Cayea. ONE song!!" He challenged me. (That's 'kay-yuh' so that you're not mispronouncing my name the whole damn book)

But yeah, I named three.

BOOYAHH MOTHERFUCKER!

With a look of mediocre satisfaction, he said to me "Oh. Nice. Maybe you *are* cool."

Holy shit.

I was making SERIOUS progress.

This was big.

I was moving up in the world. I raced back home and studied a few more bands they would be impressed with if I knew about. I was on a roll.

Then after school one day the three of us were shooting hoops, well I wasn't actually allowed to play, cause I was such a fuckin imaginary loser, but they let me watch and every now and then I'd give these dumb compliments like 'Damn! Good shot!'

Then the subject of Ryan's father, who had just passed away, came up in conversation. Ryan was one of my good friends as a child when I played in the Albertson Soccer League. I was on the traveling all-star team too. I was pretty damn good. That's when I thought to myself, they're gonna make fun of Ryan after his father just died. I can feel it. What do I do then? How should I react? Would they not spare *anyone*? But Jon said "shut up man his dad just died." And Robby agreed they should move on.

Whoa. I couldn't BELIEVE they had actually shown a glimmer of compassion. Hmm, maybe there was hope for these two, my BEST friends. I was so happy. They did have a heart. Maybe this would work out after all.

And so my days went... For two very lonely years I lived in Robby and Jon's shadow and hated every waking minute of life. Well, maybe not *hated*... after all, they *did* kinda protect me *plus* they only called me a faggot like once or twice a day. So that was pretty good I guess.

Then in October of eighth grade, everything changed.

CHAPTER 2

OVERNIGHT SUCCESS

I was standing in the parking lot where all the buses picked us up after school one day. It was the beginning of the school year in eighth grade and my social status was the same, if not worse. I was the loser sidekick to the two other losers that were slightly less of losers than I was.

So I was standing alone, well, Robby and Jon were talking a few feet behind me, God forbid I was included in an after-school-conversation... And then you know who came up to me?

Fuckin BROOKE AVERY.

Remember I was telling you that only the best of the best were allowed to talk to Brooke? And the select few that were considered her friends had attained nirvana? I *still* remembered that first day in sixth grade staring at her down the hall, wondering if my chance to say hi to her would ever come. And it all happened while I was waiting for the school bus in the parking lot.

She came up to me and said, "Soooooooo my friend Olivia thinks you're really cute."

Wait, what?

I couldn't believe she was trying to talk to me. Did she just call me cute? I don't know how I got my lips to move and vocalize a response, it had been years since I had any confidence at all, but it just came out, "Oh. Really?" My heart was pounding outa my chest I was so nervous.

"Mmhhmmm!" She confirmed while putting all her weight on one of her legs, one of those things that only hot chicks can do, and then she just stood there with this smile on her face as if she was givin me this gift of life, which she was. "Sooo… Will you go out with her?"

Go out with her? What in the fuck was— I couldn't talk. I just– I don't know what happened, but it just– I, well– "Sure. I would love to." I said without hesitation.   "YAY!" she smiled, *as if I was gonna say no…* she coulda asked me to pick up her little sister on my bicycle every day for a decade and I woulda said yes. But so she grabbed my hand and ran me all the way to the 'cool' side of the parking lot, yeah, there was a cool side of the parking lot for sure, but I hadn't ever seen it, or been there even though it was only like twenty feet away from where I was standing.

So she brought me all the way to the cool side of the parking lot and dropped me off in front of Olivia. Olivia was Brooke's best friend, remember? The girl from homeroom in sixth grade who witnessed my "YO you STINK" episode on the first day of school? She was Brooke's *best* friend, which made her the second-to-most-popular girl in school, and she was also the first girl to have these enormous, gigantic, amazing, luscious, breathtaking breasts that everyone stared at and probably jerked off to every night. Yeah. She thought I was cute.

So there I was, in front of Olivia, with Brooke right behind her, waiting for me to say something, but what the fuck do I say? This was foreign territory for me to put it lightly. The moment couldn't have been more uncomfortable. We were just standing there, staring at each other. What do I say?

Brooke intervened "Ask her out!!!"

So I did. I said something like "So, umm, will you go out with me?" cause that's how these types of relationships formed. You just ask that question, the answer is either yes or no, and then that's it. Life changes.

She smiled and said "Yes".

Then Brooke said to me, she was so pushy, she said to me "Ask for her phone number! She's your girlfriend now!!!"

"Right, no, yeah I know, so, ummm, what's your phone number?"

And she wrote down her own line. She had her *own* line?! I guess that's what happens when you're popular. Of course we were in a rich town in Long Island and I suppose lots of kids had their own line in their parent's house but I just never knew to even *ask* my parents for my own line… I mean why would I? I had no one to call.

"He'll call you later!" Brooke told her for me.

"Yeah, I'll call you later for sure" I said like an idiot.

And then them two just whisked off to their bus, like a pair of angels. Of course they were on the same bus, they lived right next to each other. And of course they lived right next to each other, their parents were best friends. And of course their parents were best friends, that's just how this town worked. It was weird like that.

I snapped outa my dream-like state and looked around the parking lot to see if anyone had witnessed that miraculous moment of transformation.

Everyone. Everyone was looking. I had attained instant popular status.

Robby and Jon watched from afar with shock, but they didn't know what was really goin on, they couldn't like hear us or anything. So I walked back towards them and waited for their reaction.

"The fuck were you doing over there Cayea?" Robby asked me with shocked
curiosity.

"Olivia and I are going out." I said with a moment of triumph.

Without even a laugh or change of expression he retorted, "No really. What were you doing over there? What did they say? Were they... *talking* to you?"

"Brooke asked me out. For Olivia. We're dating."
Silence.

"Are you kidding?" Jon asked me like a Martian had just offered him a hand job.

"Nope. I'm serious."
More silence.

"How? How did that happen?" Robby asked.

"I mean, she just came up to me, Brooke did, and said that."

I remember thinking to myself that I probably couldn't be seen talking to them anymore. I was moving up in the world and middle school was a war zone.

"I gotta go home. See you guys later" I said as I walked to my bus.

"WAIT" as Robby hustled over to me, "You got to take us with you. Make us popular. Will you?"

What the fuck was going on? I was on a tidal wave of success and wasn't about to blow it talking to a bunch of losers.

"I'll see what I can do." I said as I quickly walked away.

Things were about to change. I could feel it. I better go shower.

CHAPTER 3

STARDOM

Here it was, stardom, popularity, fame, power. I considered myself lucky to have known the darkness so well before tasting the light. It was a new day, a Friday, the most wonderful Friday I had ever met. Pre-

Olivia life was already a distant memory, though it was no more than twenty-three hours ago. A colorful landscape of possibilities loomed on the horizon as I cruised down the hallway to last period, gym class.

Gym class was the only period I had with Olivia. I had waited all day for it. I walked into the boy's locker room and took a seat on the metal bench in front of my tiny locker. I un-coded my combination lock and took my gym clothes out, bright orange nylon shorts, almost gold actually, and a white Toasters tee-shirt that my mom had bought for me at this head shop in Hicksville, Long Island called Utopia. Orange was, and still is my favorite color. Utopia was one of those half porn shops half head shops and definitely one of those shops a thirteen-year-old kid felt extremely weird walkin into with his mom... but as far as I knew, it was the only stupid store that sold those stupid ska band tee-shirts that I had to wear just in case this all didn't work out. So I got dressed for class. Three lockers down from mine was Jake's locker, Jake Stern. This was it. I waited for him... and then, he walked in. There he was. Jake Fucking Stern.

I was ready. I was armed with my arsenal of popularity, eager to engage in battle. The days of some mediocre moron pushing me around were done. And then it started. A jockstrap blindsided me and slapped me right on the side of my face. I could feel years of oppression and anger and fury erupting to the surface.

I looked at him. He laughed. His fucking friends laughed too... though aside from Dave, he really had no friends. So he was really just providing entertainment at my expense to a buncha kids that didn't really like him to begin with.

I snapped.

I picked up the jockstrap from the floor and without any control over my muscles, as if it had been engrained in my muscle memory since birth, I thrust the jockstrap through the air with as much force as I could muster up, I thrust it straight back at him, aiming for his face, and nearly pummeled him in his temple, but Jake ducked the flying cock strap as it slammed his metal locker.

That was the moment I changed.

I slammed my locker shut, still pissed, letting him know that I was still pissed, letting him know that I was a ticking time bomb ready to fuckin explode. Letting him know for the first time not to FUCK with me as I buckled my combination lock back up and walked out past his fat head and into the tropical sun of the gym, where all at once, my anger was lifted and replaced with serenity.

It was five or so minutes before class was scheduled to start and Olivia and Brooke were sitting on the floor of the indoor basketball court waiting for my entrance. They had no idea what I had just went through.

"Sup homie?" Brooke shouted to me as soon as she saw me walk outa the boys locker room. She was talking to me like she was a fake gangster, playing around with me like we had been friends forever.

No idea what to say I just said, "Heyy!"

"I like your orange shorts" Olivia told me.

They were kinda hard to miss...

"I like them too! Can I wear them Monday?" Brooke asked.

Then came a miracle: A *real* conversation was born. I kept it going...

"Then what do *I* wear?" I said nonchalantly, yet bursting inside with excitement and fear.

"Can't we all share?" Olivia flirtatiously suggested.

They wanted to share my shorts. This was great.

"I think we *should* share!" Brooke giggled in a wouldn't *you* like that kinda way.

"Which pant leg do I get? I want the left one." She finished.

"No I was about to say that! I want the left!" Olivia proclaimed.

"Okay, you two can share the left and I get the right all to myself." I chimed in.

Brooke laughed.

Olivia smiled.

I felt loved.

THEN

"Wanna hang out later? We're having a get-together at my house." Brooke said.

I played it cool...

"Uhh... Yeah. What time?"

"Well the boys will probably get there at eight."

Oh no. That's right. They had friends. Guy friends. No way they're going to accept me. No fucking way. Then the teacher started class.

"QUIET!

We waited as the teacher, a woman of lesbian nature with enough muscle and height packed onto her person to kill a whale with her bare hands, gave us instructions. She had a basketball tucked under her massive armpit as she talked, she probably coulda palmed it with half a hand… Anyway, she started class.

"TODAY IS THE START OF SQUARE DANCING. THE NEXT FOUR WEEKS WILL BE SPENT ON DEVELOPING A ROUTINE."

There were snickers around the room, but woman-Goliath continued…

"EVERYONE WILL FIND A PARTNER AND FORM A GROUP OF SIX. THE BEST GROUP THAT I CHOOSE WILL PERFORM AT THE BROADWAY MALL IN ONE MONTH FROM NOW. PICK YOUR GROUP CAREFULLY. GO!"

Everyone got up and scurried to find a partner.

"The Broadway Mall?" I heard kids say with repugnance. The Broadway Mall just wasn't that fancy… not like the Roosevelt Field Mall… Anyway, I looked at Olivia. Of course she and I would be partners. AND WE WERE! SHE CAME RIGHT UP TO ME!! I couldn't believe this wasn't the worst day of my life. If this woulda happened yesterday, holy shit. I'd be the last kid standing, like that invisible leftover kid at all those recess football games that everyone is praying won't end up on their team.

Brooke grabbed the most popular guy she could find in the class, James, who wasn't even *that* popular, but was the best she could find I suppose, and called over one more pair to join us, Steph and Mike. She arranged our group within seconds while everyone else meandered the room nervously looking to see who would want to dance with them. My worrying days were over. Here I sat at the most popular Square Dancing circle in the room.

My eyes fished for Jake to see who he had paired up with. He was sitting with some fat girl he barely knew. He caught my glance. It was then that he got the picture.

I was cool.

He was not.

I had everything.

He had a fat chick.

My thoughts were interrupted when Olivia and Brooke burst out laughing. They were looking down my shorts but I pretended not to notice. The teacher looked in our direction and the laughter subsided. I quickly checked to see if I had anything funny going on under there, maybe my underwear was showing or—oh no.

Oh no.

My dick was stickin out from my underwear givin the girls a clear shot of it through my bright orange gym shorts as I sat on the gym floor. It was sticking out from my boxers, fully exposed, cause I had my knees kinda tucked in towards my chest and so the leg holes, they were droopin down a bit. Oh my god.

"OKAY! EVERYONE UP!" The man-woman teacher told us.

There was no time to think, I tucked my dick back into my boxers as the teacher told us to get up. I felt humiliated. HOW STUPID? All the girls were still laughing. My face was flush red. They didn't know I knew what they were laughing about, but I did. But then another miracle happened. They all looked at Olivia as if to approve, a little look of "Not bad Olivia!"

Whoa.

I was the man. I'd passed the size test.

Class ended and Olivia told me that she would wait for me while I got dressed. Was this real?

I put on my cargos pants and Mighty Mighty Bosstones tee-shirt, another stupid tee-shirt that my mom bought for me at Utopia, and tightened my skater-lookin belt. I grabbed my backpack and waltzed out past all the losers I could no longer be seen associating with anymore. Olivia was waiting for me.

"Ready?"

I sure was.

SEVEN HOURS TO GO TO THE PARTY.

SIX HOURS TO GO TO THE PARTY.

FIVE HOURS TO GO.

FOUR HOURS.

THREE.

TWO.

ONE.

CHAPTER 4

SECOND BASE NIGHT

I walked up the fancy slates of stone steps leading to the dark mahogany front doors of Brooke's house. Large glass windowpanes bordered both sides of the door allowing a clear view all the way to the kitchen. I was wearing my best Pietasters tee-shirt, another stupid fuckin ska band tee-shirt that my mom bought for me at Utopia. It was all I had... I was pretty sure this one was "cool" though... so I tucked it into my Diesel jeans, a brand new addition to my wardrobe that my mom had bought for me earlier in the evening since I was now popular and told her that since I was now popular, I would no longer be able to wear what I was wearing before. So that and a black leather belt with orange New Balance sneakers. Orange was my favorite color, not even popularity could change that. It was my best outfit. Except for this fucking Pietasters tee-shirt. Whatever, it looked good. Maybe. I had no idea what good actually looked like.

I wasn't sure whether to knock or ring the doorbell. So I did both.

Knock Knock.

Ding Dong.

The movement of a shadow in the kitchen could be seen. I jumped back in front of the door to conceal myself from the big ass windows. I turned in circles, pretending to be occupied. Occupied with what? Turning in circles? Anyway the door opened. A woman in her early forties wearing tight leather pants, a low cut sweater, leopard print high heels, a collection of delicate jewelry, and a plethora of plastic surgery stood in front of me.

"And you must be... Olivia's new boyfriend!"

"Uhhh—HI!! Yeah! It's me!"

How stupid.

Keep your game Greg.

I couldn't believe how gorgeous this woman was. She must be on the board of the Long Island Society of MILFs.

"Please come in. What's your name sweetie?"

"Greg. Hi. I'm Greg."

"Hi Greg. They're in the basement sweetie! You just go on down there and have fun! So excited Olivia has a new boyfriend!"

Oh God. This woman was worse than I thought… and the basement? I gotta go to the basement?!

Okay. Just… Walk down.

Remember, Greg: You're popular now.

I stepped inside the house and looked around. I stood on a marble-tiled area with a spiral staircase that led to the second story of the house, which was directly in front of me. To my left was a room that nobody ever went into, a room full of expensive décor and exquisite furniture that had probably never been touched. All the couches looked uncomfortable as fuck. To my right was the dining room, also a bit too formal for any sort of human interaction, *maybe* for holidays. The only two rooms that seemed as if they had any use were the kitchen and an extravagant TV room right next to it. The TV was blaring loud as hell and every single light in the house was on. I searched for the basement door.

I was lost already.

"Where is it again? The door? To the basement?"

Brooke's mom hadn't heard a word I said, or maybe she had, but she was far too busy scrounging around in her purse looking for something.

"Hold on honey!"

I waited like an idiot until she said, "Sorry sweetie, what did you say?"

"The door? To the basement?"

I followed her through the dining room into the kitchen and around the bend to the basement door, which was cracked open just a sliver. I could hear laughter, talking, fun.

I was terrified.

"Thank you."

"You're welcome sweetie."

I tried to keep my footsteps quiet but then came a creak. SHIT! They all musta heard that. SAY SOMETHING GREG! FIX THIS! "Hey! I'm here!" That's what I said. I sounded like a moron in my head. Those stupid words—fuck. Ah, okay, whatever, keep going.

"Whoaaaa it's Greg Cayea! The newest popular kid in our grade! Wearing a *Pietasters* shirt!" said this kid named Marks. Marks was the most popular boy in our school. The dude version of Brooke. He was tall, good-looking, and all the chicks seemed to like his eyes. He was a fucking asshole in an endearing typa way. Anyway, "Whoaaaa it's Greg Cayea! The newest popular kid in our grade! Wearing a *Pietasters* shirt!" Marks shouted with arrogance in front of the other five or so dudes and like nine girls.

Dammit! Why'd I wear this fuckin shirt? How do I recover from this? Getting in good with the girls was one thing, but these guys were a whole new ballpark. I had to play my cards with strategy. I looked around the room. My thoughts were running wild.

"Come sit Greg!" Brooke told me. "Do you guys know Greg? Marks! James!

Chris! Harris! Johnny! Brad! This is Greg!" Brooke announced.

"Yeahhh!!! Wuttup Greg?"—the dude named Brad said to me. Brad was actually my neighbor, he lived a few houses down from me and we used to play basketball… until I was a loser and he was "cool". But he was this ugly kid that somehow got popular. I had no idea how it happened. But he mutated into dickhead status soon after that and so who gives a shit. He asked me "Where's your crew? Robby and— what's that other kid's name?"

"Jon?" I finished his sentence… as if he didn't actually know Jon's name. I mean come on, the school was tiny as fuck and everybody knew everybody. But then he carried on as if he was grateful I had given him the missing name that woulda never popped into his ugly head.

"Right. Why are those kids such losers?"

I knew what he was doing. He was playing hardball. That's fine with me, this was do or die and I wasn't about to let a few cocky lines throw me off track.

"Not sure actually. You should call em up. Ask them." I think that was a pretty solid response.

I found my seat next to Brooke, who was sitting next to Olivia. Then James, this blonde-haired blue-eyed sculpture from a couple school districts over opened his mouth, "Aren't you three like… best friends?" To be friends with the popular kids from *another* school district like James, well, that was a whole new level of popularity. That's where *I* wanted to get to, to where James was. He looked like a handsome Nazi, but he was Jewish. Anyway, he asked me

"Aren't you three like… best friends?"

He and Marks laughed at me.

I kept calm.

Fucking asshole…

"Best friends? Nah man. You're my best friend. Yo can you pass me the chips?"

They were eating chips and salsa. I knocked them both off balance as they passed those damn chips my way.

"Greg Cayea. Making a strong entrance. I like it." Marks said with approval.

"Glad you like me Marks."

"I'm glad I like you too man, it would really suck if Olivia's new boyfriend was a loser." Marks added with a jab. I think he won that round. Then Brooke said

"You guys ready???"

Ready for what I wondered.

The night had apparently already been planned out. It was Second Base Night. The theme was arranged by the B.O.P.S., the clever acronym the eight most popular girls in school gave to themselves: Brooke, Brittany, Olivia, Pamela, Pristine, Sherry, Sarah and Stephanie… The "BOPS".

Second Base Night? You mean… I get to grab Olivia's tits? But I didn't say that out loud. I said it to myself, in my head. I looked at them again, her tits. They were insanely huge. I bet all the kids from my school were in their rooms jerking off to them right now.

Stop looking.

No big deal.

Second Base Night.

Cool.

Whatever…

Brain pause.

Back to life:

HOLY SHIT!

Contain yourself Greg.

My thoughts were so racy. Just relax. I had not even dreamt of this. I never even considered it a possibility. Three more guys showed up, Mike, Mike and… Mike. *Three fucking Mikes.* Each one of them paired off with an equally popular BOP. After Brooke announced the rules, the basement broke up into pairs and everyone went their separate route to the backyard. I hadn't even said hi to Olivia, I mean my girlfriend, since I got there. Now I was supposed to lead her to some big tree outside and squeeze her tits then come back and say mission accomplished? Jeez… I was a fucking wreck.

Anyway Olivia and I walked up the stairs and found the backyard door and out we walked… Fresh cut grass, a gigantic yard with a stunning garden and the scent of light mist from the sprinkler filled the air. In the near distance was a lagoon-shaped pool that looked as if it belonged at some tropical hotel. The hot tub lit up the night with Caribbean-like colors, illuminating a pathway to the prim and proper tennis court sitting on a plethora of pricey acreage. I had never seen anything like it. So *this* is Long Island…

Olivia and I found the perfect spot, next to a big tree, out of sight from the world. She looked at me and waited for me to do something. I put my hands on her waist and moved them down to her faded blue jeans and grabbed her ass. It was so nice and plump, but it was Second Base Night, so I diverted my attention back to her breasts. She looked at me. I looked back. I jumped right into a sloppy, terrible, horrid French kiss and rounded first base. HOLY SHIT I KISSED HER!

Keep going Greg. Keep fucking going.

So I kept going. I moved my hands up to her chest and gave a squeeze over her shirt. They were so big. Second base was in clear sight. I kissed her again and slowly brought my hands back to her waist, where I found the entrance underneath her tight shirt to her bare skin. I felt her belly button. Oh my God. Up and up and up I went until I hit a barrier, her bra. I had never taken a bra off before, so I just winged it. A couple tugs later, actually coulda been like seventeen tugs later, well, at some point it snapped off... or broke off. Whatever. I did it.

I pushed it to the side and found her nipple. They were soft. Her nipples. They were the first nipples I had ever felt. They were amazing nipples. I would have held them all night, but apparently we were all supposed to reconvene in the basement to report back to the group exactly what had been accomplished as soon as we had accomplished it. So literally, that was it. I gave her tits one last squeeze and then we stopped and walked back to the house. It was fucking weird but I felt a tingle overcome my soul. I was confident. I had struck gold. I was a winner, not a loser. I was fucking awesome. It was a high I never forgot.

We were the only ones in the house as we stepped foot back in the kitchen. I had accomplished what no man on Earth had accomplished, and I had done it first! Before any of the other kids had even made it back to the house! That's one small step for man, one giant leap for Greg. The final frontier: Olivia's tits. I was still thinkin about it in my head. Then I saw the clock. Shit. It was my curfew. Should I just ignore it? Nah, not tonight. I made a huge move and now I just wanna get the fuck outa here. So when Olivia ran downstairs to report back to the BOPS once they returned, I called my mom from the house phone.

It was midnight.

"Mom?"

"I was getting worried about you."

My mom was always worried. "Can you come get me?" I asked her. But then Olivia came back and sat next to me.

"I gotta go mom, see you soon." And I hung up the phone.

We sat awkwardly next to each other in silence as if there was a big kangaroo in the room… we had made tit contact and now everything was different. We sat on the couch in silence for almost twenty minutes. Her eyes were closed. Finally, I gathered enough strength and courage and I whispered "You're really pretty…" She opened her eyes. "I like you too, Greg."

"And ummm… you've got really nice—"

HONK HONK.

Shit my mom was here.

I kissed her goodnight and left. I felt free as I quietly shut the door behind me and walked down the stone steps and onto the driveway where my mom was. She was parked on the street in front of the house in her red Mercedes station wagon. I opened the door and got in, full of energy.

"Did ya have fun?" My mom was always nervous like I said, so when she asked, it was more like "Greg *please* tell me you had some fun". But anyway, I didn't answer that question. I had a demand.

"Mom I really need new tee-shirts and some nice sweaters and a pair of nice shoes and maybe even a cool belt."

"Since when do you want to go shopping?" She asked me. Her look was priceless. Clearly I had shocked her. She had always dreamt of going shopping with me, so the next day, no questions asked, we hit every store at the Americana Shopping Mall. The Americana shopping mall is one of those malls where every store is so expensive that they think you're stealing shit every time you make a right turn to try something on. But yeah:

BOOM!

My closet exploded! Shopping bags scattered all over my room. Orange Polo crew shirts, Kenneth Cole dress shoes, another pair of orange gym shorts. It was like I was a completely new kid… And all it took was clothes.

BUT THEN…

But then none of that mattered. Everything was about to fall out from beneath my feet. It was the worst thing that could have *possibly* happened.

My eight-year-old brother, Eric, delivered the news…

CHAPTER 5

BAD NEWS

My brother is about to come to my door, but before he does, it's important to take note that during this time I was living in a moderately sized house in a moderately nice neighborhood, upper-middle class I'd say. My mom is a Jewish accountant from Levittown, a slightly white-trashy part of Long Island, and my dad is a half French-Canadian and half Sicilian radiologist and came from an even shittier part of Long Island called Babylon. They had met at Hofstra University at nineteen and got married when twenty and pumped me out at thirty then had my brother when I was five and we were living in a small condo till I was about six or seven then moved to the house we were now in, in a quaint development not too far away from Brooke's house, in a town called

Roslyn on the North Shore of Long Island. I just had to say that real quick before my brother got here, but here he is:

KNOCK KNOCK.

"What's up?" I screamed over the music. My brother Eric opened the door and stared me up and down...

"Mom told me to get you."

"Why?"

"What are you *wearing*?" he looked me up and down again.

"Clothes. Why? What does she want?"

"She said we're moving to a mansion."

"What? What's that even mean?"

So I rushed after him to the kitchen, the heels of my new Kenneth Cole shoes clanking on the tile floor as I walked in and saw my mom and dad sitting at the kitchen table on these wooden kitchen chairs with these country-looking cushions that only a home behind a white picket fence might have. They were staring at each other, giving each other the 'should I say it? Or should you?' look. I had no idea what was going on. My brother Eric stood next to me. He and I were close, I think. Like we were close and got along and were friends, I think, and aside from the fact that my mom and dad worked a million hours a week and were never home and always kept my brother and I with our housekeeper, Carolyn, or my black mom as I call her, they really didn't fuck up all too much. Pretty solid family I'd say. But that night, that night changed it all.

Back to the kitchen table.

We were all waiting in silence for someone to say something. I just wanted to get to the bottom of this whole mansion business real quick.

Mansion? What the fuck does that even mean, *mansion*, we're movin to a *mansion*... WHAT THE HELL DOES THAT MEAN?

Whatever, I had no time to fuss around, not with my new very busy and very popular schedule and all. So I immediately asked

"We're moving to a mansion?"

"We are?" My mom replied in this kinda phony surprised typa way.

"Eric said we're moving to a mansion."

There was an empty silence in the room until my mom said

"Well, would you like that?"

"Like what?"

My dad let my mom do the talking. He was a silent typa guy, kinda intimidating at times with his unspoken word... So yeah, my mom continued, "If we moved to a bigger house, would you like that?"

Turns out that day my dad had gotten BIG NEWS... He'd finally attained everything he'd been working his ass off for since he and my mom got married and were living in small apartments in Boston and Hershey Pennsylvania and now back in New York. His dreams had finally come true and he had been named partner that day at his firm.

I shoulda been happy for him, right?

But now that he was a partner, and not just a regular doctor, he went from making under six figures to a whole lotta figures. In other words, we were now officially wealthy. There was just *one* thing... This mansion, this so-called mansion my mom and brother spoke of, which my dad had picked out to celebrate his promotion, it was in the town of North Shore, out of the Roslyn school district, which meant I'd have to switch schools.

SWITCH SCHOOLS!

Everything I'd worked for was about to be taken away from me.

So I snapped.

"NO FUCKING WAY."

The thought of going back to loserdom *terrified* me and for the second time in my life, the first time being when I chucked a jock strap at Jake Stern's face in the locker room during gym class, for the second time in my life I had a violent outburst. My brother grew cautious, my mom fearful, my dad angry. I cursed and threatened to do something awful if ever that became a reality. The thought of moving me to another school was just unacceptable.

"FUCKING BITCH!" I yelled at my mom. I couldn't control my temper. There was a very black Hyde to my Jekyll that'd fostered since birth. A side of me I hadn't seen before, nor my parents, nor my brother. It was frightening. I didn't know what to do so I ran to my room and slammed the door. Maybe I should call Olivia? Nah, that'd be weird. But she was my girlfriend. I was supposed to share shit like this with her, right? I dunno, it was a weird night. My head was twitchin a bit. I wasn't sure if it would go away, but it started really botherin me. Goddam it, go the fuck away! Chill the fuck out Greg. Relax. I can't. I can. Stop thinkin.

Then during the middle of the night, when the house was dark and quiet, while I was in my bed, pacing around my mind, still a bit twitchy, I needed something to make me feel better, something to soothe the anxiety. I couldn't take it any longer. So I left my room and snuck past my parent's master bedroom and I walked through the carpeted hall then tiptoed across the wooden-floored living room to the tiles of the kitchen, which were heated tiles and made my feet tingle, and quietly opened the basement door that was tucked right next to the entrance of our two-car garage.

I treaded down the basement steps as lightly as possible and opened the door at the bottom of the staircase to a section of the house that had never been finished. We referred to it, cleverly, as the 'unfinished part of the basement'. It was a cement room with clutter everywhere, but it's also where my dad kept his wine cabinet. I had never drank alcohol before, other than this one time at Passover when I was seven. I went around and finished all the grown-ups' Manischewitz, you know that Jewish wine, then catcalled my mom like 'OOOooooWWWeeeeee!' and she looked at me and said, "I think you've had too much to drink." Anyway, that was the only time I'd ever drank... so I'm not quite sure what drove me to the wine cabinet on that night. But something did.

There were about thirty bottles of wine in my dad's cabinet. I grabbed one of them, shoved it down my pants and gripped the bottleneck through my pants pocket with my right hand, even though the entire house was asleep and I probably coulda just walked it back in clear view to my room. But no, I snuck it back in secrecy. I closed my bedroom door behind me and put a chair against the doorknob in case anyone had heard me, not like that did anything. All you'd have to do was push the door open and the chair woulda fell over. But anyway, I stared at the bottle. It was a white wine. I didn't have a bottle opener, so I unwrapped the foil and jammed the cork through the bottle using a Bic pen from my desk and I got broken pieces of cork all in the wine, but I didn't give a shit. I took a sip.

Mmmmmm.

Yum.

Another.

And another.

After drinking a third of the bottle, I was better. The medicine worked. And that was my first drink (aside from Passover). I felt invincible. From that day forward I slept next to a bottle every night, it was my only real friend.

I was thirteen-years-old and felt unstoppable.

CHAPTER 6

THE BATMITZVAH

I drank every night from that night forward and told all the kids at school about it and how they had to try it with me, but no one accepted my invite, so I just drank alone. Until my mom was makin my bed one night cause it was a mess and she was tryin to be a good mom by makin the bed... And there was this shelving unit next to the bed with three shelves but one of the shelves, the bottom shelf, it was kinda hidden from view because the mattress blocked it from sight. So that's where I hid my bottles of wine that I was still stealin from my dad's mini wine cellar thingy, which mind you was getting real hard to make it look like no bottles were missin. I had to scatter the bottles I stole and choose their positioning really carefully so that the empty holes where there was no wine stayed in unison with how it looked before. Yeah, so that shit was hard after eight bottles or so, but anyway, like I said, my mom was makin my bed. And she lifted the mattress up to tuck in the final sheet and that's when she saw the bottle.

I was caught.

She picked it up like it was toxic and might turn her into a ninja turtle.

"What... what's this?"

She was already startin to cry. Fuck.

"Uhh... I just was havin a little. I'm not like, you know, I just like the taste and do it sometimes." I told her with my heart pulsing outa my chest. She looked like she didn't believe me. She looked like she thought I might be an alcoholic or something, so I reassured her I wasn't. "It's not like I'm an alcoholic or nothin." But she still looked like she didn't believe me! What the fuck? So I let her know the truth. "I can stop whenever I want, I just don't want to right now."

"THAT'S WHAT EVERY ALCOHOLIC SAYS!" And she started cryin real loud, so loud that my dad walked by.

"What's up?"

"I found this." My mom said as she held up the bottle with tears flooding my sheets. Now my bed was really fucked up. All wet and messy and shit. But yeah, my dad looked pretty indifferent as he stared at the wine for like ten million minutes then finally said

"He had to drink *that* bottle?"

It was a $300 Chateau Margaux... oops? Then

BOOM! My mom shrieked at him to

"GET OUT!"

And he left. Then it was like, you know, a thing. I was this potential alcoholic alla sudden just from one bottle. I was real angry about that. An alcoholic? Is she nuts? I'm fuckin thirteen. It's just a bottle. At least I appreciated fine wine. This is totally normal. What a lunatic she was. But it got even worse when we finally *did* move.

So it was this three-story house that they found that was still in the Roslyn school district… phew. Didn't wanna hafta do all *that* over again. You know, build my reputation an all. I guess my violent outburst worked… So after ten million fights, I had won, we stayed in Roslyn.

The house they bought was the last house on the street at the end of a cul-de-sac. It had this extraordinarily long driveway that buried it behind all the other houses. It sat on top of a large hill overlooking a duck pond and there was this clock tower right next to it that gave the suburb a quaint little town typa feel to it. And it wasn't *really* three stories, cause the basement was built above ground, so it was kinda like a two-story house with a high up basement. It was really intimidating lookin, like the house always felt like it was towering over you in this very condescending fashion, like it was better than you or somethin.

My parents painted it Federal Blue for some fuckin reason, which is the type of blue that has a few teardrops of grey mixed into it so as to not make it *so* pronounced that it looked like a clown house from a Dr. Seuss story. But, let's be real, to the rest of the world it was the big blue fuckin house at the end of the street. I actually kinda liked that color now that I think of it.

Inside the home were six bedrooms, and here's the best part, *it had an elevator.* Now the elevator wasn't this show-off typa elevator, it wasn't there cause of all the billions of stairs that were far too steep to walk up, but because the previous owners were handicapped and in wheelchairs. But who cares, I still had a fuckin elevator in my house. Wait till Brooke and Olivia and Marks see this! I rode it up and down from the basement to my new room on the third floor all day when we first moved in. So anyway, that was the house, but it didn't matter. I wouldn't be in that house for too long. The downfall started at Pamela Reed's bat-mitzvah.

It was the middle of eighth grade and it was the first important bat-mitzvah I had ever actually been invited to. Even though I was now newly popular, the invites for most bar and bat-mitzvahs had already been picked, chosen, printed and ready to send out, so by the time Olivia and I had started dating earlier that school year, which was no more than a couple months or so ago, I had already missed the boat for some of the more important bar and bat-mitzvahs, important meaning they were the bar and bat-mitzvahs of the other popular kids.

And make no mistake, to be *not* invited to a popular bar-mitzvah was a deeply insulting and eye-opening reality, but, on the contrary, when you *were* invited to one of the popular kid's bar-mitzvahs, well, you were a *somebody*. Pamela Reed was popular. I had been invited. This was a big deal and it officially marked the beginning of my new life and clearly showed the world I had done the impossible and made a complete 180.

So I was at the Garden City Hotel, this fancy ass hotel, and she had fancy ass catering, some fancy ass DJ, and the theme of the Bat-mitzvah was *shopping*. Yes. **Shopping.** There was a big glamorous table with two hundred or so miniature shopping bags on it when I walked in, each shopping bag with a name and table number on it. I found my shopping bag. I was at table twelve.

Shit.

Table twelve. Who was at one through eleven? Were they in order of popularity? A not-so-popular girl named Tara came up beside me and said "Hey Greg!"

"Hiiiii"

I wasn't sure if I should talk to her. Would that affect my popularity? I didn't wanna take any chances in front of Olivia. I tried to make it quick and asked her, "What table are you at?" As she looked for her name and grabbed her shopping bag.

"Table twelve, what about you?"

TABLE TWELVE?! ARE YOU SHITTING ME?! BUT... BUT... THAT'S WHERE *I'M* SITTING!

Had word not gotten around to Pamela Reed that I was popular now? No no no, I was NOT supposed to be seated at the *semi*-popular table. No. THIS WAS ALL WRONG! This could ruin everything. I crumpled my shopping bag with my hand and slipped it in my pocket without her seeing.

"Greg?"

"Yeah?"

"What table are you at?"

"Oh, I don't remember, maybe like... five or something?" The fact that this semi-popular chick was even talkin to me woulda been like a fuckin dream come true some months ago, but now, well, now it was risky. I walked away with my head down. This was bad.

I didn't sit down once the whole night. I was the only one standing against the back wall, staring at my empty seat at table twelve from the back of the ballroom. Waitresses began to walk around the room to take dinner orders so I took off for the bathroom and hid for the next twenty minutes on the toilet hiding my legs every time someone walked in.

By the time I came back out, the fancy ass professional dancers that the fancy ass Pamela Reed parents had hired were doing their thing on the dance floor where they try and get the party started. Well, I dunno how it is around the rest of the country, but in Long Island, the chicks wore slutty ass dresses and lots of makeup and danced like whores. But this was all new to me. The dudes were grinding the girls and the girls were all throttling the other *girls*. It was fuckin lunacy, and awesome, but then I spotted Olivia with Brooke, I don't know if she even knew I was there, I had been hiding in the bathroom, but anyway, I saw Olivia with Brooke on the dance floor and—wait. What in the fuck—ARE THEY KISSING?! Cause sometimes the girls kissed each other for extra attention I guess.

Marks waved me over, by now we had become 'BEST friends', "dude, I didn't even know you were here! LOOK at your girlfriend" he said with a dipshit grin. I still thought he was an asshole, but maybe when you get *that* popular you're *supposed* to be an asshole? I dunno. He didn't ask about what table I was at. So that was good… but my girlfriend… she was… she was—

"DUDE! THEY'RE KISSING!" Marks shouted.

I tried to play it off like it wasn't bothering me. "Yeah man… looks like she's having fun."

"A LOT of fun" he added.

I looked at the center of the table Marks was sitting at. There was a large Versace shopping bag as the centerpiece. I hadn't realized every table had a different name brand designer. I looked at table twelve. It

was only J Crew. I really got fucked on this whole table situation. Marks
kept going, "Dude, this is awesome! She's practically fucking Brooke!" I
wanted to punch him in the face, as if I didn't see what the hell what
going on. But I just said

"What? Oh, yeah."

"Go dance with her man! Get in on that!"

It had been weeks since Olivia and I had even talked. That's just
how these fake eighth grade relationships seemed to work… but what do
I know?

The song stopped. The dance ended. Olivia started crying.

What the fuck?

Marks looked over at me and said "What's that all about?" But I had
no idea what was goin on. Olivia ran off the dance floor in tears as soon
as *I Will Survive* started blasting. What the fuck? This was weird. I stood
up to chase after her, I hadn't even said hi to her since I got there, fuck,
that probably looked real bad. Maybe that's why she was crying? So I
started skip-running in this weird horse trot typa way after her but came
to a halt when I realized Brooke was walking in my direction. Why was
she walking towards me? What was going on?

Someone help.

"Greg"

"Yes?"

Brooke wanted to talk to me about Olivia. What? What about
Olivia? Were my clothes not nice enough? I can buy better ones. It
must be the orange, too much orange? Is it too much orange? And the
cologne, it's not like I'm married to the cologne, I can change it! And
The Pietasters tee-shirt, in the trash, done, finito. Of course I said none

of this out loud. No. I was wrong. It wasn't the clothes, or the cologne, or The Pietasters tee-shirt, or the color orange.

It was me.

Apparently I wasn't living up to their standards of newly appointed affectionate popular boyfriend. I had failed. And as quickly as Brooke had gifted me the life-altering present of popularity, she took it right back away as she delivered the news that Olivia no longer desired to see me. She had ripped my stardom off me in a matter of seconds.

Then Brooke walked away. I was alone... again. I stood there for a moment, mortified. Time stopped. My whole popular life flashed before my eyes. I rushed to the popular guys I was supposed to be friends with to see if they would still talk to me now that I was a nothing again.

"Olivia and I broke up" I said, waiting like a nervous wreck for their reaction.

Marks laughed, "That was QUICK! Well, at least you're not a total *loser* anymore"

Then I had a moment of complete clarity.

He was right.

But I had to act fast if I wanted to abolish loserdom for good. I was mad, real mad about this whole situation, and I knew exactly who I was mad at. I was mad at Brooke, at Olivia, at Marks, at Robby and Jon and my parents and Roslyn and at Long Island and at those damn twitches that came outa nowhere and at Conner's fuckin shoes. I dunno why I just thought of Conner...

But Conner was this on-the-rise almost popular kid who wore these really fancy stupid fuckin shoes to school every day. Those fucking shoes, I hated them. They all had these square tips that just annoyed the living shit outa me. And his dumb cashmere sweaters too. All he wore was cashmere. And *I* was the faggot?

Then my mind got all weird again, I mean- Why would this all be happenin to *me*? WHY WAS THIS ALL SO HARD? WHAT'S IT ALL MEAN??? WHY IS OLIVIA A LESBIAN? WHY DIDN'T BROOKE TELL ME WHAT I WAS DOING WRONG!? I just got so damn angry. Maybe that's why I was obsessed with Eminem. Cause he got it. I loved Eminem. And I hated Conner's damn sweaters.

Olivia didn't want me? Fine, take your big tits elsewhere. I'll take care of this myself… So I made some changes to my life agenda to ensure I wouldn't lose my momentum.

CHAPTER 7

A NEW WAY OF LIFE

I knew I wasn't goin nuts and that I really was losin my momentum cause the next day at school was if I didn't even exist. Brooke and Olivia were just fine without me. They were doin what they always did, bein hot and popular with all their other friends, the resta the BOPS, and I was a nothing again. They all ignored my existence. It was like popularity had broken up with me. Marks still talked to me, which was a positive, but I was losin my stride. I was slippin. I had to do something fast, something wild to get the attention back on me… so I decided to rob Conner's house, at least his dumb shoes and faggy cashmere sweaters.

How much fun would it be to steal every fucking sweater he owned and burn all his shitty ass shoes? How would the BOPS feel about *that?* Yeah, that'll show em I don't need their meaningless popularity, their stupid BOP crew or Olivia's big nice perfect amazing juicy tits. Fuck. Now I'm horny. Okay whatever, stealin those sweaters and burnin Conner's shoes'll make my dick go down. Or maybe up? I dunno it *did* sound real juicy. Robbery. Had a nice ring to it. I was in some class when I thoughta that, dreaming of what that might look like.

So I found Marks at the end of the day and told him to wait with me till after all the buses left and the school was empty then convinced him to come with me on a walk. I told him that I had a surprise idea.

"Where are we goin?" He said.

"You'll see."

Conner lived right by the school, so we walked on over about a mile to his house.

"What are we doin Cayea?"

"It's a surprise."

I could tell Marks was uncomfortable. Well good. Now you know one fiftieth of how I felt my whole life. Time to get to work.

"Let's go", I told him.

"Are you seriously not gonna tell me what we're doin?"

Was this kid serious? Don't be such a chump. Maybe he thought *I* was some kinda chump. Wait, did he just call me a CHUMP? Or was that me thinkin out loud. Was this all in my head? Ehh—fuck it.

"Yeah I'm seriously gonna make your day awesome. It'll be fun. Just fuckin come on." Cause he was laggin a bit, like all nervous and shit.

"You okay man? You sound a bit... I don't know, mad."

WE'RE JUST STEALING HIS FUCKIN SWEATERS AND FUCKIN GAY SHOES AND IT'LL BE FUN! OKAY?! **THIS IS FUN!** But I didn't say that as we walked by the cookie cutter houses.

"I just wanna go see Conner for a sec."

"For what?"

"To say hi."

Marks looked at me all skeptical-eyed. "Dude. My mom and his mom are like best friends."

"Relax. He'll never know. Just watch."

"Never know what?" Marks asked.

But we were already there, so I ran ahead of him and rang the doorbell.

DING DONG.

"Don't worry dude", I told him right as Conner's mom opened the door.

"Marks! How are you?" Then she looked at me like a stranger, "Oh, Hi!" She said in that fake 'I'm nice' kinda voice. Then she switched her attention back to Marks, "How's your mom? Does Conner know you're here? I don't think he was expecting you, hold on."

And she yelled up the stairs. I walked in quickly before Conner came downstairs and questioned why we were there. Marks followed like a little bitch, well, maybe he walked in regular, I dunno, I was still mad about him bein such a dick all those years I was a loser. I can't believe he and I were friends now.

Conner answered from his room upstairs "Whhhhaaa?"

"You boys just go on up" his mom said.

So I walked upstairs to his room and he was lying on his bed with his backpack freshly thrown to the side of him, the kinda thing you did after a long day of school when you finally get back to your room, and he was so uncomfortable with the fact that I was in his house that his eyes lit up with surprise when he saw me.

"Hey man, what's up?" I said.

Conner looked up even more from his bed to see what was goin on, "Oh. Hey man. Uhh…"

"Marks is here too" I said quickly to reassure him that everything was alright. Marks wasn't even up the stairs yet.

"Oh. Cool." He said a bit confused. Good. Now you know what confusion feels like bitch. "Yeah I saw you guys hang back after school together and was wondering what you guys were doin, didn't know you were coming over, did you tell me you were coming?"

"Surprise!"

That's when Marks walked in. "Hey Conner. Tough day at school?"

"Why do you say that?" Conner said.

"Cause you look beat man."

Great, Marks was doin his job. It was time to do some work…

"Dude, that's a nice sweater." I said without a shred of sincerity. And mind you, I really didn't *hate* him. I just wanted to get even with life, and he seemed like an easy target. Am I turnin into Jake Stern? No… I was just havin some fun and more than that, more pristine than revenge, it was my first 'I don't give a fuck moment', and it felt damn good. I think I'll do this forever.

Anyway, after I told Conner I liked his sweater he was like "Thanks. I've got them in like three colors, they're in the closet, check em out".

Good idea. I think I will check em out and I walked into Conner's closet.

Marks and Conner had some bullshit convo while I was in the closet lookin for sweaters to steal, Marks sounded like a dick. He always sounded like a dick. I guess he was just a bit of a dick my nature. Whatever I was busy and he kept Conner distracted, probably still befuddled why we were there in the first place. I mean, it's not like Marks and Conner hung out. He just wanted to go home, I bet.

I found those two other sweaters, cause Conner was wearin the third, and I picked out two other of the most expensive sweaters I could find in his overly priced wardrobe. I wish I coulda grabbed his shoes and burnt them on his front lawn but they woulda been too hard to get.

Every time Conner's head was turned I shoved another sweater in my backpack. By the time Conner looked to see what the hell I was still doin in his closet, all his sweaters were gone, well, four or five of em were at least. I could hear his mom downstairs doin whatever dumb jappy moms do. I had to be swift on my exit. But then Conner was like

"What the hell are you doing?"

"Just lookin at your clothes, cool sweaters you got. But I'm tired. Marks. Let's go" I said as I walked outa the room.

Conner got up off his bed, "You guys are leaving?" Something was off. He could feel it. I casually walked down the stairs hopin Marks was behind me and opened the front door without saying shit to his mom and left the house and waited till I got to the end of his front yard before I started sprinting like a madman and dove into some bushes on one of his neighbor's lawns. Marks was right behind me. Good boy Marks.

"DUDE" He was out of breath. "WHAT THE FFF— [catching his breath] WHAT
THE FUCK WAS THAT?! DID YOU JUST TAKE HIS CLOTHES?! MY MOM'S FRIENDS [out of breath again] MY MOM'S FRIENDS [still out of breath] --FRIENDS WITH HIS MOM!"

At least he didn't care about Conner's fuckin sweaters. That's the good news. The bad news is he was actin like a little baby about it.

"Just say it was me." Shit, that was all I wanted anyway...

Well... here's what happened the next day. I wore one of the sweaters to school cause I wanted to rub it in his face and I figured, shit, how would he even be able to prove it was his? Not like Armani only made one sweater in that one color.

But Marks *did* say it was me, like I told him to do, and little did I know Conner's mom was the most popular mom in Long Island, shit even moms were fuckin popular in this town. She knew every other mom in Roslyn and within HOURS there was not a house that I was allowed to step foot onto the property of. I couldn't even go over to Marks house. I had attained instant notoriety, mission accomplished. Conner's mom even showed up at school, which musta been embarrassing for Conner, and threatened to call the cops on me in front of the whole parking lot while everyone was looking at us. So I said

"Fine, I'll give the fuckin sweaters back." And she let me off with a warning. But then she wanted me to apologize to him and so I said "fuck no". Yeah that made a BIG scene right in front of *everyone*. But the big scene was exactly what I needed to raise my bar of social status from popular to threatening. If the BOPS feared me, they'd never forget who I was. Yeah, I could do this on my own. And so started a new chapter of my life.

CHAPTER 8

I DON'T GIVE A FUCK

Turns out that sweater incident was a bit bigger of a deal than I thought it would be, but I suppose that was the point... I had officially been inducted to the popular scumbag club. The only kid I was still kinda hangin out with was Marks. So, he kept me popular, and my PR stunts kept me a scumbag. But everyone knew who the scumbags were, in fact, the chicks seemed to like it.

One day Marks invited me to this party that was in Jericho, another school district away. That was a HUGE deal, cause when you start gettin noticed by the chicks at other school districts, that meant you were beyond Roslyn popular. That meant you were on your way to becoming a legend. So I knew I had to take this party seriously.

I walked in drunk as fuck from another bottle of my dad's wine and fell into the swimming pool. That was my plan. And it worked. I was the cool drunk kid, or maybe I was a joke? No, I was rad. I met these other kids from these other schools while I was there who drank the way I drank and liked to steal shit too. So I started hangin out with them.

That's when I realized I had done the impossible *again*. Now I didn't even need Marks. Everyone knew exactly who I was. It was *awesome*. I was like, you know, even more famous than that Jewish lookin Nazi kid James I was tellin you about at Second Base Night. I had become exotic, the best typa popular, the handsome outcast. The kid that stole Conner's sweaters then wore em to school the next day and the only kid that cut class in middle school.

Right, I stopped goin to my last period class when I realized I could just walk out the door of the school and wander around the neighborhoods. I'd leave the school in front of all the teachers and kids and wander around the neighborhood till school let out for the other kids and eventually find someone to invite me into their house before their parents came home. Usually I walked in and asked for some booze and we'd steal some from their dad or whatever and I'd get all drunk and show back up at my parent's big blue house at like 8PM and my mom would be like 'WHERE WERE YOU?!' So I'd be like, "Damn, chill mom. I was out." I had come a long way from that pussy I was at that bat-mitzvah. I was becoming a sociopath.

So anyway, I was gettin tired of goin through the neighbor's backyard to get to the sliding glass doors that led to whatever popular kid's living room was hosting whatever party was goin on that night and then havin to crawl through those small basement windows to leave when it was over so that nobody's parents found out I was there, so that's why I sat at home drinkin my wine for a while before I went into this one party this one night.

It was a normal night and another dumb popular party that I wanted to make memorable, so I went to where the closet was, where all the girls kept their Versace purses and jackets and shit, and I stole all the wallets outa their bags and gave the money to my friend Nikki from this other school district. I don't even know why I did that. I guess I wanted to be worse than I was. If I was labeled a scumbag, I certainly wanted to exceed my reputation. That's another thing that also turned into this really big deal. Even my mom told me she was startin to get looks around town just for bein my mom. I don't know, but by the time summer rolled around, right before high school was about to start, it got so bad that nobody would even talk to me anymore... which made these feelings that felt odd, bizarre even, build up in my head. Like I was gonna explode, or maybe pop. Or maybe just drop dead, no—don't think like that Greg. There's too much to get done before I clock out. Like become a fucking legend. I'll just take this as far as I can. No matter *what*, nobody will ever forget me.

It was the summer of 1998 when I was sitting in front of my computer this one day in the big blue house and I was staring into my computer at my AOL screen cause it had just been invented and I was lonely as fuck and I spent hours staring at that damn AOL screen waiting for that magical "YOU'VE GOT MAIL!" sound. When finally, it came.

"YOU'VE GOT MAIL!"

YES! SOMEONE WANTS TO TALK TO ME! It was this girl Samantha, one of the girls I was friends with at Camp Echo, the sleepaway camp I spent a few years going to when I was a loser, and in the email she wrote to me "I heard you moved to The Pines! You have to meet my friend Delson! He lives right by you! He lives in The Pines!" The Pines was the name of the development that my parent's big blue house was in.

So I wrote back and said, "ehhhh… I dunno". The reason I said that was cause I knew exactly who Delson was… or rather I knew *of* exactly who he was. I had never met him. He was a year older than I was and all I knew about him was he was some fat druggie that no one liked. That's all I knew, that he was a fat druggie loser. I kinda liked the druggie part, but no way was I gonna associate myself with a loser from an even higher grade, that was just a solid no. But I called him anyway cause I was desperate and figured no one would find out about it.

"Hey man. This is Greg, Samantha's friend. She told me to give you a call cause I just moved to The Pines and you live like down the street."

"Dude! Yes! You wanna come and drink in my garage?"

It was a Wednesday afternoon.

Without even giving me a chance to respond he countered "How bout we smoke a bowl at the pool club?

That sounded much better. Something about drinking in this fat druggie loser's garage on a Wednesday afternoon felt not cool. And cool was all I cared about. Gotta stay cool.

"Sure." I said.

So we met up and he wasn't fat at all. He actually wasn't a bad looking kid. That made me feel more comfortable being friends with him. Cause that's all I knew. I knew that life sucked when you were a fuckin loser and life was *way* better when you were cool.

We hopped the fence of the pool club that The Pines development was built around and he showed me how to properly smoke a bowl as we sat atop the pool shed like a couple misfits. It was like the fourth or fifth time I tried smoking pot but I lied to him and said I got high all the time. My heart was racing outa my chest and I was having a full-blown panic attack after one hit.

Then we went to his mom's house and opened his food cabinet but there wasn't shit to eat. His mom was lactose intolerant so he had—oh wait, no, his *sister* was lactose intolerant, so he had all this dope cereal with all this whack ass milk. So I poured some Rice Crispies into this massive bowl and figured out that I could replace the milk with some whipped cream, cause he had whipped cream. Real whipped cream and not some fake whipped cream. So anyway, I ate this disgusting ass bowl of whipped cream and Rice Crispies then found some American cheese in his fridge and ate that. Then I felt fuckin sick.

So we went to his room and I basically passed out while Delson was listening to N.O.R.E.A.G.A., some rapper that was big at the time. I looked at Delson through my blurry vision and he was still all hyped up dancing and rappin along to the lyrics. Then he popped the big question.

"Do you know JD? Or Gavin Wick?"

JD was a junior who drove a black beamer. Gavin Wick was the *man*, a senior that ran the high school. Everyone knew him. He had exactly the type of infamy I needed. I mean, I was finally building a nice name for myself, the fucked up outcast handsome cool kid thief that the chicks all still liked but hated and if I could be seen with JD and Gavin Wick, man, that would *really* be all I needed to take it to the next level. I had no idea Delson was friends with them. Maybe he *is* cool? This was fuckin exciting news and I *needed* some clout going into high school or else I might drown and not be slightly badass anymore. I had to think about my career.

"No, I've never met them" I said. "Are they cool?"

"You have to meet them!!!" he was always so enthusiastic. "They are AWESOME".

So he called Wick up and they picked us up in JD's black beamer. JD had this burnt-out, high-pitched laugh that could be recognized in the middle of an Aerosmith concert, and Gavin, well... I'll introduce him in a second. Point is, they immediately lit a joint.

"Bubble gum kush" JD said as he took a hit and passed it to Delson.

"AAAAHHHHHHHH SHHHHIIIIITTTTTTTTT" Delson was so excited. And he started singing the name "BUUUBBBBLLLLEEE ggggUUUUMMM KUUUUUSSSSSH". Kid was a lunatic. Then JD told him to shut the fuck up with that singing shit.

"Yo why you always singin everything I say to you Delson?" JD asked with a snicker.

But Delson sang his answer right back "Cause this is the motherrrfffuucckkkinnnnggg [higher pitched] SHHHIIIIITTTTTT"

"Just hit the joint man and stop with the singing, you're making my ears… uhh… not feel good." JD said with a stoned-out laugh. "And who the fuck are *you?*" He looked at me.

Delson interrupted, "Yo this kid is the [singing again] SSShhhhhIIIITTTTT".

JD looked at me. He didn't seem so sure about some would-be freshman being in his car. Then Delson fell into a fit of coughing and passed me the joint and I took a hit and breathed out the smoke and when the smoke cleared I could see that JD hadn't so much as moved a muscle in his face. He was staring straight at me.

"Dude. Are you not… *inhaling?*"

I had no idea what the fuck that meant. Not inhaling? I mean, didn't you see it go from the joint into my mouth? I was confused. I passed JD back the joint but he gave it right back to me.

"Nah man. Take another hit."

Wick eyed me from his side view mirror, but I couldn't really make out what he looked like. I mean, I had heard all about him, and I was nervous as shit to be in the car with him, but he hadn't said one word and for the first time I could see a glimpse of what he might look like. And now he was watching me.

"Do it. Take another hit. This kid ain't inhaling." JD said to Wick.

Delson stuck up for me and said "Yo he *must* be inhaling cause this kid gets higher than anyone *I KNOW!*" and he kinda sang that last part a little bit like he always did. I took another hit and I had no idea how or what I was doing wrong, but I spewed out the smoke without letting the smoke go into my lungs and a big poof cloud fogged up the car.

"DUDE. YOU'RE NOT INHALING" and JD burst out laughing. Wick gave a sneer from his mirror than went back to being cool. "Aright son, look. I want you to suck the smoke from the joint like this, and when it's all in your mouth, do this." And he took a deep breath to show me how to clear the smoke from outa my mouth.

So I took the joint again, I'm feeling fucking twacked out with anxiety and nerves and still stoned from before when Delson and I were smoking atop the pool shed and now this and fuck. So I took another BIG hit and then did exactly what JD told me to do and BOOM: I coughed for about an hour. I couldn't stop coughing. JD cracked up. Delson cracked up. Wick sat still. Then JD asked for the joint back and said "Now *THAT'S* how you smoke!"

As soon as I stopped coughing, I panicked. I was too high. I was so high I needed to get outa the car. I had to get free. I was trapped. Someone please, someone help. But then JD's pager went off and we took off in the car to some kid's driveway and sold him pot. I *had to get free.* I promised myself I would never ever ever smoke pot ever again.

It was 6PM when I got back home to the big blue house. My mom was like

"Whose car was *that?*"

'Oh just this kid that I met." And I ran up to my room terrified of the high I was still on. I had to make it go away. And that was the first time I ever got high. But I still hadn't met Wick! I realized I spent like an hour in that car without him ever even turning around.

But that was all about to change.

CHAPTER 9

WHO IS GAVIN WICK?

It was the first day of high school. I stood still, confident, slightly high, a little drunk even, and searching for someone in my grade that I hadn't yet alienated and that actually still liked me but couldn't find anyone.

Then I saw this tall good-looking guy wearing casual attire with a distinguished hairdo of messy-hair and sly grin looking at me. He looked familiar. Everyone seemed to know him and everybody seemed to have something to say as they passed him by. Hot chicks, weird skaters, homies from the projects, jocks from the wrestling team, everyone seemed to know him. He was leaning against the radiator in the center of the hallway and through all the chaos was staring at me like a predator. He lifted himself off the radiator and left his spot and with a confident walk, approached me. As he walked it seemed like everyone on the planet was still chucking dialogue in his face trying to be his friend, but he didn't get sidetracked, he just kept on walking as he made his way to where I stood. He was like, pretty much everything I ever wanted to be in life. And he was right in front of me. But then I knew immediately who it was when he said

"Sup Cayea."

It was Gavin Wick.

"Oh, hey man. What's been goin on?"

"You ready?" He asked me.

"Ready for what? High school?"

He laughed. Then stared down at me.

"Nope."

"Ready for what?"

He smiled.

"Tonight."

"What's tonight?"

"Oh tonight is... well—fun. Tonight is fun. You're gonna have fun." And then he walked away.

I couldn't stop thinkin about it all day. I wandered around that strange building full of rich Jewish and Italian kids and black kids from the projects. It was an odd mix of ethnic inequality, but whatever, yeah, that's just how Roslyn High School was.

Anyway, I couldn't stop thinkin about what Wick said to me. What the fuck was tonight? I started getting real anxious and nervous and shit.

I was just scatterbrained as fuck. The haunting feeling of calamity, that something terrible was about to happen loomed over my psyche all afternoon and consumed my mind.

At 3PM in the parking lot, where all the juniors and seniors parked their BMW's, Mercedes, Audis and SUV's, as I smoked a cigarette with Marks, JD's black BMW pulled up in front of us. Gavin Wick was in the passenger seat.

"11 ****** Lane, right?" Wick shouted at me from the window. That was my address.

Marks was confused, as was I. I was freaked the fuck out.

"You know them?" Marks inquired. But I didn't pay much attention to him. I was fixated on the beamer in front of me.

"Why?" I asked Wick.

"Cause Cayea, we're gonna give you a ride home. Hop in."

This was strange. I didn't really say bye to Marks as I got in the car.

Inside the car it was dark and smoky and even though the volume was set fairly low, the bass pounded Busta Rhymes into my eardrums as we vibrated our way outa the parking lot.

JD lit up a joint. We drove in silence as the two of them glanced back and forth at each other and laughed like a joke was just outa my reach. Wick looked at JD, JD looked at Wick. But nothing to me. I was all fucked in the head about it. Then I had to ask

"So… What's going on tonight?"

"Nada." Wick said like a cool dickhead.

"How'd you know my address?" I asked.

"Cause—" and he took a hit from the joint—"We live in the same neighborhood."

JD started laughing as Wick passed him back the joint in a fit of coughing.

"Okay, well, but—what about tonight?" I kept asking. I didn't see what was so funny about this.

Wick shot his head back to me and looked into my soul and said "What about it Greg Cayea from 11 ****** Lane?"

JD chimed in with his sinister laugh and high-pitched drugged-out voice, "I'm sure you'll find out!" And gave another weird off-toned giggle.

We got to my house and they didn't bother pulling into my long ass driveway.

"Get out." Wick said.

So I got out. My heart was racing with uncertainty. I paced around my room after ignoring my mom in the kitchen when I walked in and then I decided to call Marks and ask him if he was free to hang out. I had a bad feeling that people were going to show up at my house that night. I was paranoid. Marks's mom HATED me, as did everyone else's parents, for like, you know, stealin the sweaters and robbin the chicks money at that party and all the other stuff by now, but she *still* agreed to pick me up and drop Marks and I off at the spot, the Landmark Diner, where the entire neighborhood hung out.

So we're hanging outside The Landmark Diner and I'm smokin a cigarette, which I thought made me look cool, when suddenly a black Jeep swerved into the parking lot and stopped directly in front of me. My cigarette went limp. Oh no. Then Lisa Monte, the most popular girl in twelfth grade, got out of the car with her best friend and rushed me and grabbed ahold of me and yanked me towards the car and chucked me in the back seat and the Jeep took off. Marks was left in the dust, again.

What the fuck—What the hell was going on?

Lisa was in the passenger seat. She climbed over the center console and got in the back with me. The car sped up full speed as Lisa got all close to me.

This was perhaps the greatest slash most terrifying moment of my life, up until that point at least... Life got a whole lot crazier a whole lot faster than I ever coulda imagined real quick, but for now, back to Lisa.

"Hey. I'm Lisa."

I knew who the fuck she was. Again, I played dumb.

"What's going on?"

"Take off your pants." She told me.

"Huh?"

"Take off your pants! Hurry!"

She grabbed my belt, undid the buckle and took my shoes off.

"WAIT!"

She unzipped my jeans and tugged at them until they came off.

"WHAT THE FUCK ARE YOU DOING!?"

She grabbed my shirt and yanked it up and I heard a rip.

"Oops. Sorry. I'll buy you a new one—" and she continued ripping my shirt off until I was in nothing but my boxers.

"DONE!" She shouted to her friend driving the car. "GO GO GO! Make a left at this light! Take the shortcut!"

"Why am I naked?"

"DRIVE FASTER! THERE'S NO COPS ON THIS ROAD EVER!" Lisa shouted.

"WHAT ARE WE DOING?" I screamed.

We ran a red light and drove into the Jewish Community Center AKA the JCC, it's like the Y, but for Jews, and we drove to the back of the building and I saw there were a bunch of cars and seniors all running around frantically. And there he was.

Gavin Wick.

Gavin stood in the middle of the back parking lot with a clipboard, easy at work.

"Is that Cayea?" Wick shouted to Lisa with a smirk.

"YEAH! WE GOT HIM!" She said, pulling at me to get outa the car.

"He in his underwear?" Wick asked without looking up.

"Get out!!" Lisa tugged at me. "YUP! I GOT HIM IN HIS BOXERS!" She responded to Wick.

Wick started laughing. "Bring him here."

They dragged me outa the car and everyone looked at me in my underwear and laughed. Wick smiled at me. He checked something off on his clipboard. "Now go get me a stop sign by the clock tower and a lock of Danny Delgato's hair."

"Let's go!" Lisa shouted. And she got back into her Jeep and off she went with her hot friends.

Then Wick looked at me. "Don't ever be a fuckin faggot again."

I didn't even know what he meant. Oh no. It was the smoking pot thing! He still remembers that? I didn't even know how to inhale! It wasn't my fault! But I didn't say all that. I just wondered how it might feel to throw a brick in his face and crack his clipboard against his ribs and steal his money and run away screaming and runnin through sprinklers.

But anyway, that was my first day of high school. I had made it onto the Midnight Madness scavenger hunt, a ritual run by Gavin Wick at Roslyn High School. 'Greg Cayea in his underwear'. That's what it said on the list. It felt good. I was off to a good start. Now how the fuck do I get home?

So I just walked. In my underwear, all the way home and opened the coded garage door and took the elevator up to my room so that my mom and dad and brother wouldn't see me. It was embarrassing and awesome. I was known in the senior class already. I was the man.

But then shit got a bit outa control.

It all started this one night. It was homecoming for Jericho, that other school district I told you about not too far away from Roslyn, and Delson took me over to some kid's house name Justin Romello. Justin was another kid that everybody knew about. He was at the top of the list of most scummy trash bags in Roslyn, in other words: my role model, and there I was at his house staring at a pound of pot. How'd I even get here? Oh that's right, my new friend Delson brought me.

So Justin was throwing this pre-party get together before the Homecoming game but the only people that actually showed up were me and Delson. Justin looked at me and said "this is what a pound of pot looks like" and he took out a nug and handed it to me. "Here ya go Cayea." He already knew my name, everybody knew my name. Then Justin opened his hand and there they were. My downfall. Two pills.

"They're called Tweetie Birds", he told us. Delson started doin that little dance typa singy thing he always did when he got excited.

"AAwwwwwhhhhh Ssshhiiiiittttt, is that what I think it iiisssssss?" Delson sang.

That was the first time I had ever seen ecstasy. I was thirteen-years-old. Justin handed me a glass of orange juice and said "drink this."

"Dude, I don't wanna take a whole one" I said. I was nervous. What if I die?

"So just take hhhhaaaaLLLFfffff" Delson sang to me.

But I was terrified. I didn't know what to do. Delson swallowed his pill immediately then kept tellin me to take mine cause he didn't wanna peak without me. Justin *assured me* that I would be thanking him later. He didn't even ask for money. He just gave it to us. So I cracked the pill in half and swallowed it while Delson called the cab to come pick us up to take us to the Homecoming game.

I sat in the backseat of the cab and told the cab driver "This is the greatest day of my life." I was rolling my head off, but *I* just thought I was in a super good mood. "You're such a great cab driver. You're like, I mean, I wouldn't wanna be anywhere else than your cab right now". The cabbie was lookin at me like shut the fuck up but in my head he seemed to be thoroughly intrigued by my compliments. I kept talkin, I wouldn't shut up "People think I'm a bad kid, but I'm not. I'm just happy. I'm finally happy and it means so much to me that you came to pick us up. Do you know where we're goin? The Jericho Homecoming game." But then I kinda forgot if that was the truth. "Isn't that where we're goin Delson?"

"That's exactly where we're goiiiinnnNNNNNNN" and he sang it with an ecstasy-influenced slowness in his voice.

"Where's Justin?" I asked. I hadn't even noticed Justin wasn't in the cab with us. "Is he not coming? I really like him. I mean, I love him. He's a really awesome dude."

"So awesome." Delson said.

"Don't you love this cab?" I said.

"It's perfect." Delson said with a large smile.

But then I remembered that I still had half a pill left!

"Oh my God!!!" I said with mad excitement. "I still have—" and I pulled out the other half of the pill.

"AAWwwwww Shhhhiiittt!!!! Take it man!!! Take it!!" Delson was more excited than I was.

And so I took it.

The next day I stole $250 from my dad's dresser and bought ten more pills. But that was it. The world began to unravel.

CHAPTER 10

CRACKHEAD CAYEA

It was April 29th of 1999, I had stopped going to school. I was fourteen-years-old and nearly done with my ninth grade year. And I guess that was a lie, I *was* still goin to class sometimes, maybe about one class per week, but I always made my entrance trippin on mushrooms and high on ecstasy and stoned outa my mind in the hallways for all to see before takin my seat in whatever class I stumbled into. I had weird friends from odd clicks of crews. I wasn't really infamous anymore, I was kinda, well... invisible again. My new nickname had become 'Crackhead Cayea' and honestly, I wasn't a huge fan of that. I never even smoked crack, but I guess that wasn't the point. It was a big day that day cause it was the day that I took my fiftieth pill of ecstasy, and I know that it was pill number fifty cause I was keepin count... So, that might have somethin to do with my new nickname. And I guess stealing all that money from those girls' purses at all those parties and takin Conner's sweaters and stealing knives and fog machines from the Roosevelt Field mall and stabbing the shit outa my pillow every night fucked up on Special K and trashing motel rooms high off whippits mighta also played some part in that name. I was also gettin kinda violent.

There was this one time I ripped the doorknob off of this kid Levin's bedroom door, some kid I became friends with from another school district, and slammed it over his back and shoulders in a fit of rage after he started beating me in a slap-boxing match. I think I mighta nearly killed him cause the doorknob was one of those old heavy doorknobs made of brass or some shit. But anyway, I *did* apologize for nearly killing him and he did forgive me... So maybe it wasn't as bad as I thought.

Yeah, I had this thing where I always started slap-boxing with kids I hung out with to make sure I had power and I always made sure to never lose no matter what it took, so when Levin started winning, I ripped his heavy doorknob from off his door and attacked him like thunder... I dunno, I guess I just got mad. Like I said, I said sorry and we became friends again. But I'll get to him in a minute...

Anyway, it was April 29th, 1999, and I was fourteen-years-old, smokin pot with this tall black kid from the Roslyn housing projects named Ollie. I always felt cool hangin out with Ollie cause he just got outa juvie after three or so years, I think he went away when he was in fifth or sixth grade for throwing a cinderblock at some dude's head. They charged him with like attempted manslaughter or murder or some shit cause the dude he hit went into a coma, but anyway he had just gotten out and everyone was scared of him and he liked me and I so I felt cool.

Anyway, we were at Saint Mary's church, the church next to our high school and it was during my sixth period Earth Science class and we were off smoking a blunt behind the church. So when the blunt was cashed, we sprayed some cologne on us and walked back over to the school together, blitzed out of our heads, and walked over the church fence, which was all bent back to the ground by all the other pot smokers walkin through it so that by now you could just walk right over it, and we walked through the senior parking lot full of pricey cars to the front entrance of the high school. The entire school watched us from their classroom windows cause the classroom windows all looked out onto the parking lot. I got paranoid. Everyone was watching us.

Wait, *were* they watching us? Yes. Everyone is watching us. Shit, does that matter?

Fuck it.

Then Ollie took off to, well, wherever... back to the projects maybe, and I walked inside, strolled by the cafeteria and through the large hallways to room 405, my Earth Science class. This should be fun, I thought. Earth Science while fucked the fuck up.

Class had started twenty-five minutes ago. I was wearing a big puffy jacket and designer jeans with a hoodie over my head to cover my bloodshot eyes. I walked in and the entire class stopped. I hadn't been to *that* class in like, three months. The entire room filled with skunk. I smoked that good shit I guess. But nobody gave a fuck about that good shit, they just shook their heads with disapproval. This kid has *really* fallen off the deep end. That's what I can imagine was going through everyone's head.

Ms. Lubel, our butch, blonde, lesbian teacher came up to me and sniffed my coat in front of everyone. I felt mortified. I didn't even *need* to be there, she was lucky I showed up to her class, I'll just leave… but it was too late. She squeezed my jacket, lifted me up outa my seat and dragged me out of class.

"What? I'm in trouble for smoking a cigarette?!"

She smiled a smile that wasn't really a smile, but a look of 'this kid needs help'.

"That's not a cigarette." She said without even looking at me.

Well who the fuck did she think she was embarrassing me like that in front of the whole class?

Bitch.

Lesbian.

Fuck!

Click.

The door was locked. I was inside the principal's office. The door opened and Mr. Brickell walked in shaking his head. He remembered when I was a cute cuddly kid. Now look at me. He shook his head with a genuine disappointment. "What's happened to you?" He asked with sincerity... and a note of respectful awe.

"Nothing. I was just smoking a cigarette."

"I'm suspending you. Your mom will be here in a few minutes to pick you up." And then he closed the door on me. I was blasted out of my mind staring out the window waiting for my mom's car to show up. I felt terrible. Nobody understood me. And then... My mom pulled up. It had been months since she and I had spoken more than a few sentences. I saw her park her red Mercedes station wagon and walk through the front doors of the high school and I heard her heels clickity clacking on the hallway floors as my heart pounded with grief.

Tick tock. I waited and waited and BOOM! The door opened. There she was. Time to leave. We drove in silence.

Those five minutes felt like forever. I got out of the car before the car had fully stopped moving and ran up the stairs to my room. I couldn't even look at her face I was so shitty feeling. I jumped in my bed trying to think what my excuse would be. But I had no excuse. I was fucked. The house was a still mist of shame.

My mom finally opened the door at around 6PM that night and sat on the edge of my bed. I made no eye contact with her. There was nothing I could say to explain.

"How long has this been going on?" She asked me softly.

I told her I only smoked on the weekends.

"What drugs are you on? Is it just marijuana?"

"Yeah mom. Of course it's just pot, and only sometimes I swear. I'll slow down with it I promise." She probably still thought I was an alcoholic...

And then shit. I heard my dad downstairs. She probably timed it like that. Suitcase down, coat off, footsteps up the stairs. His footsteps grew nearer and nearer and nearer and more powerful and slower and slower until...

The door opened.

I had never seen my dad look so upset. But upset to him came off as more disgusted, more of a look of, 'I tried, and I failed'. He couldn't even open his mouth. I mean what was there to say? I was a mess.

"You need some help." And then he stood there, searching for the words to help me, to make me better, to fix the family, to soothe my mom... but I guess he couldn't find anything to say so he slammed the door shut and left.

I felt like I crushed his heart. I knew I was tearing the family to shreds. My brother was too scared to even walk by my room anymore for fear I'd flip out. My head sunk in. My eyesight bled. I was sick and everyone knew it. I agreed to go to substance abuse counseling, but on my first session I convinced the therapist I was only experimenting... truth was I had done every drug under the sun and I was only fourteen. My parents decided maybe public school wasn't right for me, so we shopped around to private schools to see if I could get back in and finish ninth grade, but we never made it that far.

Then came a very dark night, the night my dad found my knife. Now, it's not the knife so to speak, but what happened after he found it.

"What's this?" He said as he walked into my room with my knife in his hand to find me searching for that knife no longer in its hiding spot.

"That's my fucking knife give it back!" And I rushed my dad and pushed him. What had I just done? Who am I? It's too late now. Just keep going. But go where? My dad looked at me, and with the heaviest words he could deliver:

"You're not my son." And he tried walking away from me, but I spewed venom at his back, horrible words to let him know how much I hated it all. I was sick of life. It had been fourteen grueling years of depression and I was ready to leave the planet.

"FUCKING FAGGOT." I said that. To my dad. "FAT FUCKING ITALIAN FAGGOT." I said that too. My dad's not even fat. My mom started crying. My dad walked away. "KIKE BITCH." I said that to my mom. I said it and I felt it and it felt wrong but I couldn't back down. I had to show how deep my wounds really were.

"But you're Jewish too!" My brother said from the kitchen counter, hiding from me, next to my mom.

"FUCK!!!!!!!" And I went back to my room and blasted Eminem. Eminem was the only thing in life that made me happy. But I wasn't happy. I was scared. I was scared of myself. I had to get away. I don't know where. But I knew I had to get away… So I woke up later that night and stuffed my bed and called a cab.

I took all the money I had stolen in the last week from my mom's purse and my dad's drawer and called my friend Levin, that kid I almost killed with his doorknob. He was a rich kid from Old Westbury who had no rules to abide by, and I told him I was coming to get him in a cab.

I bypassed the alarm system, popped the garage door open a sliver, and rolled underneath it to the outside of the house.

I ran down the long ass driveway and got in the cab.

The driver asked me where I wanted to go. I gave him Levin's address and we picked him up and he got in with a bunch of weed and Corona and money. He told the driver he wanted to go get a motel and an escort.

Silence.

"A hooker?" I asked him.

"Well... an escort", Levin said as he handed me the cut out girl from the yellow pages. He had obviously thought this through.

So we went to the Gold Coast Inn. Levin paid for the motel and the escort, and in exchange the cab driver put the room in his name, and agreed to let Levin pay for him to fuck the hooker too. That was the arrangement.

I sat at a shitty desk in the room waiting for the hooker to show up with a twenty-two ounce of Corona and joint and stared at the wall.

KNOCK KNOCK.

A pimp and hooker showed up at the door. I sat and watching it from the desk in a blurry haze. Money was exchanged, the pimp left, the girl stayed. She walked in. It was awkward at first... she was maybe in her late thirties, early forties, dyed red hair, Brazilian... much different looking than the cutout from the yellow pages that Levin had showed us.

Levin looked like he might blow his load just from her walkin in. His eyes were like, you know, a little fuckin kid as she sat next to him. He put his hand on her thigh and started makin out with her like he'd done it a million times before. Fuckin weird from where I was sittin, which was like five feet away. Jason, the cab driver, paced around and waited for his turn.

I had to watch Levin take off his clothes, not like I wanna watch this hairy ass Persian kid get naked, oh right, he was Persian, anyway it was hard not to look cause I was in a small motel room with two dudes and a hooker and a pimp outside, you know? There weren't many other places to look. So in the grossest fashion possible, they had sex. But like that uncomfortable odd bizarre forced sex, not that he raped her or anything, it was just that kinda sex where you know that's what's supposed to happen, sex, and so you do it even though the timing is all fuckin weird an shit.

So he fucked her, or she fucked him, I dunno, who gives a shit… There was insertion for all I know, and it all happened five feet away from me while I was sitting in my chair smoking my second joint and finishing the 22oz of Corona while Jason sat on the opposite side of the bed. He sat with his back turned, as if that gave them more privacy.

So Levin came, or finished makin whatever nasty noises he was makin, and then she looked at Jason. So Jason took off *his* clothes and *he* fucked her. I watched *that* too for a sec. What the fuck was I supposed to do? So I switched directions and started watching the TV but the screen was all staticky. I watched that small broken TV that was bolted to the top corner of the shit-ass motel room to try and block out the moans and grunts coming from the bed five feet behind me.

It was 4AM and I kept staring at my pager, oh right, I had a pager, hoping to God that it wouldn't start buzzing. The pager I had was this red pager with a black transparent case giving it a black raspberry kinda look. I liked that pager. It was a good color at least. I had to listen to

Jason finish up too… And then you know what happened? Before the hooker… I mean escort… Before the Brazilian thirty-five or thirty-six-year-old escort left, she stood before me.

I turned to her.

"A young little bit, no?"

"Oh… No… I'm not… Doing it. It's just for them."

She was waiting and didn't seem like she was on her way out. There were three dudes in the motel and as far as she was concerned she was fucking each and every one of us…. But not only was I fourteen, I looked twelve. And I was nervous as fuck.

"No… No thank you."

"Okay, maybe when older you are."

And she left.

I looked at Levin through a hazy vision. A 22oz and two joints will do that to a hundred pound ninth grade dropout.

"Should we buy some whippits?" I asked.

Oh right, money was never in question when Levin was around if you didn't figure that out. He lived in a gated estate that was comprised of like three houses and twenty million acres of property. It was a Tuesday night. He was supposed to be in school in three hours, but not me, I had no school.

BUT THEN

bZZZZZZZZZZZZ

Shit. It was my pager. I looked at the number. Fuck. It was my mom.

"Uhhh… Jason, you gotta take me home."

So he snuck us out cause the motel clerk had no idea there was anyone other than Jason there, any kids there for that matter. The whole situation looked pretty bizarre to be frank. But first we had to pay the pimp *again*, I thought we had already done that, but he was still there askin for money, so Levin gave Jason a few hundred more dollars for the hooker and Jason gave it to the pimp and the hooker smiled as if to say 'well… that was interesting' and then they both left.

"Just turn your lights off", I told Jason as we got to The Pines. "Don't pull into the driveway." As if he didn't already know the deal. But it was too late. All the lights in the kitchen were on. The front door opened. My mom stood at the top of the wooden stairs that led to the house. She was in her bathrobe. She looked like… Fuck, well she didn't look good. She was sobbing. I was clearly a fuckup, even more so than I was earlier that night. For the rest of the early morning she slept in front of the front door with blankets over her so that I couldn't leave again. Pretty heartbreaking really. My tenure as a loser-turned-popular-turned-bad-boy pothead-turned scumbag was about to come to an abrupt end. The last day was approaching. The last day I'd ever be home ever again.

It all started the next morning…

CHAPTER 11

NO MORE GREG

It was 8AM. My mom was sitting on the edge of my bed and my dad was standing over me in his work clothes, a suit and tie.

"Greg." My mom whispered to me while I was half asleep. "Greg."

I was barely awake when I finally opened my eyes and delivered my last but pathetically weak apology:

"I'm sorry about last night."

My mom looked at me and said softly, "You cannot live here any longer. We're taking you to a treatment center."

HUH?! WHAT??? For smoking pot and taking ecstasy and snorting special K in the school bathroom and cutting class and dropping out of ninth grade and eating mushrooms up and down the hallways and takin speed in the gym locker room with random druggies and stealing sweaters and buying hookers and robbing houses and getting thrown outa class and getting suspended and threatening the family and callin my mom a kike and pushing my dad and running away in the middle of the night and earning the nickname 'Crackhead Cayea' and getting banned from all the houses on Long Island?????!!!!

But that's not what I said, shit, I mean, I wasn't about to tell em *all* that- they'd never understand. But whatever, I had nothing left here to live for anyway. I just asked:

"Where?"

"It's called Hazelden, and it's in Minnesota." My mom said. Then I looked at my dad. He looked like he might cry. He felt like a failure. He didn't say that, but I saw it.

"Wait, WHAT? A different state?! YOU'RE SENDING ME TO MINNESOTA????? What in the FUCK is wrong with you people??? IT WAS JUST POT!" ...And all those other things I never told you about.

I had no idea what a humungous thing this was all turnin out to be. I mean I didn't know it at the time, but Hazelden wasn't just *some rehab...* it was a *serious* fuckin rehab. IN FUCKIN MINNESOTA!

"It's only thirty days. You'll be back before summer."

It was May 3rd. I guess summer isn't *that* far away, I thought to myself. "We don't know what else to do." My mom finished off.

Silence.

"You'll be home by summer." She re-affirmed.

But that sentence ricocheted against my skull. I didn't react how you think I might've cause I had no more fight in me. The struggle felt like it might be over finally. I had given up. So all I said was:

"Can I have some friends over tonight to say bye? I'll stay here the whole night. Just a few of my friends over to say goodbye, that's it, I promise."

I'd never seen such a strong stare down between my mom and dad. It looked like they were playin tug of war in their heads but so that only their spirits could feel the conflict. It was like, well, if we say no, he might flip his lid, but if we say yes, he might destroy the house. After what felt like five million school years, my mom looked at me and with a sad face, said:

"Okay."

It was my farewell present.

My last farewell present for a very long time... cause I was NOT home by summer. In fact, I never came home ever again...

They agreed to allow me to have a *few friends* over, but the night turned into a massive open house party. Kids walked around making out in every room of my parent's house, cigarettes were being smoked all over, there were strangers in the basement holding cardboard boxes of beer, wannabe thugs in the kitchen, drugs everywhere... my mom and dad and brother hid themselves in my parent's room with the door shut as tight as it could seal. It was the fitting farewell salute to the legendary fuck-up I had become I guess.

And where was I?

I locked myself in my bathroom in my room while all this was goin on outside in the house and lied down in my bathtub with a forty-ounce of malt liquor. Marks sat next to me on the toilet, also drinking a bottle of malt liquor. Next to the sink, an-almost-empty-bag of mushrooms and remnants of the last of the ecstasy, which was now completely gone. A bong, of course, sat on the bathroom tiled floor with a half smoked bowl of pot still in it.

Marks took a hit, his eyes rolling all over his head.

"Am I too high?" I asked him.

"Not at all. I'm just as high as you and I'm perfect."

Cause "I feel too high." I said.

"We did a lot of drugs.

"I know, is that bad?

"I love you." Marks said.

"I love you too. Is that bad? Are we too high?"

"Everything is just the way it should be right now." He told me.

"I'm sad."

"It's only thirty days. You'll be back before camp."

"Should we do more K?" I asked.

"Yeah." He replied.

Marks took out a small vile of powder from his cool-enough-to-wear-to-a-party sweatpants pocket and untwisted the small lid. He grabbed a plastic pen cap from a Bic pen that rested on the bathroom sink counter and scooped up as much special K as he could fit on the end of the pen cap and held it up to his nose.

"I'm rolling really hard. I don't even feel the mushrooms." I confided.

"Yes you do. It's just blended in so well you don't notice."

He handed me the vile of special K after he snorted it all off the pen cap. I felt my body nearly give out. I was about to die. "I can't do any more." I told him.

"Yes you can. It's your last night. Do it."

So I dipped the pen cap in the vile of powder and stared at it. It took all my will power to sniff the drugs off the cap. Then something happened. Something so vivid I can't but shake the horridness from my memory after all these years. My body and soul separated. I stared at my lifeless body from my soul, which was now floating in the top corner of the bathroom. My body went limp, but my soul was astute and aware. My soul looked down at my body. He was talking to me. *I* was talking to me. My spiritual being was criticizing my physical life.

"Look at you dude" my soul said.

"What?" I tried to talk back.

"You're too high." Said my soul.

"Am I?"

Marks looked at me, "Who are you talking to?" But my soul continued:

"This is why you are the way you are."

"Am I too high?" I asked my soul politely.

"You're nothing." My soul said back.

Tears formed.

"Are you okay? Who are you talking to? Why are you crying?" Marks was starting to bug out. He kneeled down next to the tub and put his hand on my body's shoulder and told me to

"Take another bump."

Then the doorknob started jiggling rigorously.

Marks hid the vile of powder and shoved it back in his sweatpants pocket, "WHO IS IT?"

Someone screamed, "OPEN THE FUCKING DOOR!" It was havoc.

Marks slowly unlocked the bathroom door. The sounds and lights and movement of a party shone through the sliver of openness.

It was Robby Deltorro, "Dude your mom is banging on the door!"

Robby is here, I thought. I'm so glad it all worked out. But where is Delson? What's going on again?

Robby looked at Marks and I... Me laying in the tub and Marks sprawled on the floor next to me with his forty, and said "What the fuck are you two doing?"

My soul came back to my body: "Huh? My mom?"

"GET THE FUCK UP DUDE! SHE'S BANGING ON YOUR DOOR! DO YOU NOT HEAR ME?" Maybe he was angry with me for not makin him as popular as I was.

The sounds were off in my head. "GREG!" My sight was blurry. I wasn't sure what was happening. My mom? I felt so bad for my mom. "GET THE FUCK UP CAYEA!" I swayed back and forth from the bathtub as I tried to stand. I was floating in my tub. I floated out the door. I floated to my mom. My eyes were shut. A terrified voice penetrated my halo. Was she crying?

"Greg"? But she sounded like she was worried. There's nothing to fear mom. She cried. I floated and swayed and slept as I stood.

My soul just looked down at the mess and shook its head sadly.

Then everything went black.

My eyes opened. My room was clear. My head wasn't. My mom and dad stood above me. I was in my bed. The night was over. The morning was here. My bags had already been packed. There was a car in the driveway. We were going to Minnesota. I found my CD player and took one CD, The Slim Shady LP by Eminem. I found my orange button down plaid shirt I had stolen from Barneys. I put on my worn out Mossimo baseball hat and cocked it to the side. I put my headphones on. I followed my Dad. He didn't speak to me, not out loud at least, but there was an entire novel between his ears that screamed silently, and the words floating in his head pierced right through my false confidence.

Eminem already blared his anger into my eardrum. I was safe with my headphones on. I was with someone I could relate to. Nothing ever made sense, and it never would. Rehab was the same as non-rehab. Maybe there'll be some hot rehab chicks there. My heart grew hopeful. I don't remember seeing my brother on my way out. I don't remember seeing Carolyn, my black mom, she mighta been crying in her room. I had made her sad too. Life was dumb. Anyway I followed the stairway downstairs and then downstairs again to the basement and out the door and out the garage and into a black car. My mom sat next to me with pain in her pupils.

"You'll be back by summer", she told me through Eminem's voice. But I wasn't interested. Who cares? My dad got in and shut the door, and off I went.

CHAPTER 12

REHAB NUMBER ONE

We landed in Minnesota and hopped in a cab and got to a pristine brick building with shiny glass doors and walked inside then down some hallway to a square-shaped room with a buncha nurses behind a hospital-like counter in the center of the room. But none of that mattered. All that mattered was there was nothing but Eminem in my ears and sadness in my gut as I looked around the facility tryin to figure out my life. I was spooked. It looked like a psych ward. I felt really lost and scared.

There was one hallway with a buncha doors on both sides of the walls. I wonder if that's where I'm going? Then one of the doors in that hallway opened and some strung out dude wearing a white bathrobe thingy and a cigarette hanging from his mouth with red around his eyes walked passed me. He didn't look at me, or my mom and dad. Or the nurses. I watched him walk across the square-shaped room to a sliding glass door, which led to a small wooden picnic table that was outside, like it had no roof, but you were still stuck between four walls. It was a tiny smoking area.

Anyway, he sat down and lit his cigarette. If there was one thing I know it was that I wasn't like *that* dude. So I wonder why I'm here? Whatever who cares. Where the rehab chicks at anyway?

The only time going tick tock was in my head. I had no idea what was happenin outside my mind, but I saw a bench against the back wall of the square-shaped room so I walked over to that bench and sat my ass down still listening to Eminem. The album was on repeat, *Still Don't Give A Fuck* was blaring loud in my ear.

My parents had my bag. One bag, my orange backpack. I love orange. It's my favorite color. I hope that's not some universe shit tellin me I'ma end up in prison one day. Whatever, they were over at the nurse station thingy in the middle of the room for like thirty minutes or whatever doing whatever they were doin, checking me into the joint and getting rid of me basically. I stared at everything and let my life play out in my head like a dream sequence. I guess this ain't so bad. No more choices. I can just do what I'm told. But what if I don't wanna do it? Fuck that they can all go fuck themselves, I'm not doin this shit. Fuck if it is I know that I'm not doin, but I still ain't fuckin doin it. I was mad as hell. Or maybe it was Eminem that was mad as hell. Maybe we were both mad as hell.

I mean I was nothing like these people, at least not like that one dude in the white robe out there smokin his cigarette, he's the only person I saw anyway so it's not like I had a lot to judge off of. But I really started thinkin my parents made a huge mistake, or maybe I was fucked in the head like I thought I was earlier in the day, or maybe I was hallucinating. Is this really happening? Where's that fuckin soul when I need him? I don't even know what I'm talkin about.

My mom looked a mile away even though she was only ten feet from where I sat. They looked back at me, my mom and dad did, and said "This is for the best Greg" or some shit like that. Actually they didn't say that with their voice, it's what they said with their eyes. I could hear it through the silence. But no, they were wrong. I thought they were right this morning, that maybe I did have a problem, but alas I concluded there was no way I belonged at this place. Then they finished up with the nurses and looked at me and all they could say was "We love you" with a glance of the eyes, or maybe they said it out loud, I can't remember. But they finished the paperwork shit and bid me farewell.

Yeah yeah, rehab, I get it, cool. Bye to you too. It wasn't a dramatic goodbye or anything. I saw them waving. Waving? Oh right. Rehab. I'm in rehab. I saw my parents walking. Walking? Oh right.

They were going home. I was staying. This was my new home. It was just me and Eminem on the bench. Then this nurse came up to me and she took away my headphones. Fine. Eminem is gone now too. Now it's just me and my head and my thoughts and my past. She asked me:

"Do you smoke?"

At the time I only smoked like two or three cigarettes a day, mostly to look cool in fronta people but I had a pack of cigarettes with me, and so I said, "yeah."

"Do you want a cigarette first?"

I was only fourteen. She wanted to know if I wanted a cigarette. Sure. That's kinda weird but I nodded and off she sent me to where the dude in the white robe sat. I opened the sliding glass door and sat down. I searched for my pack of cigarettes in my baggy jeans.

"Need a smoke?"

But I found my pack. Before I could find my lighter he lit my cigarette for me. We sat and smoked for a moment before he asked me, "What's your D.O.C.?"

"Huh?"

"Your poison."

"What do you mean?"

"Your drug of choice."

"Oh… uhh… maybe ecstasy? You?"

He showed me his arm, but I had already noticed. He told me to feel his veins: "Feel this" and took my hand and placed it over the inside of his elbow, where your veins are, and let my fingers touch his skin. But his skin was not soft. His veins felt like they were frozen.

"Like rope", he said to me. "They're like rope. That's what heroin does to you. You do heroin?"

"No I don't"

"Good."

It was like he was coaching me through life as a drug addict.

I asked him "How long you been here?"

"Two days. But this is my third time here. So I know the deal."

"What *is* the deal anyway?"

"Three or so days here, in detox, then they move you to the other side and you actually get sheets and pillow cases and good food. It's not bad. But the first few days fuckin suck. At least you don't have to detox like I do. Detoxin ain't fun" as he got up and opened the sliding glass door and moped on back to his room with his robe dragging across the carpeted floor.

I put out my cigarette and followed his lead. I was lightheaded from the nicotine after only three drags. The nurse took me down that hallway I had a feeling they were gonna take me to and opened the door to a room where everything was plastic, like the junkie dude just told me. Is junkie a bad word? I dunno I felt bad for thinkin he was a junkie. Anyway the pillows, the bed, the sheets... all plastic. There was no shower curtain either cause the nurse said sometimes people try and hang emselves in the shower using the curtains to make a noose. They took away my q-tips too so I couldn't puncture my eardrums.

"Someone punctured their eardrums?"

"Only takes one to spoil it for the bunch."

What a cliché that was. But still it intrigued me.

"On purpose they did that?"

"Not as strange as it sounds." The nurse said as she finished goin through my bag.

So yeah, I spent three days there without Q-tips. In fact, they never gave em back I don't think. Every three or four hours they took my blood. Blood drawn every three hours, even in the middle of the night. I would wake up at three in the morning and see the nurse. Then the needle. Then my blood. Then my door closing. Then it was morning, but it wasn't bad, cause I was so sleepy all the time, especially when they took my blood. Then the nurse came back for more blood. They gave me nothin but pencils and cigarettes for those three days. I don't even remember eating. I never had signs of withdrawal, but the nurse told my parents I had jitters throughout the night for all three days. I wonder what Marks and Robby and Wick and JD and the girls back home must be thinking? I was consoled with the fantasy that my legendary status was probably iconic by now. I wondered where Delson's mom sent him, cause he got sent away just like me, but I bet he was somewhere terrible, like in the middle of the pacific cause his parents *really* over-reacted about *everything*... Especially those bunk checks he wrote from his dad's account. He was writin these eight-hundred-dollar checks from his dad's checking account and cashin em in every week and we were stayin at this fancy hotel in Roslyn, called The Claremont, and throwin all these parties full of whipped cream and trashy chicks and scummy dudes and ecstasy and, well, you know, all the stuff that the cool kids did. Cause we were the cool kids now.

I must be a hero, I thought. I bet everyone is talking about me. I bet I am a legend. I felt powerful. I couldn't wait to get to the other side and meet some rehab chicks. I bet they are so hot and trashy and lonely and just how I am. There was no better place to meet the love of my life than in rehab. That much I was sure of. I made it my goal to find a rehab girlfriend that understood me and that would run away with me and live with me forever, with or without drugs. I wasn't so sure I needed the drugs as bad as I needed a girl to run away with. That was more exciting to imagine. I had all these dreams of a better life. Life on the run.

Then I finished detox and was taken to the other side of the building, just like the junkie dude said. So far he was right on point.

The other side of Hazelden felt like an Aspen lodge. The rooms were cozy with four beds each next to a desk. And the beds had sheets and pillows with pillowcases made of cloth, so that was good. Then there was this sliding-glass door that looked like you could open it and go hang outside in the peaceful looking park-like yard outside the window, but you couldn't. The doors didn't open. They were locked.

The first friend I made was Sargon. Sargon was my roommate who claimed to be a witch. He practiced this religion called Wicca and spent time with these cards called tarot cards and would do these readings every night. He wore black eyeliner, black nail polish, and had long stringy black hair. He looked at peace, yet there was something dark and ominous about his outlook on life. I liked it. I watched him practice his witchcraft stuff every day and pray to the Goddess, that was like, you know, the God of Wicca, every evening before lights were out. He gave everyone in the rehab tarot card readings and said his psychic powers were gifts that he was given by the Goddess. I thought he was crazy, so this one time, I asked him to prove his powers.

"Pick a number between one and a hundred and paint the number in your mind as big and as bright as you can", he told me. "Now project it to me in your mind."

Okay lunatic.

So I did. I picked some weird two-digit number and visualized it and he guessed it right on his first try. Maybe God *is* real? I dunno but that was the beginning of my spirituality. It became a hobby of mine to test his magic. I told him to do something else. He laughed. I begged. He said:

"Fine, in ten seconds someone will walk into this room. Start counting down."

10, 9, 8, 7, 6, 5, 4, 3, 2, 1... Then the door opened.

"LIGHTS OUT GUYS!" The light switch flipped down, the door closed behind the staff member dude and all was dark. I never questioned him again. Shit was dope. Sargon is the reason I still believe in everything. After meeting him, I knew anything and everything was possible. Maybe I should become a witch like him? Hmm... I'll think about it.

Anyway that was my first night there, in that side of the rehab, and for some reason I pulled out a sheet of paper and wrote a poem. I had never written a poem before. I never read anything. I hated any and all educational anything. I wasn't a fan of literature. I have no idea what in the world possessed me to write a poem, but it was almost as if it was the only thing for me to do. I had to write it. With no drugs or girls, I needed something. So I wrote poetry. All Sargon had was Wicca. All Stevens, my other roommate, all he had was cuttin his wrists, dude kept cutting himself. All Jeff, my other and final roommate, all he had was bein a fucking dickhead. Man was he a *fucking* dick-fucking-head. He was all short and his face was always red and he wasn't a bad looking guy I just think he was pissed he wasn't the *best* looking guy. He was always talkin about pussy. Always tellin us how much pussy he got. But he was also always tellin us he'd beat the shit outa whoever blah blah blah and he was, you know, kinda short. So I think he was just mad about that. I could be wrong.

Anyway, so I just kept writin poems.

The days were all the same: Wake up early. Do chores. Smoke break. Breakfast. Smoke break. Lecture. Lunch. Group. Recreation time. Shower. Dinner. Chores. Spades. Smoke break. Bed. Finally, I found what I was looking for, a girl.

I met Lacey during one of our ten million smoke breaks. She was a nineteen-year-old heroin addicted hippie with dirty blonde hair from Indiana and a scholarship or somethin to Purdue University. She had a petite figure and slightly sunken in eyes. We spent hours tellin each other stories in the smoke room... I did this, well I did *that*, well listen to THIS, okay now check this out... I had to make her love me and run away with me. I had to plan a life that was a fairy tale that could actually happen.

I drew pictures of what fairy tale life looked like. Then I wrote poems about it. There would be forests and fluffy grass and big trees and peaceful sheep. Nobody but us would live there other than the wild horses roaming free. We'd have cigarettes, a trailer, there'd be birds and plenty of sex—not that I knew what sex actually felt like... but it would most certainly be there. Nothing but love would surround us. There weren't even any drugs involved. There was no need for drugs if I had what I needed, which is why I took the drugs in the first place, to find that fairy tale land.

I did everything for Lacey. When I knew I wanted her there was nothing that would stop me from getting her. I wrote her love letters without ever professing my love, cause I knew I couldn't tell her our future just yet. That much I knew. I'd keep it a secret and surprise her one day. In my head, the relationship had already started. I even told all the guys that she was kinda my girlfriend.

I was the youngest patient there by a long haul, and I always spiked my hair up and wore that bright orange expensive shirt that I had stolen from Barneys and talked with a thick New York accent, so my nickname quickly became New York and I quickly became a rehab favorite amongst the older dudes. They all thought I was cool. And now I had Lacey. I was really enjoying myself. Rehab was kinda cool.

This one day I really wanted to open those sliding glass doors and frolic in the park-like grass outside my room. So I figured out that there were two magnetic strips, one attached to the door, the other to the wall, and as soon as the door opened the magnetic strips were pulled apart and it would sound the alarm.

So I fixed that fairly easily by ripping off the magnetic strip from the door, which was kinda hard cause I had to pry it off with homemade tools without the magnetic strips separating during each tug and sounding the alarm… but finally I did it and got my hands on some duct tape and taped the two magnetic strips together so the door was now free to open and close without the alarm going off. Now, the door didn't open. It was screwed shut… so that was the next task at hand. Unscrew the door so it'll open. Easy. I used a dime that I found. Done.

Every afternoon during rec time I snuck out of the room and climbed up on the roof to the second story of the building, where Lacey's room was… I taught her how to rig the alarm too… and we would meet to smoke cigarettes with each other on the roof. It was a glimpse of what true freedom might actually feel like, and it was glorious.

When I got back to the room I told the guys I made out with her. I lied cause I had to. If I didn't make out with her, then what the fuck did I rig the alarm for and sneak up to her room for every day? Was I a pussy? Did I just wanna smoke cigarettes with her? If that were the case, why didn't I just do that in the smoking lounge like I did anyway every two hours between scheduled rehab activities? Well… That's why I lied. I wasn't a pussy. I was just… you know, nervous.

I hadn't made out with her *yet*… but I mean, she was my future hippie runaway wife. What was I supposed to do? Lie about *that*? Lacey was mine. She made me happy and nobody better fuck that up.

One day she asked me, "Did you tell anyone that we were hooking up?"

"Huh? Why would I do that?"

"Cause someone told me that you told him we'd been hooking up."

"Oh."

"We're not."

"We're not what?"

"Hooking up. You and I. We're not together."

I knew she didn't mean that. I knew she loved me. She was just nineteen and I was fourteen. It was just a hard justification for her to make to herself and I could understand that. So I just played it off like it was no big deal.

I wrote her more letters but she responded less and less.

The staff saw what was going on and Lacey and I were placed on FOCUS. Focus meant we couldn't talk to each other, sit next to each other, or even be seen in the same room as each other. Relationships were a no-no. But I was happy at first. At least now everyone will know I was telling the truth. That we *were* together and we *were* in a relationship. I mean, why would they put us on Focus if we weren't? We had been together for nearly ten days before being placed on Focus and nothing coulda made me happier.

But after three-and-a-half weeks she had finished the program, cause she had gotten there before me… But our love wasn't yet written in the stone I wanted it written in before she left. In fact, I wasn't quite sure how we were supposed to run away and live together once she went back to Indiana. I had to talk to her. I pled with the counselors to take Lacey and I off Focus.

"I can't talk to my friend for TWO weeks??!? WHY?!"

"You've been on Focus for three days Greg."

"YOU'RE A FUCKING LIAR! YOU'RE A PIECE OF FUCKING SHIT!" I blurted.

Oh no. It happened again. I lost my cool. That wasn't that bad though, right? I mean—yeah, that wasn't that bad. And I was right anyhow, I mean, three days? Three days was two weeks in rehab years. But *then* I got word that she and Jeff… my dickhead roommate I told you about, I got word they made out with each other.

WWWHHHHHHHAAAATTTTTTT????!!!?!??!?!?!?

I asked her if it was true. She said no. I confronted him, who mind you could have beaten the living shit out of me. I mean anyone coulda beaten the livin shit outa me, I think, I was like ten years younger than all the other dudes there. But I asked him:

"Dude. What the fuck?"

He told me she and I were not together and she was the one that kissed him.

WWWHHHHHHHAAAATTTTTTT????!!!?!??!?!?!?

So I broke our Focus and ran over to Lacey in the smoking lounge.

"YOU FUCKING BITCH"

Shit. Everyone heard that. The counselors were livid. Lacey was getting really pissed. I was fucking angry. What a dumb bitch.

Then the day came when she and Jeff were officially together, out in the open, even though she lied to me every time I confronted her. Jeff didn't give a shit. But on her last day I *had* to make a move. So I wrote another fuckin letter professing my love.

She surprisingly responded and wrote me back and told me she cared for me too, but that she was not in love with me. She loved me, but she made it clear she was not *in* love with me.

Well, that just wouldn't fly.

So I found her and I smiled. She smiled. I grabbed her and threw her on my back, piggy-back style, not rape-style… and I ran with her up and down the hallway as the counselors were having their Monday morning meeting. They all looked at us breaking Focus cause we weren't supposed to even be in the same room as each other. I paraded up and down the hallway with her on my back in front of the weekly counselor meeting anyway and stared them all in the eyes to let em all know, the counselors that is, to let em all know how fuckin *stupid* they all were. It was also my last attempt to show Lacey how much fun we could have with each other.

"Greg... put me down." She said affirmatively.

So I did. She left later that day and I knew my plans were ruined.

Summer camp was just around the corner. Life was going to be good again I guess. I would return home a complete legend and my stature would speak for itself. Only a few days left and my life would be better than it had ever been.

But Lacey, I just wanted Lacey. Fuck Lacey. No, I love her. Do I? I was fuckin tired. I need a nap.

On the day of my scheduled release, I was ambushed by my parents and my counselor in this small room, it came outa nowhere. I wasn't expectin to see them all teary eyed and shit like they were. Nobody had been too pleased with my performance at the rehab I guess. I mean, the joint was a fuckin joke. So what *they* said was that I was not taking my recovery seriously. Then my counselor did this thing where he made me list off all the drugs I had done in front of my parents. It was like, uhh, why? But so he kept tellin me to tell em everything. So I was just like okay:

"Weed, forties, shrooms, ecstasy, painkillers—well, only sometimes painkillers, ummm speed I guess, some special K—you know, that cat tranquilizer? Or was it horse tranquilizer? Whatever—That stuff", I told them. "And umm, well, I think that's it. I never did like coke or anything." I said with excitement, like I should be given a medal. But my counselor looked at me as if to say 'Look at your parent's Greg'. So I looked at my dad. He was blank. But he was sad blank, like so sad he went blank. But I don't know why? I mean, they *knew* I was on drugs, right? I looked at my mom and she was *balling* her eyes out. As if this was all some big surprise.

Then my counselor suggested another program with a bit more 'structure' to help me follow the rules.

So they made me board this small plane. I didn't really have anywhere to go, so when they brought me to the airport and I walked through security, I just... well, got to the plane that said Lafayette, Louisiana and boarded it.

And that's how I got to this town called Opelousas in southern-as-fuck

Louisiana. It was supposed to be a *really* good rehab full of *amazing* counselors and all this shit. But the place wasn't so nice... Bad as life was, it was nowhere *near* as bad as it was going to get.

CHAPTER 13

THEY FOUND OUT I WAS A JEW

I landed in Lafayette Louisiana at a small airport with Southern twang all around me. Some Asian kid named Jack met me in the baggage claim section while a white van waited for me outside.

Jack told me he had been there for six months. He was from New York also. He was like some trusted rehab kid I guess that they sent in to retrieve me from the small shitty airport. Anyway, he was from New York, and I was from New York, that's about all we had in common. I still only had one bag, my orange backpack, and I didn't check it or anything, so off we went to the white van that was waiting for me outside.

I wondered what everyone back home was doin… I felt like I might break down and freak out. But what good would that do? Whatever, every new rehab I go to is securing my iconic stature in even more iron-clad steel. Just keep your mind right Greg, keep cool. So I fake-told myself, 'Eh, whatever. New rehab chicks. Let's go.'

So like I said, Jack took me outside the baggage claim area to that white van that was waiting for me in the arrival section of the pickup lane, not like it was really a pickup lane, it was a road, a road outside a small shitty airport, and the door to the white van slid open and my life flashed before my eyes. It was over. My whole life was over. SNAP THE FUCK OUTA IT PUSSY! YOU ARE MAKING HISTORY! So in the white van I went.

Inside the van were two other kids, both white southern dudes with socks hiked high up to their knees and basketball sneakers and thick twangy accents. They looked kinda silly. In any fashion, we didn't really match. There could be no bigger difference in what we thought was cool. I was pretty sure I was right though, and they were wrong. Hiked up socks? Yeah right. So they were all patients at the rehab… I guess it's not that bad? I mean, if they let em out to come get me and all…

In the driver's seat was a woman named Ruthie. I liked Ruthie. She was nice:

"Hi sweet pea."

Yeah, I just liked her.

She was a Cajun woman, maybe like sixty or somethin, she looked like she'd been through a thing or two in her life. She told me to

"Shut the door sweet pea."

So I shut the door and off the institutional-lookin white van went into the rural suburbs of Lafayette.

We got to this shithole town called Opelousas. No red brick or shiny glass doors at *this* rehab. Nope, this rehab was called New Beginnings and there was dirt and wood and shitty benches painted green with splinters sticking out all over. The entire facility was outdoors, with the exception of our apartments. It looked like a broken down summer camp for drug addicts. Which is what it was.

When I walked under that 'Welcome To New Beginnings' sign that was pinned up outside the joint, there were more white southern dudes, a whole plethora of them, like another species, a buncha white wannabe gangsters smoking Newports everywhere I looked. Maybe they weren't wannabe gangsters, maybe they *were* gangsters, how the fuck should I know? All I knew is they looked like they were tryin real hard to be *something* and they looked kinda silly. Why would they try so hard to be someone they're not?

I was still fourteen when I got there in June. The bugs were so thick in the air I couldn't even open my mouth for three seconds without catchin a bug on my tongue. Everybody was around eighteen or nineteen. This one guy had third degree burns all over his body. He was from Tulsa, Oklahoma. There were no Northerners there except for the Asian kid, Jack, who grabbed me from the airport. I felt like an alien that came from North of the Mason Dixon line.

Right off the bat nobody liked me. That's why they called me Yankee. Staff took me inside some room and made me sign ten million papers. One of the papers I had to sign made me declare that I would presume everyone in the rehab was infected with HIV so I couldn't talk to the girls for longer than five minutes at a time. That was the rule. 'The Five-Minute Rule', they told me.

I looked out the window of the room with the millions of papers I was signing and wondered if my parents knew all this shit was happenin to me. Like, did they see a brochure of this place or some shit and say 'YES! THIS PLACE IS FREAKIN AWESOME!' Like how in the *fuck* did I end up here?

Then I saw the rehab chicks. They were AWESOME-lookin. Trashy and skanky and slutty lookin as fuck. It was damn near perfect. Anyway, it felt like I was walkin a plank as they showed me to my apartment. Everyone was lookin at me. Everyone stared. I wasn't one of them. I was different. I was far more different than the different I was in Minnesota. Down here felt unsafe. There was no security. It felt like I was on my own. I was alone again. Where was that fuckin soul when I needed him? He must be busy.

Inside my small bunk-looking-apartment were four small rooms and one bigger room with a kitchen. Inside each small room were two beds. Each bed took up one third of the room, which meant there was only enough room to stand up and lay down. Kind of like a prison cell. And guess who my new roommate was? Stevens.

Remember him? My roommate from Hazelden? The dude who kept cutting himself all over? The last time I saw him was back at Hazelden when we all walked back into our room after lunch and there were bloody towels poking out of his drawer. It looked like a murder scene. He had carved "Love Hurts" into his arm and was sent to a mental institution and now apparently to New Beginnings, and so he was my roommate, again.

Weird.

They put me on this chore wheel and showed me how to do all the chores. The chore wheel had all eight dudes from my apartment on this paper plate, and every day you'd spin the paper plate to see what chore you had to do. We had three inspections every day, after each meal, and it had to be SPOTLESS or else they gave you PWD hours. PWD stood for Prolonged Work Detail. They told me that's where you gotta pick up cigarette butts or gather pecans or empty out trash or spread mulch or whatever yard work needed to be done around that place.

I couldn't sleep that first night. I was depressed as fuck. I lay awake thinkin about how it all happened so quickly. Life sucked more now than it ever did. And my first morning that next morning was so bizarre I couldn't imagine doin this every day for however many months they wanted to keep me here for.

So what happened the next morning was they woke me up early as hell and made me go to this thing they called 'Morning Walk', which is where I had to walk up and down this dirt road until they thought I was awake enough. After Morning Walk they took us to some other room in some other building for 'Morning Meditation'. The shit sucked.

So I sat in Morning Meditation in my pajamas with a buncha fake white thugs while they read from this daily meditation book then they asked me to talk about it. I didn't wanna talk about that shit so damn early in the morning, or ever for that matter. Fuck. I felt like everyone was lookin at me. I think they were. Why'd they ask *me* to read that shit? Maybe cause I was new? I couldn't even remember what the fuck the passage was about so I just made some shit up. Then came the cigarette break, which was HUGE, cause it was the first cigarette of the day, and by then I was smokin a pack or so a day so cigarette number one was important. After that, they sent me back to my apartment and we all made breakfast in silence and quickly did our morning chores for inspection, but everyone was always in a bad mood in the morning so it was always all uncomfortable and shit, then we went straight to group therapy after breakfast and inspection then we went to an AA meeting then lunch then chores then inspection then another meeting then mandatory volleyball- yeah, we *had* to play volleyball. I got real good. Then dinner, chores, inspection, meeting, and since everything took place outside, I started smokin *over* a pack of Newports by *dinnertime*. I was officially a heavy smoker and I was fourteen-years-old.

I made friends with that dude who had third degree burns all over. I thought he was cool. He was a 'Blood' and had gang tattoos all over his body. In fact, all the white dudes there were 'Bloods'. I didn't know that was a thing, maybe it is and I'm racist, maybe it's not, maybe it is, I don't really give a shit. At the time, if I even SAID the word 'Slob', which is a bad word for a blood, he got real upset, which seemed kinda silly to me.

One day during chores I was singin "What if God was one of us, just a Slob like one of us", that song by Joan Osborne, I was singin it while I was sweepin the carpet to see if it would piss him off and he FLIPPED THE FUCK OUT. So I stopped singin that shit. He nearly killed me. He backed me up into this corner and stared me down and I got scared so I slapped him in the face and his face turned bright red, not from my slap, but from his anger and shit and I thought I was about to get the pulp kicked outa me but all he did was point his finger in my face and tell me I was lucky.

And so was life for about two months or so until one day…

My bunkmate Tom, some annoying-ass Midwestern kid that probably talked the most outa anyone in our bunk, more than anyone in the hemisphere maybe, anyway, he asked me this one day:

"Hey Greg, there's a lotta Jews up there in New York right?"

"Uhhh… yeah." Uh oh. Is that bad, I wondered? I started to feel weird. Then he asked me

"You're not a… a… a Jew… are you?"

The word Jew dripped outa his mouth as if it tasted like vomit. Maybe being Jewish is bad? But I mean shit, everyone in New York is Jewish… so I just said:

"Well, my mom's Jewish— but… My dad's Italian Catholic—"

"YOU'RE A JEW?!?!?!?!?!"

And that was that. I had been the cute Yankee that all the girls thought was handsome and guys thought were cool, but once word got out I was a Jew, none of them would even talk to me. Even Milton, my leather-skinned cowboy counselor with a Marlboro red eternally hangin from his mouth… not lit, just danglin always, even *he*, my *counselor* that was supposed to be helpin me or whatever, even he called me *Juden*.

Juden is German for 'Jew'.

It's what the Nazis called the Jews in the Holocaust. I don't think I heard my real name for the entire six months I was there. Everyone called me Juden.

Then one day this pickup truck wrapped in confederate flags pulled up to the rehab and two bald-headed men exited the truck. Weston and his father. Two skinheads from Lake Wales, Florida. He was like some kinda meth-head or whatever, Weston was, and so he and his dad checked him into the joint and his pops took off and Weston and I met.

"A JEW?!?!" he said. "IN HERE?!"

I said nothing for a few weeks. I was scared to do anything. It was like whatever I did made someone mad. But then one day Weston walked outa his counselor's office while I was sittin on a bench smokin a Newport waitin for the next AA meeting and he looked right at me and screamed:

"YOU!" Like an uneducated hick: "YOU, YOU FUCKIN KIKE FAGGOT JEW BASTARD!" And he marched toward me like he was gonna take a swing.

"Better do something Juden" the dude with third-degree burns and gang tattoos all over his body from Tulsa, Oklahoma said.

But he didn't have to tell me to do anything, I knew damn well what I was about to do. Kill him. I had just about enough of this fuckin bullshit. And I don't mean just rehab, but life. I was sick of it. I dropped my cigarette and walked inside.

"Where ya goin Jew?!" Weston shouted.

I'm gonna kill this fuck.

So I looked around the living area and the first thing I saw was a broom. So I grabbed the broom and walked back outside. Everyone was watching. There was a fight about to happen.

"Dude! Juden's bout to get wild on Weston's ass!" The dude with third-degree burns shouted to the rest of the rehab like it was a bit of a joke. Like what the fuck could a *Jew* do anyway?

Weston looked at my broom like it was a toy and said "Whatchyou gonna do kike? Huh? Sweep me? Sweep the dirt off your dirty Jew face?"

I was red fuckin angry and so I wound up and cocked that broom back as far as I could and I smashed that damn stick part of the broom right into his goddam fuckin face and started raging and screaming:

"YOU FUCKING—"

I cranked my arm back again then I cracked it as hard as I could again over his back and head and shoulders until he charged me and threw me on the ground. But I kept slamming the broomstick into his face even while I was on the ground again and again and again until a crowd had formed and I was makin his nose all bloody.

"Break it up Juden!" Some staff shouted and broke us up. I was still mad cause Weston was still alive. I hadn't killed him yet. Then the dude with third-degree burns said:

"Didn't know you had it in ya Juden".

Finally, I had stuck up for myself. After all these years, I had found my answer. Just slam a broom over everyone who made fun of me. It worked with Jake Stern when I flung that cock strap back at his face and

now it worked with Weston. Fighting was the answer. So I lunged at
every single person from that day forth that even mouthed the word Jew,
which happened a lot. I got into a fight pretty much every day for a
small bit of time until they all got the picture. I wasn't some fuckin
chump. I got pretty good at it actually, fightin that is.

Then came my first institutionalized birthday.

I turned fifteen on September 29th 1999. That's right about the time
Lisa from Lawrence, Massachusetts showed up in her tight black pants,
lip ring, purple hair and bright red lipstick and blew me a kiss as she
walked under the 'Welcome To New Beginnings' sign. A new goal of
mine was born:

Fuck that chick.

Make her mine and get the fuck outa here and fuck her head off.
The idea of sex made me kinda nervous. Wait, kinda? Very. Very
nervous. I was a virgin, but nobody knew that. In fact, everyone
thought I had slept with numerous girls because whenever they asked if
'Juden's got laid' I ripped into them like a wall of ignorance and carefully
described just *how* much sex I'd actually had. So yeah. I was a virgin that
had to play the role of a sexual God. Which was hard, cause I had no
idea what sex felt like. BUT I was determined to have sex with *her*, Lisa
that is, and to not just make her another imaginary notch under my
imaginary belt, cause I had started to believe my lies by that point. Am I
even wearin a belt? Anyway, *this* was the girl. I was sure of it.

True love.

I jerked off to her every night.

The next day I ripped out a piece of loose leaf paper from my
notebook and wrote her a note. The note told her how beautiful she

was and that I was determined to have her. I folded it up and slipped it to her while we were all sweeping the pavement and doing our morning chores.

Then at mandatory volleyball, we both sat out, it was a million degrees outside, so we sat under a tree, Lisa and I, not lookin at each other, as I slipped her another note I wrote her at an AA meeting. I looked at her after I gave her the note and in her full-lipped lips she mouthed the words to me:

"I want to fuck."

And she bit her bottom lip with her top teeth as she said it as if to say 'I'm comin to get you and you better fuck me like you promised you would.' That's how I interpreted it at least. She probably said that cause I had told her how skilled at everything I was in that last note I gave her and just how erotically I could truly please her.

Now she actually wanted me to do it. Shit. I didn't know how to respond so I went back to the apartment and jerked off and tried to forget about it for a moment but I couldn't. The scene replayed in my head on repeat forever and ever and ever and she won. I was beat. I was ready to do anything to have her, even though I was terrified that I didn't know what to do with her once I figured out how to get her. I could visualize how it'd all go down, but I felt like a pussy when I realized I'd have to actually do all that shit in real life. I wasn't sure I could deliver. My heart raced with anxiety just thinking about what would happen if the opportunity actually arose.

But it would never *really* happen, so I was safe. So I kept on telling her how hard I'd fuck her and how sophisticated my moves were.

But I was wrong. The opportunity *did* arise.

It was a Friday afternoon. My counselor, Milton, came up to me and said **"Juden! Git 'ere!"** So I followed him on the pathway behind the apartment to the rec center where his office was located. He brought me into an empty room with a TV and VCR and put a VHS tape in. He told me to **"Sit an watch. This where you gon be you don't git that attitude right boy. You hear me?"**

It was a 20/20 TV special on this place called Paradise Cove in the Samoan Islands. Paradise Cove was a labor camp for fuckup kids like me where they beat you and locked you in wooden boxes and duct taped your mouth shut for three days. Google it.

"THIS WHERE YOU GOIN JUDEN. ONE-MORE-THANG. ONE MORE ANYTHANG!"

Yeah... Milton was a real fuckin cowboy. I bet he didn't even know what Juden meant. Whatever, by now it was just my name, so I guess no hard feelings attached to it, I guess. I'm not sure. Actually, I hated that name. I dunno, whatever...

Later that evening I was walkin to the institutional-lookin white van and it looked like it might rain. It always rained in Opelousas. My gangster jacket was on, cause by now I was tryin real hard to be a gangster like all the other people there, especially the dude with third-degree burns all over his body, and the jacket pocket was stuffed full of Lisa notes. She and I were passing ten trillion letters a day by then and I had about half of em in my pocket.

We were gettin ready to file into the white van to go to another AA meeting in some broken down house in the ghetto in some broken-ass neighborhood that they always took us to and it was a bit cold outside, or chilly rather. It's never really 'cold' in Louisiana.

Ruthie was waitin outside the white van waitin for us to all get our asses in gear and what not so she could take us. Remember Ruthie? The woman that picked me up from the airport that I really like? Yeah, so she was waitin outside the white van for us all to get ready when she started to look chilly. Well I didn't want her to be cold or anythin, she was like sixty-five, so I gave her my jacket to warm up. I really did like her. She was always so nice. She even cooked us a Cajun gumbo after my apartment had won cleaning inspection this one day. Those damn cleanin inspections, they never stopped no matter where I was, Hazelden, now here at New Beginnings and—Wait.

FUCK.

THE LETTERS!

GIVE IT BACK! THE JACKET, GIVE IT BACK! RUTHIE GIVE ME THE FUCKIN—but I didn't say that. Just calm the fuck down Greg. Everything is fine. Maybe she won't put her hands in the pockets.

Yeah.

Pray.

Pray.

Pray.

"Juden? What're these?"

And there they were. My stack of love notes. I felt like I was lookin at my death sentence starin at those letters. This was bad. This was *real* bad. I started gettin terrified. I thought of those Samoan Islands and the duct tape.

SHIT.

Maybe she won't tell on me. She likes me. She won't do it.

I begged and begged and begged her to not tell Milton, but she said: "I'm sorry Juden. I gotta report this."

You're kiddin me. Was she kidding me? I looked at her. Nah, she was def not kidding with me. Holy fucking... FUCK! I *had* to get the fuck outa here before the weekend was over and Milton came back and found out about it. This was for sure my *'one-more-anythang'*. I had to get the fuck out. What if he *did* actually send me to that place? Oh no. Shit shit shit shit. THINK GREG, THINK! And so I made a decision: No Samoan Islands for me.

I devised a plan. A shitty plan. Here it is:

RUN.

FAST.

So that night I slipped Lisa one more note, the final note, and told her we *had* to run that night and she *had* to come with me and that I had it all figured out. I told her we were gonna leave later that night and not wait one more second. I was proud as fuck of myself for all I was accomplishin ever since I was a loser in sixth grade. I was a real go-getter I suppose. Anyway...

It was October 30th, 1999, Devil's Night, a month after my first institutionalized birthday, the night we broke out.

I was fifteen-years-old.

CHAPTER 14

WE MET BY THE DUMPSTER

"Ready?" I asked her.

"Yeah." She said, already nervous as fuck and seemingly outa breath from hauling the trash to the dumpster.

"Okay. Just run as fast as you can and follow me. K?"

"I'm nervous. What if we don't make it?" She said.

What a silly thought, "Of course we'll make it!"

"Thehr's no way we'll get cwaught?" She asked in her New England accent.

"No way at all. Never. We have to do this. Okay?"

"Okay."

"Ready?"

"Yeah."

THREE, TWO ONE:

RUNNNNNNN!!!!!!!!!!

We sprinted outa rehab and ran into the bushes and onto this dude's front lawn that was about a hundred yards away from the exit of the rehab. His lights went on. The front door opened. He came out with a gun.

"OH MY GOD HE'S GONNA SHOOT US!!!
RRRUUUUUNNNNN!!!!!!!!!"

BOOM!!! A shot was fired.

We jumped into a ditch on the side of the road and covered ourselves with leaves. Holy shit. This was off to a rough start.

Lisa asked, "What the fahk do we do now?"

"Shhh!" She was already pissin me off. Lemme think woman, SHIT! Oh no. A truck turned onto the street, it was coming towards us. Was it the sheriff? Already?! No way they already knew we were gone. Dammit I can't believe how bad I was fuckin this up so far! Then the truck stopped, almost as if it was looking right at us. Its lights went off. Then it slowly pulled closer toward us. I told Lisa:

"Don't move."

"What tha fahk man??????"

"Just SHHHHHHHHHHHHHH!!!"

The truck pulled up, lights off, we both froze. I felt like I was gonna pee. I felt dead already, like someone was gonna hop out the truck and blow my head off. I couldn't make out what was going on through the dark glass of the truck window, who was in the truck? Then it stopped RIGHT in front of us. FUCK! They're gonna shoot us!!! I was sure of it now!!

FUUUCCCCKKKKK!!! But I didn't say any of that. I was frozen with fear and didn't make a move.

THEN…

Mysteriously, the truck pulled away. Huh? What the FUCK was that about?! No time to explain miracles, we gotta go. So I told her, "Okay. We gotta move again. You okay? You ready?"

"I'm tired." She said.

Was she fuckin serious? Already?!?! But I didn't say that. This is what I said: "Just a little more. We're gonna run there", and I pointed to the forest surrounding the rehab, "cause no one will expect us to hideout so close to New Beginnings. Then we'll bolt again later tonight."

"Will that wehrk?"

"Absolutely. Ready?"

"Ugh… yeah. Can we wait for ten minutes?"

"Ten minutes?" Was this chick fuckin nuts? OF COURSE NOT. But I didn't say that. What I said was

"Nah we gotta go now. Come on, just follow me. Ready? 3, 2, 1…
GO!"

We dashed down the street we had just run down, then ducked into
the thick trees and bushes surrounding the rehab. Branches flung back
in Lisa's face as I ran over rocks and spikey bushes and maybe poison
ivy.

Then police sirens sounded and flashing lights could be seen through
the trees. We had only been gone five minutes. What a clusterfuck this
already was, jeez. We jumped down. Does that make sense? Jumped
down? We *got* down and watched cop car after cop car drive into the
New Beginnings dirt road. I peeled off a few layers of clothing to make
a blanket over the rocks and sticks and shit and we laid down outa sight.

We were safe for now. NO WAY anyone could see us. All I could
think about was THIS IS MY CHANCE TO LOSE MY VIRGINITY!
I have to fuck her. If I don't fuck her I'm like… how I was in sixth
grade. The biggest loser in the world… and that was *light years* ago.
Yeah, I don't wanna backtrack here. I'm not a loser anymore. I'm
like… you know, famous. Right? Everyone is thinkin about me back
home. I'm sure of it. Okay, yes, I'm a legend. Get back in the game
here Greg… Do it.

But should I? Do it now? I looked over and her eyes were closed.
No she's sleeping. She's not really sleeping. How could you fall asleep
right now? Whatever, maybe she is. It's not the right time. I'll close my
eyes and worry about it later.

So I woke up at what seemed like might be 2AM, but I didn't have a
watch or anything. Where am I? Oh right. We ran away from rehab
and my life is on the line. Lisa was right next to me. The cops were all

gone. Time to go. I woke her up and she smiled. Ah! She still likes me! Good. Okay, still on track to fuck her a zillion times in all different positions and from all different sides and directions then run away to heaven with her and never come back. Fantastic. I'm about to be elevated to such an elite fuckin status of existence my head'll fall off.

Let's do this.

We couldn't *run* down the street, it'd raise too many eyebrows, so we casually walked through shitty Opelousas. It really was a shithole town.

Outside a motel there were remnants of a Halloween party. We stopped inside to see if there were any drugs or alcohol we could get our hands on. I *needed* to get high and *then* I could make my move on Lisa. Maybe I am a drug addict? Hmm. Maybe I'm just a pussy? Nah, I'm not a pussy, I'm the man, remember?

Whatever, we walked inside the motel lookin thing and followed some sign in the lobby that directed us down to some basement where it said on some other sign: "Halloween Party" outside this shitty lookin door. So we opened that shitty lookin door and walked into this saloon lookin crack den. Nobody was there. There were a few bottles of empty beer with a few sips left, so we drank them but they tasted like backwash. Maybe I *am* an alcoholic? So we left and went back upstairs.

Should I try and fuck her now? Nah. Not now. Too much to do. Freedom first, wild mammal sex later.

So we walked back upstairs past the front desk where the front-desk dude was starin at us wondering who in the fuck we were, but we walked right by him like we were absolutely supposed to be there, cause we were, and we walked to where the outdoor pool was and sat on the dirty white beach chairs surrounding the cement pool. I stared at the vending machine right next to the pool. I was so fucking hungry. For a moment, I felt free. The motel clerk dude came outside and asked who we were. So I said:

"We're leaving."

Then we walked more and more and more, but the ground below the road we were walkin on all of a sudden became this swampy marsh type thingy and we got stuck on that road and there was no way off it cause below us was alligator infested swamp and there was all this baby alligator roadkill all over the road. Then this possum came outa nowhere and scared the shit outa me.

Then I saw these two people.

They were on the other side of the road, which was kinda far away cause there was that big wide swampy median separating the two different directions of the road, and on that other side of the road were these two people dressed in white. White robes.

"LOOK!" But she didn't look.

Anyway these dudes, or maybe chicks, or maybe both, shit I dunno, but those two fuckin people in the white robes, they were dancing these weird fuckin dance typa movements. Like modern dance for hillbilly Cajun hicks.

Then I realized it was the fuckin *KKK!!!*

I couldn't believe that shit really existed! DOPE! Or wait, no, not dope. But uhh—COOL! Wait, no, not cool. Not cool at all. I just thought it was interesting I guess.

Lisa and I hadn't said a word to each other in like an hour. So I broke the silence:

"Good thing we're on this side of the highway… huh? You know, cause I'm Jewish an all?"

But she was tired and pissed off. "All I want is a fahkin couch", she said. Her accent kept gettin thicker.

The bridge finally stopped and the swampy median went away and we were again on solid ground and it started pouring rain. Dammit it's always fuckin raining here. Anyway that put Lisa in an even *shittier* mood. But then we spotted a rundown RV park and get this… you know what was *RIGHT* outside the RV park?

A FUCKIN COUCH!

She had *just* said she wanted a couch! And we hadn't seen any civilization except those KKK characters for like… I dunno! A long time! And then there was just some random couch underneath a random tarp smack center in front of some shitty RV park!

"Are you kidding me? Do you see that?" I asked her.

"It's a fahkin couch." And she started walkin over to it. Man, she was in such a bad mood. But I was enthralled by the coincidence:

"I know! We were just talking about a—You *just* said all you want is a—"

But she didn't give a shit about 'signs' or miracles. To her it was a fahkin couch and all she wanted to do was fahkin sleep.

So we ran through the three-foot high grass to the couch. The grass was soaked with heavy rain and tickled my hands and made me all itchy as we ran through it to get to the soggy cushions of the couch. Then we hopped up on it, tryin to get comfortable, and somehow I shut my eyes even though I wasn't sleepy and fell asleep. I'll fuck her tomorrow, I thought as I fell into slumber.

It mighta been 4 or 5AM when my eyes opened. Someone was starin down at us as we slept.

It was a little girl.

She was holdin a blanket. I woke Lisa up.

Lisa smiled and said in a sleepy voice, "Hi there." Then she did that high-pitched 'I'm talkin to a little girl voice' when she said "What's your name? What do you have with you?" Lisa's slutty lipstick musta spooked her cause the little girl gave us the blanket then ran the fuck away. "Awww" Lisa said as she dozed back off into sleepiness without even sayin hi to me. Dumb bitch.

We woke up again and the sun was bright and hot and the air was wet and sticky and humid. The RV-park was in full swing, everyone was lookin at us. I couldn't *believe* I *still* hadn't even kissed her. We got up and searched for that little girl and found her outside an RV playing in the dirt. She got all shy when Lisa and I gave her the blanket back and thanked her.

"Thank you so much honey." Lisa said. "Is this where you live?"

The little girl nodded.

"Sweetie, do you have anything to drink?"

We hadn't wet our throats since the backwash we chugged at that motel last night. The little girl nodded and took us inside her RV.

When we walked in the little girl's RV her grandma or some shit was in the back of the RV sittin on some ledge starin at us as if she didn't speak English or wasn't sure how to communicate to us that we were imbeciles. Who knows, maybe she *didn't* speak English, but who the fuck cares. I was so thirsty.

The little girl showed us to a cruddy white camping cooler that was sittin on the floor by the kitchen area of the tiny RV and opened the lid and my eyes fell on a beer. There was beer. I hadn't even thought of that, so I grabbed one. Maybe I *am* an alcoholic? Lisa looked at me funny. Was I not supposed to do that? The little girl looked at me funny too. Yeah, maybe I shouldn'ta done that. Her grandma or whoever that old cranky woman was looked at me funny too and said, "Aright time t'leave."

Man, I *really* shouldn'ta grabbed that beer. Anyway, I guess our time had expired. *Was* it cause of the beer? I don't know, probably not. So we left and walked on over to the payphone by that tarp and soggy wet couch we slept on and Lisa picked up the phone.

It was time to make some moves.

So Lisa called her boyfriend collect, oh right, she had a boyfriend, to tell him about her new life plan to run away and live with me and to ask if we could just stay with him for about three years till we were eighteen. She assured me he would understand.

I muttered an Eminem rap to keep my nerves tranquil as more and more eyes gathered around us. We looked insanely not local, me with my baggy jeans and cocked hat and Lisa in her slutty ass everything and lip liner and eyebrow ring and purple hair. We *really* didn't blend. Then, without warning, Lisa erupted and started screaming into the payphone:

"PIECE OF SHIT! YOU MOTHERFAHKER!! I ALREADY TOLD YOU—"

Whuh oh…

Then she slammed the payphone down and walked away furious. I chased after her to make everything okay. But then some woman shouted at us from the RV office thingy:

"Ah think it time fer ya'll to git awn gone! Ah don need that kin'a language roun mah lil girl! Cussin like that! Ya'll git faive minutes fore ah'm callin th'Sheriff!"

Our brisk walk turned into a full on sprint as we ran off again into the million-degree heat, drenched in humidity, and dragged ourselves back to the road we had trudged late last night and ran fast, till we were out of sight, out of breath, out of water, and out of life.

By that point we were beyond starving. And thirsty as fuck. The beer was gone and I had never even grabbed a water. I dunno if I even got to feel it, the beer. I mean it was only one of em and now we had to figure out how to survive without food and water in the middle of the summer heat of central Louisiana so my mind was focused on that. I just wanted to get high. And laid.

"PUT YA FAHKIN THUMB UP" she kept tellin me.

Her thumb was up. My thumb was not up. We were covered in sweat already.

"PWUT YA FAHKIN THUMB AHP!" She yakked at me again louder.

Her accent kept on gettin thicker and thicker the more pissed off she got.

"I'M THA ONLY ONE DOIN THA WEHRK!"

So I put my fuckin thumb back up to shut her up. She was *really* startin to get on my nerves. Maybe I don't even *wanna* fuck her.

We saw a church on the side of the highway. YES! A car was pullin outa the parking lot. It was the second car we had seen in like an hour. I think. I mean I had no idea what time it actually was. But so we jumped up and down trying to get the car's attention. AND WE DID! YES!! It's comin our way! Then the car stopped! YAY!! So we got in and got in the backseat and saw that she was a nice church lady who said, "Where ya'll goin?"

So I said "Massachusetts."

"That's a far ways away."

"Yeah it's okay, we're gonna grab a ride from a truck driver." I told her. Right, I had decided we would hitch a ride at a truck stop… I dunno why. Not sure where I got that idea.

She looked at me from her rear view mirror with suspicion, "Ya'll ain't runaways now are ya'll?"

Lisa stared out the window as if she wasn't enjoying this one bit, this whole runaway idea that I'd come up with.

"No ma'am. We're not runaways." I said, keepin our game together.

"Well… there's a truck stop up here I can drop ya'll off at, but… You sure everything's okay?"

"Totally."

As we pulled up to the dingy truck stop, she said to us "Ya'll mind if I say a prayer with ya'll?"

Uhhh… So she got outa her car and ran around to us and she grabbed our hands and asked Jesus to keep us safe then she slipped me a twenty-dollar bill and said:

"May God be with you."

Then she left.

TWENTY BUCKS! **YES!**

Through the doors of the truck stop was a small diner to our left and a dark and tiny empty casino room to our right with a few slot machines not in use. Down the hall was a sloppy room with a washer and dryer and a little TV bolted to the top corner of the room. It reminded me of that TV at the Gold Coast Inn when Levin bought that hooker for Jason, our cab driver. The TV was just small enough so that you had no idea what was playing and just large enough to squint and read what channel it was on.

We sat on the floor of that room next to the laundry machines and the floor of that room was dirty from all the trucker boots tracking in all that dirt from their lives on the road. We were dirty as fuck and I still hadn't fucked her. But now I wasn't even sure I wanted to anymore. But then I looked at her. Yeah, I definitely wanna fuck her. Like, hard. And messy. Yeah. Uhh… Should I do it? *Can* I even do it? Does she still wanna fuck me? Of course she does. I'm awesome. Okay… not now, but maybe in a sec.

So we were sittin on the ground trying to figure out our next move when an older gent, a black trucker dude with a kind face and stern grin, walked in. He looked at us in confusion and said:

"What in the hell ya'll doin?"

Uhhh…

"We *really* need a ride to Massachusetts, will you give us a ride?" I pled… But now I wasn't sure about this whole livin with this chick till I was eighteen in Lawrence Massachusetts thing. Whatever, we made it this far, might as well. But then the trucker said:

"Massachusetts?? Ah headed t'Shreveport."

The fuck is Shreveport? Then Lisa talked for the first time in like a month "Where's that?"

"Shiieet. Not ba Massachusetts! It in the ova diirection. Ba Texas."

Hmm, I thought real hard. I can figure this out.

"Ya'll alone? Ya'll can't be lyin down here, this ain't no good neighborhood." Then he looked at us real hard. "How old you two?"

He seemed pretty cool about it all so I told him the truth.

"We're fifteen. Well, *I'm* fifteen, she's actually... uhh, she's fourteen. I'm fifteen."

I had forgotten all along that Lisa was a year younger than I was. She was *fourteen* not fifteen. Anyway, I continued:

"We ran away from a terrible place. We have to get away from here. You have to help us."

So he bought us showers at the shower booths outside. They were like two bucks per shower. Then he took us for cheeseburgers at that small diner I told you about that was in the truck stop, he bought us two packs of Newports from the gas station and stayed with us that whole night, sleepin at this small table next to us with his head propped up against the grimy wall.

I really like this trucker, I thought. What great people we've met. I wanna do this forever. But we still needed a ride. I think. Yeah, we did. There was no choice anyhow. So we asked every truck driver that walked in for a ride but everyone turned us down. I *really* assumed it woulda been easier than this. Why did I think this was gonna be easy again?

The cool truck-driver was asleep. Then the thought of Lisa crept back into my mind. Holy shit. We were in a fucking truck stop. Safe. Together. This was my chance! FUCKING DO SOMETHING GREG! This was my time to shine and fuck her blind. Lisa was awake. I was awake. It was silent. I forgave her for bein a whiney bitch. She musta done the same. We were in that weird moment where she was waitin for me to finally make a move, I was waiting for myself to finally make a move, and there was discomfort and anxiety and pressure in the air.

Finally I said, "I could really use a blowjob."

Oh my God. Did I really just say that? Lisa smiled an uneasy smile and said nothing back. I pretended like nothing had been said and made a comment about the TV. I kept talking about the TV. For like ten minutes I talked about this fuckin TV.

"I could do that." She said.

"Do what?"

"Never mind." She said.

OH NO! THE BLOW JOB! SHE WAS TALKING ABOUT THE BLOW JOB! NOOOOO!!! HOW DO I BRING IT BACK UP?!?!

FUCK!!

I had *never* felt so ditzy. I blew it. I ruined my chance. I had to do something to numb the idiocy outa my head, so I went to the gas station and stole a bunch of Tylenol PMs and came back and we both took a bunch of them and tried to stay awake to get that sleep deprivation high and all the while the cool truck driver slept at that table right next to us. He was passed the fuck out. I still felt like an idiot. But then the Tylenol PM kicked in and I felt better. Ahhh…. I should keep some of these around all the time. We were up for like thirty mins or so and then POOF. I was asleep.

I woke up mid-night and the cool trucker was gone. Oh no. We're alone again. I'm alone. Where am I? I was still so fucked up I fell back asleep.

THEN…

Game Over.

I woke up and saw cowboy boots in my face.

It was Milton.

HOW'D HE FIND US?!

"I'm gonna give ya'll a ride to one'a two places, juvie hall er New Beginnings. Which you want Juden?"

And that was that. *And* I never made a move on Lisa. I was a failure, and now I had to go back and lie and tell all the guys that I fucked her. I was the cool Jew that everyone liked and I didn't wanna let em all down or anything, so when I got back I did what I had to.

"Yo, I fucked the living SHIT outa her! OF COURSE I DID!" And I made up this whole fake story about how I fucked her.

"PLEASE tell me you fucked her more than once Juden. *Please.*" Tom said.

So now I had to tell em all that I fucked her all over Louisiana. I could see Lisa pickin up cigarette butts on the girl's side of the rehab through the window blinds of my apartment while I was lyin my head off to the guys about the sex we never had. What if she found out? How could she *not* find out? This lie would be too hard. What was there to REALLY worry about though? After all, they were obviously gonna be kicking me out anyway. All I had to do was make it a few days till they shipped me away to the Samoan Islands. I accepted my fate. Even the Samoan Islands would be better than gettin caught in a lie that might ruin my legacy. Man that'd be horrible. After all this work to build my name to where it was. I was feelin like dog shit. Maybe the Samoan Islands wouldn't be that bad...?

But when I was called into Milton's office an hour later, he said "Juden, we givin you *one* mo' chance."

WHHHAAATTT?!?!?!?!? NNOOO!!!!! YOU NEED TO GET ME OUT OF HERE!!! ASAP! But I didn't say that. What I said was this:

"What?"

"We ain't givin up on you just yet. Maybe now yer gon see."

"Well. Um. Okay." I said.

"That's it." Milton said.

"I can go?"

"Juden. Don't make me regret this."

I walked out of his office and into the hot and long and damp grass that surrounded the office and I didn't even bother scratchin my shins that itched like mad from the damp weeds and insect bites I got every time I walked through that damn field back to my apartment. All I could think about was being exposed of all my lies. I couldn't afford it. I had to do something to protect my reputation. So I made an executive decision.

I decided to get myself kicked out.

Like, immediately.

I wasn't about to let Lisa and all the guys find out that I was a Juden fraud. I had to get out of there, and fast. There were only so many hours that would pass before one of my apartment-mates would say somethin to one of the girls about what I had told em. I was sure the *entire* girls' side already knew what a fuckin pussy I was. This was already bad for business. I couldn't even look any of em in the eyes. My legendary status here was depleting by the second. I watched like a hawk every time one of the guys had any interaction with a girl. If one of the guys found out, boy, would *that* be bad. They'd probably kick the fuckin shit outa me.

Then I saw Tom talkin to this chick.

Shit. Was he telling her what I told him? Was she replying with a completely different story that Lisa had told her? I was paranoid as fuck. I had to get out. My heart was about to explode.

They called us all into one of the rooms that they held the on-campus AA meetings in and everyone filtered into the room. Were they all lookin at me? Did they already know? Was I the only one still fakin it? I only had one choice:

To act like a raging lunatic until someone threw me out of that damn place.

"FUCK THIS MEETING!" I shrieked. I just started cursing outa nowhere in the middle of the meeting and bein a moron.

Ruthie looked at me like I was puttin on some shitty show for everyone and said "Juden? What's wrong with yew?"

"THIS WHOLE FUCKING PLACE IS A FUCKIN…" Uhh… I wasn't even angry at all. So I just got louder to hide my non-anger… "WHATEVER. FUCK YOU RUTHIE!" Which *really* felt shitty cause I did like Ruthie a lot, even though she ratted me out. I know she was just doin her job. Was she? I dunno, whatever:

"FUCK YOU RUTHIE."

"Juden what'n the heck wrong with yew?"

I got up and walked out and picked up the payphone. SIDENOTE: You are *not* allowed to pick up the fucking payphone, so I thought that was a pretty smart move. I caused as big a scene as I possibly could but like I said, I wasn't really mad at all. Weird AA-outbursts were definitely not my style.

Luckily, I made it to bed without anyone finding out what a liar I was.

But then someone woke me up at some haunted hour of the night.

I heard someone say:

"Wake up."

I opened my eyes slowly while on my cot-like bed.

"Wake up Juden."

Huh? It was this one staff member guy. He had a weird look on his face as he said:

"Come with me. We're taking you to the airport. You're going back to Long Island."

GREAT! IT WORKED! I CAN'T BELIEVE IT! I'M GONNA BE SO DAMN FAMOUS WHEN I GET BACK! YES!!!!

Then I started thinkin... Don't I need my clothes? Yeah, something didn't feel quite right. So I asked him:

"Wait... what about all my clothes?"

"Don't worry about it." The staff member dude said.

Don't worry about my clothes? What's this dude talkin about? He must be tired too, so I started packing my backpack. Then he grabbed me.

"You don't need that right now."

"But it's my backpack, I need my backpack, I swear."

"No, you don't." And he pulled me up to my feet. "Follow me."

"But I love my backpack."

Whatever, I'll come back in a minute and get it. So I followed him outa my room and out of the apartment and walked along the rehab pathway to the administration office. The door slammed shut and two large men in dark suits blocked the exit.

Shit.

I stared at them, as tough as I could.

"We're legally allowed to break any bone in your body during a restraint. It's up to you how you wanna go."

Well that kinda hit my funny bone...

"Go where?" I asked.

They told me "Don't worry."

"Wait... what?"

They told me "No questions."

"Where is my luggage? My things? I need my backpack, I'll be right back."

But they blocked the door and told me to "Relax, it's all electronic."

All electronic? What the fuck does that even mean?

"Can I grab my backpack?"

"Do we need to handcuff you?"

Keep cool, I told myself. Keep cool. You are strong. The man. A legend. This will only increase your stature. Everyone will know about this. I'll be respected for counties and counties throughout Long Island.

"Fuck it. I'm fine. Let's go."

And so my dreams of going back to Long Island were crushed as they stuck me in a car, no—wait, I got in the car myself, they just locked the doors and then they drove me for two hours to the New Orleans airport.

"Where are we *going*?" Just cause I'm a legend doesn't mean I wasn't curious… I was flying somewhere. That much I knew, I just wasn't totally sure if we *were* going to Samoa. Cause I mean, if we were goin to Samoa… well, I might just kill myself. Don't talk like that Greg. So I asked again, "Where are we going?"

Still no answer.

We got out.

They handcuffed me.

Everyone watched as the men brought me through the airport security like I was some kind of prisoner, which I guess I was. That's even cooler. I hope someone finds out about this.

We arrived at our gate:

Atlanta, Georgia.

My heart slowed down. This wasn't the gate for the Samoan Islands! GEORGIA! I LOVE GEORGIA! Actually I'd never been to Georgia. And as it turns out, Georgia wasn't so nice…

Welcome to Hidden Lake Academy.

PART II

HIDDEN LAKE ACADEMY

CHAPTER 15

HELLS LITTLE ACRE

And so that's how I landed myself in the middle of the woods, in the middle of The Appalachians, in a small red pickup truck with two large men, one with a fat face and tight ponytail pulling his skin smoother than it oughta be, wearin these limo-tinted sunglasses and the other one with a face full of wrinkles and silent eyes hiding behind his heavy eyelids.

They both guarded my movements, with their peripheral vision, as we all stared straight through the windshield and drove to the soundtrack of staticky white trash country music. I couldn't move. I was stuck in the middle seat and that was all I really knew. After a while, even the staticky white trash country music station filled up with so much static we had to turn it off. I knew I was goin somewhere bad, where even the country music couldn't play. I just didn't know quite how bad... So when we pulled up that last tiny road and drove past that torture chamber-lookin small cabin I told you about at the beginning of this story and parked in front of that small admin-lookin building, all I had was a head full of questions and mind full of fear.

But then those two private investigator dudes left, like I told you in the beginning, and some burly mountain man and older Vietnam War Vet told me to take my clothes off after puttin me in the bathroom. I wasn't even sure if that was legal, but what good was illegal here anyways? It felt pretty lawless and I knew there was no one to actually help me, so I had to talk my anxiety down from the cliff it was about to drop off of and simmer my nerves.

They want me to get naked... so what? Maybe it's just—fuck. There was no makin this prettier than the ugly it was. This could be *real* bad. The only thought that really plagued my mind at that very moment was how in the FUCK my parents could let this happen to me. What in the FUCK were they thinkin? Do they even know where I am? Did they send those two guys to get me? Where are they? Are they on a cruise somewhere in the Bahamas? While I'm here? Locked up in some… well, wherever the fuck I was??

So they stripped me naked and made me jump around like a frog while these two grown men looked under my balls to make sure there was no… uhh, well whatever it was they were lookin for down there. The good news is all they wanted was to search me. I thought I might have a dick in my ass at any moment.

The Colonel, who I later found out was a Colonel in the Vietnam War, which is where he picked up that clever nickname, he and the burly mountain man threw me the official Hidden Lake Academy uniform and trashed away my hat and chucked my baggy jeans and loose tee-shirt that I was wearing at the time, the clothes that I had been transported in, and they threw it all into some trash bag I was sure I'd never see again and told me:

"This'll be your home for the next two years."

HA! Yeah right!

I knew that *one* thing was absolutely for sure. This would *not* be my home for the next two years. In fact, I doubt they'll be able to keep me here longer than two weeks. Yeah… I'm bouncin the fuck outa here like, tomorrow.

But that's not what happened next…

CHAPTER 16

WHAT HAPPENED NEXT

So the burly mountain man took me outa the bathroom and made me put on that shitty prep-school typa uniform and he walked me outa that hillbilly administration room and with all his anger about life spread wide across his face, he led me outside and down this long, neatly paved road that looked like it had been paved earlier that week for the seventeen millionth time.

On both sides of that perfectly constructed road were these pristinely-built dormitory buildings made of brick and colored light colors that might make you think it was a happy rural boarding school, but at closer look it appeared more like some religious mental institution hidden in the woods.

Nothing could be seen behind the dormitory buildings except thousands of tall pine trees leaking in from the vast Appalachian

Mountain range around us. Disturbing images kept sweeping my serenity to the side every time I wondered what might go on at this new place.

There wasn't a speck of trash in sight. I didn't like that one bit. And what made it worse was the fresh-cut grass in front of the dormitory buildings cause it matched the cleanliness of the cookie cutter colored paint that was freshly painted on those psych-ward-lookin dormitories that they were taken me to. The mountain man walked behind me to make sure I didn't run maybe, I dunno, but he steered me to one of the brick dormitory buildings and opened the door and in we walked.

When we walked inside my heart nearly popped at the sight. Nothing could look more sad and pathetic and depressing and terrifying. It was just this one long hallway with bland yellow paint on the walls with rooms on both sides from one end to the other. It *really* looked like a mental institution. Oh man, what if this *is* some sorta mental institution? Am I crazy? Do they think I'm nuts? Keep cool Greg, you're not mental. You're normal. You're awesome. You're gonna be remembered forever for this.

He walked me down the hallway to a room in the middle of the hallway, in the middle of all the other rooms, which there were no doors on the hinges of. We walked swiftly inside to an empty cell—I mean bedroom—I mean cell—and he showed me to my bed in the corner of the room. There were three other beds in the room, four total, and each bed was made so damn neat it looked like they were on display. Mental institution for sale. The room was so boring, so bland as fuck that I wanted to cry. Each bed had these paper thin and depressing flowery blankets and these paper thin and depressing inch-thick pillows with a desk right next to em. And the desks were all empty. It looked like I was the first kid to ever walk into that building. The mountain man told me to:

"Lay down. The kiddies'll be back at four."

Yeah, he said the word *kiddies,* which creeped me the fuck out even more so.

When he left me I realized I was the only one in the building. Maybe I should run now? But I looked in the hallway and there were surveillance cameras all over the ceiling and the Plexiglas doors were locked shut from the outside.

I had no idea what time it was or how far away from four in the afternoon it was so I had no idea when the 'kiddies' would be back or what to do or how to act... So I just climbed up on my bed that he told me was my bed even though there was no way I was stayin at this fuckin place and there's no way I'll ever call this my bed, and I closed my eyes and wondered if maybe I had taken this whole legacy thing a bit too far. I wasn't even sure the kids from Long Island would ever even find out just how weird this all was and if *that* was the case, then this was all for nothing, right? Nah, I'm sure they'll all find out. Actually, who gives a fuck. Wait—I do. It sure felt like I mighta made the wrong choice here, well, made a buncha wrong choices here... Hmmm... How in the fuck did all this happen again? Wasn't I the most popular kid in Roslyn like a year ago? Didn't all the girls like me and all the dudes think I was cool and wasn't I the fuckin man? What in the *fuck* had I gotten myself into?

Anyway I closed my eyes and fell asleep, I think I fell asleep at least, and woke up or came back to life or whatever was happening in reality to the sound of forty or so voices thrashing together at once.

Three kids walked into my room. Two white-bred country lookin boys and one black kid without an accent. Or maybe he just had *my* accent? Wait, did I have an accent? Where the fuck am I again? Georgia?

Anyway when my roommates walked in they all started laughing. What were they laughin at? Good fuckin question. I got no idea, but it made me real mad. And they all looked so young compared to Louisiana. Stupid young fucks. Maybe they don't hate Jews here at least?

Nobody had on anything other than the stupid uniform that I had on too, but they all ripped certain parts of the sleeves and shredded the bottoms of their paints a bit to give em some character I suppose, not much character though cause the variations were real slight, but I guess it was the only way to keep what little individuality they had left. So point is, I couldn't really tell who was a gangster and who was cool and who was a nerd and who was what, cause they all looked the same in that dumb uniform, so I just had to go off of personality I guess… I had never seen any place like this, not even in the movies.

The hallway ricocheted with meaningless banter as I lay on my bed feeling more outa place than ever. I had to get out.

Not one single person in that room said one single word to me and then everyone started rushin around cleaning shit. I didn't know if that meant I should be cleaning shit too and I didn't really wanna talk to these fuckheads if they didn't wanna talk to me, so I didn't ask and I just continued to lay on my bed and not do shit.

All of a sudden everyone in my room stopped talkin and shut the fuck up and moved quietly and swiftly and their demeanors all changed and I had no idea why but then I saw that there was this guard-like dude, a black dude with a shaved military haircut and broad shoulders and big muscles and a sly smirk about his face in the room. I hadn't even notice him walk in. He was in an army lookin uniform as he looked me up and down and said casually:

"New YOHK, huh? You from New yOHK?"

I looked at my hands and I had written the words 'New York City' on them, even though I was from Long Island. Long Island wasn't quite fitting for the wild narrative that I was building so I thought Queens worked much better, so I wrote 'New York City' and 'Queens' all over everything I owned, which was nothing anymore, it was all gone I think, forever maybe. I don't think I'll ever see my backpack ever again. Anyway I had written that shit all over my hands, so that's what he was lookin at, my hands, and he just kept sayin in this thick Georgia accent:

"New yOHK!" And he emphasized the 'OHK' at the end of every time he said it, like he was tryin to make fun of my state, like I was the one that named it. Then *he* started laughin too!

WHAT THE FUCK IS SO FUNNY DICKFACE?

But I didn't say that. I just said:

"Yeah. I'm from New York."

"Well", and he chuckled, "Wehlcum tah tha durty South, New yOHK."

And then he walked out and screamed in the hallway to all the other kids "OUT OUT OUT OUT OUT!!!!" And then all the kids scrambled outa their rooms and into the hallway, including my roommates, who were still amused at my existence for some FUCKIN reason, and they all went into the hallway too and everyone got in a line in the hallway by one set of the Plexiglas doors at the far end of the dormitory and waited for something. So I just followed suit cause I didn't have anything better to do. It was just another place to add to my list of places that would add to my list of legendary institutions I could tell everyone I had been at.

But by the end of the day, I realized this place might be a bigger problem than I thought.

CHAPTER 17

THAT NIGHT

My sheets were covered in sweat. It was now nighttime, or maybe it was early the next morning, or maybe I was still asleep, or maybe I was awake and hadn't ever been to sleep, or maybe I was still in Louisiana— fuck. I was confused. The dormitory was dark. Everyone else was asleep, or were they? Yeah, they definitely were asleep. I musta been awake. Then the reality struck me...

Holy shit, this is real. This is where I am. I'm fucked.

Then a heavy switch sounded and the lights all went on at once in the hallway.

BANG!! BANG!!! BANG!!!!

My eyes stayed still. No more, I thought. I'm done already. I wanna go home.

My roommates got right the fuck up and started doin shit. Obviously I had no idea what to do.

"Should I be doin somethin?" I finally said to my one country-lookin roommate that was in the corner straightening out his toiletries and shit cause it was the only thing it looked like he owned. But he didn't even look me in the eye when he said:

"Shut the fuck up FNK".

"FNK? What the fuck is *your* problem?"

This stupid piece of fuckin shit, who the hell did he think he was? Who the fuck did he think he was talkin to? But then he stopped what he was doin and walked over to me and looked at me in the eye. Up close he was much taller and more muscular than he was from across the room, which kinda scared me, but I stared the hillbilly back anyway to stand my ground. Then my other roommate, this black kid named Boogie, he ran between us and said to the hillbilly:

"Yo homie chill the fuck out with the FNK, aiight?"

And then he backed away and everyone retreated and I still had no idea what the fuck a 'FNK' was.

I looked into the hallway through my door-less room and saw those damn surveillance cameras. They were everywhere, all over the ceiling. Somebody was watchin me, my every move. Then again:

BANG!! BANG!! BANG!!

WHAT THE FUCK IS THAT? It sounded like pots and pans maybe. I wish somebody would just tell me what was going on and how this can all stop.

BANG!! BANG!!! BANG!!!!

Yeah, definitely pots and pans slammin together.

My roommates were all dressed in their uniforms already and their beds were made perfect and everything was cleaned and they hustled into the hallway but my bed was still not made and I was so damn confused as all the kids threw themselves onto the ground in the hallway and got into a pushup position. I had no clue what was happening but I wanted no part of it. This place was way too fucked up and I wasn't gonna play into it. I wasn't gonna do what they were doin, fuck that. No way. And while we're at it, I was done with all this bein shipped around shit too. I'm goin home, I thought. I was tough enough to go home and make my iconic reappearance at The Landmark Diner and watch the gasps and aw's and ah's of everyone as they laid eyes on me for the first time in almost a year.

HOLY SHIT! IT'S GREG FUCKIN CAYEA!

Damn right it is...

That's what they'd all say. They were all sophomores by now. Man, I been gone a while. Even better. What a scene it'll be when I show up at Levin's party in Old Westbury at his father's mansion and all the kids from Roslyn and all the other school districts all drop their jaws and rush me and ask me:

Where you been?

What the fuck happened?

When'd you get back?!

Then I could start clearing up the rumors...

I heard you were in juvie!

I heard your parents sent you to an orphanage!

I heard you robbed a bank with your COCK!

Yes, yes, ladies and gentlemen, there's a bit of truth in all of that...

But then I 'd be interrupted by Leslie, some hot chick from some other school that I never told you about cause she doesn't serve the story except for the fact that I'm tellin you she was hot. So yeah, Leslie, she'd run over to me in the midst of it all and be all hot and shit and grab me and pull me aside and ask me to be her boyfriend.

"Boyfriend? But I just got back Leslie!"

Then she'd blow me in front of all of Long Island and ask her friends to take pictures of it on her Polaroid and then she'd hang the photos in her locker a few school districts away then all the guys in her school district would walk by and ask who that fuckin kid was, and it'd be me. And they'd all know my name but not know me in person. Yeah, this'll be awesome. Then all the freshman at Roslyn would find out and worship me. I'd be the coolest thing to touch the school since Gavin Wick. People would talk about me for years and decades. It would be a spectacular return and all the girls would—

—"HEY!!!!"

Huh?

I snapped outa it.

"HURRY!"

The other one of my roommates that I hadn't talked to yet, a smaller, also hillbilly-lookin kid, he was flippin the fuck out from the hallway and screamin to me in a whisper to:

"HURRY!"

A large waspy guard with a square face in complete army fatigue carefully stepped over each kid, inspecting every room to make sure nobody was still sleeping as he walked through the hall. His name was Gary. Another dude in the same uniform, a black dude, muscular, bald and terrifying was right beside him. His name was Harris. But you already know Harris, cause you met him yesterday. The dude who kept sayin 'New yOHK'.

Gary and Harris marched down the hallway together lookin into each room. I got outa my bed and threw myself on the ground and crawled into the hallway and onto the floor like everyone else. I had no time to think of anything else to do.

"FRONT LEAN AND REST!!" My roommate said to me again in a loud whisper.

"Huh?" I had no idea what that meant.

"Like this!"

So I followed his lead and got into a pushup position. I dunno why he didn't just tell me to get into a pushup position.

I watched Gary down the hall as he stopped. He was starin into a room. A creepy smile painted his face.

"GET UP YOU LAZY MAGGOT!" He screamed into some room.

I tried to hold myself up but could see nothing but the floor as I struggled to keep my arms straight. Harris took a seat in one of the two chairs in the middle of the prison-like hallway, keeping an eye on us and chuckling to himself while Gary fired off another round of drill sergeant shouts:

"GET YER BUTT OUTA THAT GADANG BED YOU!"

I kept my head down. Gary walked in the room. Then I heard:

PLUNK!

It was the sound of a body smacking the ground. Grunts and groans came outa some kid's throat. Then came a yell from a voice:

"AHH! STOP!!" as Gary walked out and waited with an iron grin. That kid came out, his red hair all over the place.

"GET DOWN!"

But the redhead kid refused. He just stood there.

Harris laughed an evil laugh in his chair while Gary looked straight into the redhead kid's pupils. Then he smiled and looked at the rest of us struggling to hold our pushup position then looked back at the redhead kid and screamed with fury right in his face

"EVERY SECOND YER NOT DOWN IS ANOTHER ONE'A YER BUDDIES WHO AIN'T EATIN CHOW!"

Then Gary looked down at some *other* kid with shaved blonde hair named Tyson who was right below where Gary was standin and Gary screamed at *him* into *his* ears even though he was only a few feet away:

"GUESS YOU AIN'T HUNGRY HUH TYSON?"

"Get the fuck down Morgan!" Tyson screamed at the redhead kid.

"HEAR THAT YOU? THAT'S YER BUDDY YOU BURNIN!" Gary shouted back at the redhead.

My arms gave out and I fell to the floor. My roommate looked at me in horror:

"GET BACK UP! QUICK! HURRY!"

So I picked my stomach back off the floor and extended my arms as best I could and held myself up with all my strength.

Morgan, the redhead kid, he finally got down. Gary looked over at us all in pain and waited for like ten trillion seconds and finally started yellin out numbers:

"ONE!" Gary screamed.

Everyone went down. I followed cause... uhhh, well, I just did.

"TWO!"

Everyone pushed themselves back up.

"THREE!"

Everyone went back down again then back up and shouted in

unison:

"ONE!"

And Gary counted again:

"ONE, TWO, THREE!"

And we all kept doin pushups and callin back numbers in unison:

"TWO!"

"ONE, TWO, THREE"

"THREE!"

It was all so damn foreign to me. And after we did like fifty

pushups, well, I was more doin these like jello-y ups and downs by the

fifteenth pushup, anyway after we did the pushups he told us to

"GET UP!"

My chest muscles felt like they were ripping apart. And it was only

like... I dunno, 6AM? Who the fuck knows...

"YA'LL GOT FIFTEEN MINUTES BEFORE

INSPECTION. GO!"

Then all this weird commotion started. Like everyone ran back to

their room and some kid went up and down the hallway throwing towels

onto the floor and then as soon as the towels hit the floor kids ran out

from their rooms and scooped up the towels and got naked and wrapped

the towels around themselves and ran back into the hallway and rushed

into one of the two bathrooms. I was left in my room tryin to figure out

what in the fuck I should be doin. My one roommate that was yelling at

me in a whisper back in the hallway and helpin me out was in his towel
when he said to me:

"Don't even worry about showering man, you won't get a shower
for at least a week."

"I can't shower?"

"Seniority man, we only get ten minutes and you're a FNK. Brand
new FNK at that."

"What's FNK?"

"Fuckin New Kid. You."

"How long *you* been here?" I asked him.

"Sixteen months."

"Are you serious?"

"Ain't that bad… well, yeah it is. You'll get used to it."

Then he rushed outa the room in his towel to the bathroom and as
he was leaving, my other roommate, Boogie, who saved my ass from the
hillbilly kid that looked like he might kick the shit outa me, he was
already rushing back into our room all covered in shower water still. He
threw his towel off and was all naked and shit and started puttin on his
uniform.

"So I don't get a shower?"

He turned and looked back at me and laughed.

"Yo don't be lookin at my ass yo!"

"I'M NOT LOOKIN AT YOUR FUCKIN ASS!"

"Yo chill dawg, I'm just playin. You just a FNK. You'll learn.
Don't be worried bout no shower though cause you ain't gettin one for
like a month, but eyo, you from New York?"

"Yeah I'm from New York."

"Word I'm from The Bronx. That's why they call me 'Boogie'. Where you at? You from like Ma-hatt'n yo? You look like you from Ma-hatt'n."

ANOTHER NEW YORKER! YES! I thought.

"Nah, Long Island actually. Right by Queens." I had to add that part in obviously.

"Word. Well, good talk FNK." And he bounced outa the room in his uniform to go... uhh, shit I dunno. I *still* had no fuckin clue what was happenin. It was all goin by so fast I had no time to think! So I took a deep breath and made my bed and waited silently, concentrating on my breathing, tryin to not have a panic attack. I think I mighta been meditating. I dunno, but I was tryin to keep calm. Then I heard Harris:

"OUT OUT OUT OUT!!!!"

DAMMIT! I was just about to figure out how to get outa this shithole! But now I gotta go again! FUCK!

I NEED TIME TO THINK!

CHAPTER 18

ONE LONG DAY

So we formed this rigid line in the hallway and Gary and Harris told us to shut the fuck up and not get outa formation and they took us outside to that overly tidy paved road and walked us to this cabin-like building that everyone called The Lodge.

The Lodge was divided into two sections, where we sat, and where we ate. And in the part where we sat were these different sections of couches and everyone went to a specific couch and sat down as soon as we walked in.

But I didn't know which couch to go to, they all filled up so quick. I was left without a couch.

"You gotta go to the FNK section new kid."

Some random dude said that to me as I was wandering around the room lookin like a moron I guess.

"Over there."

And he pointed to this one section of couches that I guess I was supposed to sit at, but I wasn't so sure about this whole playin by the rules bullshit. These kids are all such pussies just doin whatever the fuck they're told to do. Sheep. I'm not like these kids. I'm no sheep. I'm Greg. But I didn't have any bright ideas at the moment other than to walk over to the FNK section of couches, so I walked over to the FNK section of couches and sat down.

Jeez… No WAY am I stayin here. I had to get out and I had to set aside some time to think or else I'd never find a good strategy, so I immediately put my head in between my knees and closed my eyes and started plannin my escape in my imagination.

Then the greatest thing in the world happened.

Chicks walked in. THERE WERE GIRLS HERE! YES!!!!!!

Sure they all looked a bit malnourished and skinny and pale and uhh, well they didn't look like the girls in Louisiana, not like Lisa… man, I can't *believe* I didn't fuck her. I bet they ALL know now that I'm a big fuckin liar… Whatever, they're there and I'm here so it doesn't really matter all that much anymore. Still though it bothered me knowin they all hated me. Anyway, the girls at this new place didn't look so good but fuck, I'LL TAKE IT! Damn. That woulda been real nice if they were all hot, but they weren't. Maybe that's cause they all had the same clothes on and no makeup and similar haircuts? I wonder if they think the same about us? About me? Am I being arrogant? Okay stop thinkin. Just figure this out Greg: How the FUCK do I get outa here?

Then at the head of The Lodge came that damn burly mountain man who strip-searched me in the bathroom yesterday with the Colonel. I found out his name was Barren, but everyone called him Bear.

"OKAY KIDDIES QUIET!"

And he was a *lunatic* the way he kept sayin *kiddies!*

He waited for like, *two* more seconds then an outburst of fuming rage:

"SHUT YOUR GODDAM MOUTHS UP!!!"

Silence.

And then, with a total change of tone, borderline multiple personalities, he says: "Now don't make me out to be the bad guy here kiddies."

STOP SAYIN 'KIDDIES'. What a fuckin psycho. He crossed his arms over his chest and said:

"Boys, after chow you'll head to the gymnasium." And *then*, with *another* change of tone, this time growing with ferocity, he growled:

"AND DON'T LET ME CATCH ANYONE SITTING DOWN! I'LL SLAP YOU WITH A WORK ASSIGNMENT SO FAST YOUR HEAD'LL SPIN!"

What's a work assignment? I thought.

But then, *again*, with *another* change of voice, he said with a softer tone:

"And the girls will clean the kitchen up then go back to the dorm till lunch. Are we clear?"

"Yessir."

"ARE WE CLEAR?!"

"YESSIR!"

"RESTRICTIONS FALL OUT!"

When he said that, like thirty kids, boys and girls, all holding these blue and black folders, they all stood up and walked outside into the cold. It was November and we were in the Appalachian Mountains so it was below freezing outside.

I dunno what the fuck Restrictions are, but they apparently all leave. Then Bear started callin out these things called Peer Groups to eat.

"PEER GROUP 23! EAT!!"

Then like ten kids got up and moved from the couches section of The Lodge to the cafeteria section of The Lodge, which they called The Chow Hall. The rest of us stayed on the couches. I couldn't think with all this yellin. Then Bear shouted:

"PEER GROUP 24! EAT!!"

What the *fuck* is a Peer Group? After like thirty minutes, when no one was left in the couches section of The Lodge except for us kids at the FNK section, Bear screamed:

"FNK'S! EAT!"

But there was barely any food left by the time I got to The Chow Hall, so the lunch lady woman behind the cafeteria line gave me whatever was left, but that didn't matter. I had no fuckin appetite. I could barely swallow air. And in The Chow Hall the eating tables were separated into gang-like sections too, so again I had no idea where to sit. I was terrified once I had my tray of food. I didn't know where to go and I had no time to figure this all out! It was so frustrating!

I saw a table that had these two kids, so I sat down with them cause it seemed the least intimidating... not that I was scared or anything. One of the kids at that table, his name was Miller, I later found out was a thirteen-year-old rapist with Hepatitis C who raped this twelve-year-old girl in the woods behind his dorm, my dorm. After I found that out I didn't sit next to him anymore. But the other kid, he was this scary lookin Egyptian kid with dark skin and a rough facial expression permanently glued to his face and emotionless eyes that seemed to have no soul and he basically looked like he would lay me out with one punch.

"Welcome to hell."

And that's how I met Rafal.

"Yeah? Hell? What do we do after this?" I asked him nonchalantly. I just needed some time to form a plan.

"Walk around for four hours" he said as he continued to eat the shitty food.

"We walk for four hours? Like... how do you mean?"

He seemed to get more and more pissed every question I asked for some reason.

"You can walk however you want, but you can't walk with me."

Silence.

I took a bite of bread. Did he just say I couldn't walk with him?

"Why not?" I asked.

"Cause we're already eating together. Can't spend too much time with anyone."

I didn't know what the hell he meant, and he didn't seem to care that I didn't know what that meant.

"Don't worry, the two years go by fast."

"Do they?"

He laughed.

"Fuck no dude, just try and get used to it."

I was startin to get a bit scared.

When we finished eating, they made us go to The Gym, which was this building next to The Lodge and it was just a carpeted basketball court. I was told to start walkin and not stop once. There was nowhere to walk, so like Rafal said, I walked alone in circles for four hours, till lunch. So for FOUR FUCKING HOURS I *had* to walk around in a circle, alone, by myself cause I didn't know anybody, and all the while Bear is starin at me and the rest of us waitin to catch someone to stop walkin. I walked alone with my thoughts till noon trying to figure out a way to escape. At least I had time to finally think, which is what I needed. Time to think.

So we walked for four hours and I didn't come up with a damn escape plan smarter than to just start runnin like bloody hell and hope to not get caught, but that didn't seem so reasonable so I kept walkin to The Lodge... they were takin us back to The Lodge for lunch—I mean 'Chow'.

But as they walked us in a line we passed this other road, a road I hadn't seen yet. And down that road I saw a lake. I stared at it and thought, huh... guess that's why they called this place Hidden Lake? I was puttin the pieces of this weird jigsaw puzzle together in my head. Then I saw a buncha kids all walkin in a line holding shovels and axes. They came from outa the woods next to where the lake was. I saw Gary, he was in the front of the line, and then I saw Harris, who was in the back of the line, and the kids all looked like blurry blobs of petrified depression from where I was standin. I squinted to make out what was goin on down there. It looked like they were walkin *into* the lake or something. Were they goin swimmin or some shit? But then they cut back into the woods and walked *behind* the lake and completely outa my sight.

What the *fuck* was goin on at this place? *Then* I met Satan.

CHAPTER 19

A SATAN NAMED THEA

It all happened the next morning when I walked into a room for what they called 'Realizations', which was their version of group therapy, but it was a goddam joke is what it was.

There were fifteen seats setup in a circle, one fucked up kid per seat. Welcome to my Peer Group, Peer Group 34. There were two other chairs and in those chairs, two very wicked people, Thea and Benjamin, my 'counselors'.

Thea was this twenty-three-year old chick that had just graduated from Harvard and was now, for some *fucking reason,* in Dahlonega Georgia. She was TWENTY-FUCKING-THREE and *already* a blithering witch with blonde hair draped over her skeletal anorexic face that probably used to be pretty before the skin started sucking the living shit outa her bones in search for some nutrients.

Benjamin was an overweight, bible-belt, pastor typa man who sweat profusely and probably beat his kids with an iron, but Thea did most of the talking.

"Hi everybody, I'm Thea. I'm excited about this!" And she was. She was like, fuckin... excited and shit. Maybe she didn't know what this place was like yet? Maybe she didn't care? I dunno but she kept talking. "Well, why don't we go around the room and share about why we think we are here and what we hope to gain from this experience."

I started talking cause I love talking and I love attention.

"I'm here cause--"

"--Excuse me, Greg, is it? Greg?"

"Yeah. Greg."

"Remember the Three Seat Rule."

"The what?"

She rolled her eyes. "Okay" already getting pissed... "Now we have here what is called the *Three Seat Rule*. What that means, Greg", in the most condescending voice known to humankind, "is that you must get up and move at least three seats away from me, so that you and I can have a proper conversation. I know you might not be used to *proper conversations*, so I'll explain. If you are too close to someone, it can come off as threatening, in which case I might have to radio for Mort to come get you. Is that understood?"

What a cunt. And who's Mort? What a shitty name... Mort.

"So you want me to move seats?" I asked in *my* condescending-as-fuck tone, but also thoroughly confused.

Then she wrote down something in her notebook. The fuck did she write down?

"Fuck are you writing down?"

The group laughed. Thea picked up her radio and I intercepted—

"Okay okay." So I got up and Jonny, this tall goofy kid from the suburbs of Detroit, he got up too and we switched seats. I dunno, after all was said and done, I didn't even feel like talkin anymore.

"Now, isn't that better?" Thea asked in her 'you're a fuckin piece of nothing' voice.

"Oh yeah. Much."

"Greg, if you're not in a place where you feel like you can speak to me without sarcasm, that's perfectly fine. We can come back to you."

"What the *fuck* are you talking about? I didn't even *say*----"

That was it. She was done talking to me.

"Jonny, is it? You're Jonny aren't you?" And she switched her attention to Jonny. But Jonny was already half-asleep.

"Huh?" He said surprised with drool on his bottom lip.

"Why don't you go ahead and tell us what you hope to achieve while here."

"Nothing." Then he put his head back down.

"And is that why you're here? Because of nothing?"

"That's exactly why I'm here. Cause the world is full of fucking idiots." And he said all that with his head still down.

Thea picked up two black folders.

"Jonny, I'm placing you on a Fall-In Restriction." And she handed him a black folder stuffed full of papers, I dunno what the papers were. There were like fifteen of em. Papers that is.

Stupid fuckin bitch…

But here's the kicker, she told us we *had* to write our parents a letter. I *have* to write my parents a fuckin letter? Yeah right… BUT IT WAS REQUIRED! This place was so twacked out… Write my parents a *letter?* Does this Satan-worshipping whore have any idea where the fuck I am? WRITE MY PARENTS A LETTER???

No. No thank you Satan.

I will NEVER write those fucking pieces of shit letters ever again. Here's my letter:

'Dear Mom and Dad. I am rotting away in institution number three now, in state number three. I am currently not home before summer, as you promised. In fact, it's almost *next* summer. Will I be home by *then?* Of course I won't, cause I'm never coming home ever again. *Then* maybe you'll get how fuckin terrible my childhood is. Love, Greg.'

Dumb fuckin cunt-lickin pieces of shit. I'm sorry. I didn't mean that. Wait, yes I did. Wait, no I didn't. AH! FUCK THIS PLACE! I NEED TIME TO THINK, MORE TIME. I CAN DO THIS. Stay calm. Stay focused. Meditate.

Okay, so Thea said I had to write them twice a week and if I didn't write them, she was gonna put me on Restrictions. Well, she said that to all of our Peer Group—fuck. I'm startin to talk like them here. I just said Peer Group. Startin to talk the way they want me to talk. Well I won't do it. And I won't write my parents a letter. AND WHAT IS RESTRICTIONS?!

So many damn questions.

Number one: What the FUCK is Restrictions?

Number two: What the FUCK are all these stupid fuckin words this place came up with?

Number three: You think you can *make* me write goddam letters?

But I was wrong. She *could* make me write letters, cause as I found out, Restrictions wasn't so nice, it was fuckin terrible actually, and all she had to do was pick up her radio and get some big guard to carry my ass wherever they wanted to put me and that was that. But the biggest pile of dog shit was the fact that Thea *read* the letters to make sure she liked what we were sayin.

"You're gonna have to redo this." She said about my first letter.

"Redo what?"

[Quoting my letter] "This place is full of rapists?"

"IT IS! THAT DUDE I MET YESTERDAY RAPED THAT CHICK THEN CARVED 'HEP-C' INTO HIS KNUCKLES!"

"And what exactly does that have to do with you, and why *you're* here, Greg?"

"Are you nuts?

"No, but I think you can spend some time on Restrictions reflecting on that. You'll have plenty of time to rewrite this letter and write a new letter that's a bit less… hmmm… manipulative. Okay? Or would you like me to have Mort take you down to Lower Left Field right now instead?"

Restrictions? Lower-Left Field? FNK? Peer Groups? Mandatory parent-letter writing? AND WHO IS MORT?! AND WHY IS HIS NAME SO SHITTY?!

"Are you proud of this Thea?"

But that was it.

I found myself sitting in a dark shack later that day. And you know where that shack was? Behind that damn lake. Behind the Hidden Lake. So *that's* where all those kids were goin with all those tools and shit when I saw them yesterday. And now I was one of them, with a shovel in my hand, walkin in a silent line to some worksite where I'd have to shovel holes and move bricks for the remainder of the day.

Point is, the bitch crossed out everything I wrote in all my 'mandatory letters' with red ink and made me write dumb shit like "I'm excited to grow emotionally" and stupid shit like that. Wait till I talk to them on the phone. THEN I'll really let em have it.

But there were no phone calls. Not for four months at least...

"Four months?!?!" I asked Thea.

"You're not even able to write your parents letters without trying to manipulate them into pulling you out of the program, Greg. I certainly don't think you're ready for a phone call. We'll talk about that when you're ready."

"BUT FOUR MONTHS?"

"Yes Greg, four months. But why don't you try and keep focused on today, and not four months from now, okay? Great. Moving on..." And the bitch moved onto someone else.

And that was Realizations. But why don't we call it what it *really* was: Group mind-fuck. This place was all one big mind fuck and Thea was the Queen of fucking your mind. She put on a strap-on cock and inserted it right into your ear till she popped your eardrum with her pricey educated satanic psychology they musta taught her at Harvard. And I knew she went to Harvard cause she said:

"I went to Harvard."

And that's what I did three days a week, for four and a half hours each day. Now what I did on those other four days of the week were even worse. Let's jump back to that dark shack behind the lake I was sent to. It was called 'Restriction Village', another one of their dumb fuckin words they made up.

It was maybe about 10PM by the time they fed us our huge feast of a dinner:

Three cheese sandwiches, a bowl of shitty soup, and an apple...

CHAPTER 20

MY FIRST NIGHT AT RESTRICTION VILLAGE

But before we ate, here's what happened.

So it's pouring rain and it's nighttime and the shack, Restriction Village, is only enclosed by this tin roof and these planks of wood on the sides that are spread two feet apart from each other so we're pretty much outside and my hands are buried in the mud below the shack, while my feet are propped up against the floorboards of the shack and Gary is screamin:

"UP!"

"DOWN!"

"UP!"

"DOWN!"

And we're doin these muddy pushups while the beads of rain blow into our faces and splatter all over our eyes, makin it hard to see and burnin my retinas and my hands are sinkin further into the soft red clay that makes up the mud in rural Georgia every time we go back down for another pushup.

There's this huge fire pit right next to the shack, and these small steps made from rocks carved by previous Restrictions kids, that lead to the small trail that runs behind the hidden lake. So that's where we were, in the middle of fuckin nowhere, outa sight and behind this big ass lake at some cracked out lookin shack. And it's nighttime.

I looked at Jonny, cause he and I were both put on Restrictions, and he looked at me. We were both thinking the same shit. GET US THE FUCK OUT OF HERE. I couldn't take it much longer and it had only been a few days. Seven hundred more days to go? HA! No fuckin way.

After the pushups, which occurred every time someone spoke outa turn or any other number of things that made Gary mad, he pointed at me to distribute the cheese sandwiches.

After I passed out the food and sat back down, Gary made us look at it for like ten minutes before he said:

"EAT!"

I was salivating like a dog by the time the food hit my mouth, even though it was barely food, but anyway it was during that first cheese sandwich that I made a firm decision: Jonny was comin with me. He and I were gonna break out this bitch. I was makin progress. I solidified my newest and only crewmember for 'TEAM GET THE FUCK OUTA HERE.' When I told him of our plan he didn't hesitate for a moment. I told him we would figure this out together.

We weren't quite sure how to do it, but we started exchanging ideas every time we could sneak in a sentence or two to each other, cause on Restrictions, nobody was allowed to talk to anyone. So, it gave us time to think. Finally, we came up with a plan. Not a great one, but a plan nonetheless. Here's what it was:

Run as fast as fuckin possible on Christmas Eve. That was it. That was our plan. And it felt slightly genius after a while. I guess we thought we were brilliant cause of our assumption that Christmas Eve would be the most understaffed day of the year.

Anyway, I still thought we needed a bigger crew, so I told Jonny about Rafal. I don't know what it was about Rafal but I knew the second I met him in The Lodge that he had to come with me. I was NOT about to rot away for two years in this shithole and I figured if anyone could watch my back, it was Rafal. He'd keep us safe and fight off the hicks and bears and shit. So I made the decision that he'd come with us too. And when I told Rafal about it, he all of a sudden seemed to like me and said:

"Fuck yeah, let's do it."

So that made three of us with a very simple motto:

DON'T GET CAUGHT.

Stories of what happened to the kids that tried to escape weren't pretty. Nobody had ever made it. I tried not to think about it. I mean, I couldn't think about it. I had no choice, I *had* to leave. What was I gonna do, stay there? No way. There was no way I was staying there, I had absolutely no other options. I was fucked either way. And still I knew all about what happened to Tyson when he tried to escape. Remember Tyson from the hallway yesterday morning? Well he tried to run like a year ago and he got close, but he didn't make it. He made it *all* the way to Atlanta then tried to steal a cab, but the cabbie locked the doors and sprayed pepper spray in his eyes. Then he got arrested and went to juvie for two months. *Then* they sent him to this wilderness program in Utah, which is *just* as fucked up as juvie, maybe worse, I dunno, and he spent six weeks there, *AND THEN* they sent him back *here! AND* they put him on 'Isolation'! For like a week! And 'Isolation' is supposedly the worst thing that could possibly happen to a human being, 'Isolation', another 'word' they used around here… But whatever happened to Tyson wouldn't happen to us. *We* would be the first group to *actually make it* and everyone would remember us forever. We'd be famous.

But first, a moment of silence for Tyson. He may have made it through Isolation, but he died not too long after leaving Hidden Lake. No one knows why. Apologies for that sad tale. Back to the story…

Then I met a girl. Her name was Lana. She was hot. I asked her to come with us just cause she was hot. She was from Atlanta so that might help us out a bit too I guess, but really I just wanted her to come cause she was hot and three dudes and no chicks is no good.

Then there was this *other* girl named Jesse, and she was in my peer group, Peer Group 34. So that's how I met her. I asked her to come also cause she was mad cool. Yeah, before Realizations one day I was like:

"Yo, we're runnin."

She was like "I'm in."

And that was that.

Then there was this chick named Sedona. Now this one is a bit puzzling cause she was in Peer Group 23, the oldest Peer Group, and had already been there for nearly two years and was *almost* done with her time, BUT, she got caught stealing wine from the school church service and they were threatening to extend her sentence. So yeah, she was pissed and wanted out too. Now we had three chicks that were gonna run with us. Fuck yeah. I was *finally* gonna get laid! Just thinkin about it gave me performance anxiety. Think about something else Greg.

Okay, so let's go over our crew again.

There was me, Jonny, Rafal, Lana, Sedona, and Jesse so far. We figured the bigger the group the better if we were all gonna live as runaways till we were eighteen.

But then we kinda fucked up and let this kid named Teddy in at the last moment. Teddy was a Korean kid from Baltimore that was convinced he was a 'Blood', like the other kids in Louisiana. I wasn't so sure about his affiliation, but whatever, the part that pissed me off the most was that it unbalanced our girl to dude ratio. Now we needed another chick! But we never got one! We were four dudes and three girls, so I guess Teddy would have to settle for not having sex, or maybe we'd just all have sex with each other and have weird orgies and shit. Who knows? Or maybe he can fuck one of the girls after I do? Already I had these crazy plans of sex with these girls that I didn't even know, not to mention, we were *still* locked up in the middle of the woods and nobody had ever escaped... so there was that too. I had to come up with some tricks to help us make this work.

TRICK NUMBER ONE:

I wrote a fake note and mapped out a fake route leading to Gainesville Georgia, a town in the other direction, to throw the guards and Sheriff off track, and left it blatantly sticking out of my Big Book, the AA book I was given at Louisiana. Oh yeah! They sent me my Big Book from Louisiana! I forgot to tell you that! But I dunno where the rest of my shit was, or if I'd ever see it again. My damn backpack... it was gone. Fuck. Okay whatever... so on my bland bookshelf next to my bed was my Big Book and in the Big Book was this fake note. Not as strategic as I had originally planned it to be. I might as well have written:

PLEASE FIND THIS. THIS NOTE IS FOR YOU.

But at the time I thought it was genius. Actually, I thought all my ideas were genius... maybe *that* was my problem? Anyway, it was worth a shot. I didn't have any better ideas.

TRICK NUMBER TWO: There was no trick number two. We only had one trick.

Okay... So we started plotting. Here are the mechanics of what was about to go down...

First we had to get both us, and the chicks, outa the dormitory. Now, the dorms were all identical and each room had a window that didn't open. Since Jesse's room faced the lake, we figured the girls would all get together in her room before lights out and we'd tap on the window to let them know when we were outside.

THEN they would sneak out just as we had—how is that exactly? I dunno yet. BUT, after we figured that part out, and figured out how to get outa the dormitory without being seen... which was kinda impossible given the one hallway and locked Plexiglas doors and surveillance cameras and guards, we'd all run down to the wilderness shed at the far end of the lake, which is where they stashed all the backpacks and camping shit, to get food. They kept Rice Krispy treats there for the guards to munch on while they tortured us, so we figured we'd take those.

THEN...

Well, *then*... we fuckin RUUUUNNNNNN!!!!

One thing was for sure: They wouldn't ever find me, ever, and my parents would never see my face again. This was exactly what I needed to add to the tale of my infamous reputation before I returned home to Long Island, on the run, as a complete legend.

We would run on Christmas Eve.

CHAPTER 21

X-MAS EVE

It was Christmas eve.

We had it all figured out except for a few minor details. My heart rattled when Gary and Harris came on shift. They went up and down the hallway and took inventory of all us fuckup kids in the dorm. They did that every couple hours. That meant we only had a couple hours before they found out we were gone. Still there was one problem: We were locked inside the dormitory and it only had that one long hallway and Gary and Harris were guarding the interior AND the fuckin surveillance cameras were all over the ceiling. A small detail we still hadn't yet figured out. I know I know, we shoulda had that down already but whatever, we'll figure it out. The answer'll come to us any moment now.

Jonny and Rafal and Teddy snuck to my room, room fourteen, all layered up with clothes. It was *really* cold out. The only thing I grabbed was my journal. I didn't even put my jacket on cause it woulda been far too obvious. That was a mistake. BUT WAIT! An idea!

I know how to get past the doors!

"Jonny." I said. "You're on door duty right?"

"So?"

Door duty meant he had to clean up all the mud and red clay and sweep the foyer and crud off the floor mats when you walk into the dormitory.

"After you sweep the outdoor mats, let the door close on the rubber of the mats so that you can't really tell the door is open, and don't let it close all the way so it won't lock. And if you do the same thing for the other set of doors, then all we gotta do is sneak out! EASY! Right?"

So yeah, not only was there one set of doors blocking our escape, but TWO sets of doors we had to get through. But this new plan of mine, well, I just fixed that problem, so we were all good.

We waited till they called chores and Jonny got it done. Atta boy Jonny! See? I told you it'd come to me any minute! We were almost there… Almost home free.

Okay, now we had to somehow sneak outa my room and get close enough to the doors at the far end of the hallway while keeping the appearance that we were in regular uniform just doing regular chores. Shouldn't be a problem, but first, I asked the guys to hold my hand.

"Hold my hand."

Jonny said "Why?"

"Cause my roommate at my first rehab in Minnesota was Wiccan. And his shit worked. So we're gonna pray to the Goddess. That's what he did. And he could read minds and shit."

"That's some gay shit dude." Rafal said.

"It's not." I assured him.

Then Teddy chimed in "I'm down. Let's pray."

They grabbed my hand.

"Here comes some weird hippie shit from Cayea." Rafal warned the group.   Yup. He was right. We formed a circle. If the Goddess listened to Sargon every day, she would definitely hear me out just this once. So I gave it my best shot. I had never prayed before so I just made some shit up.

"Keep us alive on our journey.

Liberate us from confinement.

Grant us freedom.

Protect our health.

Heal our wounds."

That was it. I made that shit up on the spot. The countdown had started. It was 9PM, maybe. We took a deep breath, sucked in our fear, and

Three.

Two.

One.

BOOOOOM!!!!

CHAPTER 22

NOT ACCORDING TO PLAN

We nearly shattered the glass doors as we kicked them open at full throttle, blasting down the hallway for everyone to see. We meant to be quiet, sly and mischievous on our way out... but the adrenaline totally fucked those plans up and we found ourselves just running for dear life. Jonny already started to crack and get all nervous as soon as we busted through the doors.

"SHIT! THEY HEARD THAT SHIT BRO! RUN!"

I mean, of COURSE they heard that! WE JUST BOMBARDED THROUGH THE GLASS DOORS IN THE MIDDLE OF CHORES!

We leapt behind the high grass and slid down the misty red clay to the trail that wrapped around the lake. In the dark, we couldn't see the rocks and tree roots on our path as we sprinted to Dormitory three, the girls dorm, to Jesse's room, like we had planned. We counted the windows until we got to room eighteen where the girls were waiting.

I said to the group

"Stay here."

And I ran up the hill and tiptoed to the edge of their window and gave a little tap. Damn it was cold outside. I tapped again, we didn't have time to stand in one place for too long, plus I had to keep moving to keep my blood hot. Where were they?! Again… I tapped.

Lana came to the window and stared at me as if she was not looking at anything in particular. Like I was a ghost or some shit.

There must be a guard in her room, I thought. Then, with a sudden burst of movement she gave me a 'JUST GO!!!' typa hand movement.

Huh? JUST GO?! WE HAD A PLAN! Then *Jesse* came to the window and shook her head.

What the FUCK was going on?!?!?

Jonny screamed above a whisper "CAYEA!!!"

But I said "Shhhhh!!!!"

And Rafal said all aggravated "They coming!??!"

And I kept tapping the window but then they both disappeared,
Lana and Jesse. I didn't even see Sedona—She musta changed her mind.

SHIT!

I ran back down to Jonny and Teddy and Rafal. Teddy was busy
tryin to keep himself warm. Fuck it was so *fucking cold*.

"They aren't coming." I told the guys.

Teddy was like "WHAT?!"

But Rafal didn't give a fuck, he just said "Fuck it bro!!! LET'S GO!"

And so we bolted down to the wilderness shed.

"STOP!"

There was a voice. We dropped to the ground and held our breath
from making any movement. This was it. Fuck. We're done. I'm done.
This is never gonna end. Then I heard the words more clearly:

"OH HELL NAH! YA'LL BETTA NOT BE RUNNIN ON MY
SHIFT!!!"

It was Harris, shining his flashlight through the trees, screaming at
the top of his lungs. We froze. Fuck fuck fuck fuck. Does he see us?

"HE SEES US!" I shouted.

So without warning the group I got up from where I was hiding and
started running but I tripped over Jonny cause he was still on the ground
and nearly knocked us both down, but I regained my balance. Then
Jonny and Rafal and Teddy got up too and followed after me and we
booked the fuck out down to the end of the lake hoppin over tree roots
and scrapin our faces on branches and nearly falling into the water a
bazillion times. But we kept going. Nothing would stop us. My lungs
were so stretched out and sore from breathing so fast by the time we got
to the wilderness shed that I thought my lung might rip in half.

Rafal grabbed a heavy rock and took a step toward the shed, ready to catapult it through the window.

Jonny said "WHAT THE FUCK ARE YOU DOING?"

"GETTING FOOD!" Rafal shouted back.

"I THINK WE SHOULD JUST GET THE FUCK OUTA HERE!" I said.

"WITH NO FOOD?!" Rafal asked like I was fuckin this whole thing up, which I was kinda. But I mean, I wasn't really *that* hungry anyway.

Teddy looked around rubbing his hands together with his sleeves covering his fingers and blocking the wind from his ears as best he could while he waited for us to decide what we were gonna do. To break into the wilderness shed, or not to break into the wilderness shed, that was the goddam question that we needed to fuckin answer.

But Jonny SCREAMED, "COME ON!!! WE GOTTA GET OUTA HERE!!!!!!"

"Ahh fuck it…" And Rafal dropped the rock.

We were completely surrounded by the Appalachians without anywhere else to go. There was a small opening into the forest blackness that looked like it might be a trail, so we darted into it with fury… But there was no trail.

All of a sudden I started falling.

"AHHHHHHHHHHH!!!

"HEEEEEELLLLLLLLLLLLLLLLLLPPPPPPPPPPPPPPP!!!!!!!!!"

THUMP.

SILENCE.

BEAT.

AWAKE.

WAS I ALIVE? THE *FUCK* WHAT WAS THAT?!

My body ached as I lay in a ditch. I heard a voice echo above me. It was Jonny. He was laughing. Then I saw Rafal. Thank God. I'm alive.

I got up and looked around. We were at the bottom of a twenty-foot embankment that I had just catapulted off, BUT, we were now officially safe from HLA... but also officially lost as fuck. There was NO way out of this now. We *had* to keep going and not die and somehow find our way outa this damn forest. We knew if we walked straight we would hit Camp Wahsega Road, the only road in town... but which way was straight? This was all a lot easier in my head a few hours ago.

FAST-FORWARD THREE HOURS.

I could see my breath in the pitch-black forest. The cold was gnawing at my bones. The wind blew right through the fabric of my pants. My ears were frozen. We huddled close together to generate body heat at the trunk of a large tree. My heart was galloping inside my chest. Maybe I made a mistake? Don't think like that Greg. Keep going.

I heard strange noises. I heard a baby. She was crying. She was shrieking.

Someone was beating her.

"Did you guys hear that?" I said.

What was it? Was there a ghost? Were we in the wrong forest?

Rafal grabbed a stick. So I grabbed one too. The sound of animals brushing through the dry leaves surrounded us in all directions. The cold gusts of wind were unbearable. We hiked through sticky pine trees and sap and I got it all over my hands. Then, at our coldest moment, Jonny and I didn't see this creek cause it was all dark and we stepped right in it and got ourselves soaking wet, which put us both in this real shitty mood, especially Jonny, cause he was already in a shitty mood. But anyway, our pants and shoes and socks were wet as fuck and my foot went numb immediately. Then the water kept seepin deeper into my pants and sneakers until the bottom of my pants started frosting over with light ice. Soon my feet tingled from the numbness.

It had been hours that we'd been trying to find our way out of that fucking forest. I was beginning to think we might die. There was no way out. I was terrified. But if we didn't keep moving we'd die just from the cold. So we kept wandering, aimlessly, looking for a way out.

And then it happened.

We found our way!

"THE ROAD, I SEE IT!!!!!!!!!!" I shouted, letting everyone know how 'right' I had been all along, but really I was thankin God, or the Goddess, whoever saved my ass from dying, in my head over and over again. Thank you God. Goddess. Thank you universe, whoever you are. It felt like a miracle as I shouted again: "LOOK!!!"

Everyone squinted. YES, THERE IT WAS! We had done it!

YESSSSSSSSS!!!!!!!!!!!!!!! My blood boiled with excitement as I carried my body over to the road. WE HAD MADE IT! IT WAS CAMP WAHSEGA ROAD! JUST LIKE WE PLANNED ON IT BEING!!

But then I looked at the "Welcome To Hidden Lake" sign. Wait a minute… It was twenty feet away? Three hours lost in the woods and we had ended up only a few hundred feet from the "Welcome To Hidden Lake" sign? *THIS* WAS AS FAR AS WE MADE IT?!

It's okay, we just… you know, get on the road and start headin to town… but where was town? I looked around. There was nothing. There were a few scattered houses that had seen better days, but other than that it was just a whole lotta red clay and dry pine needles crunchin beneath our feet. I had no idea where to go.

We weren't gonna make it. We weren't even close. Fuck, what the hell was I thinking? And I told all the guys that I had this all figured out just like I told Lisa. Remember her? I wonder what happened to her… huh. And Lacey! I can't even really remember what she looked like by now, but whatever, now there was this! Fuck! Now the guys are gonna hate me too just like Lisa and Lacey hated me!

I didn't tell anyone about this monstrous fear, I just kept tellin everyone, "almost there". But that was a lie. We were almost nowhere. We were almost in jail. That was the truth but the truth never seemed to be interesting to say out loud. More than that, I was fuckin STARVING.

WHY DID WE LEAVE THAT WILDERNESS SHED WITHOUT THE RICE KRISPY TREATS?!?! WHY DID WE *NOT* DO THAT?! Oh wait, I think that was my idea to not do that. Shit. Man, everything was goin wrong. But we kept walkin.

I got so hungry at one point that I sat down and ripped out a patch of grass and shoved it in my mouth. It tasted horrible.

"Are you eating… grass?" Teddy asked me.

"Yes, I am."

It had only been ten hours since we ate, but I was so damn hungry. I spit it out and there was green shit all over my tongue from the grass and it was nasty. Then I tore out a sheet of paper from my journal and crumpled it into a ball and chewed *that* down as best I could and swallowed. *And*, believe it or not, it actually *worked*. I wasn't hungry for like ten minutes! Then Jonny screamed:

"TRUCK!!!!!!"

Headlights gleamed ahead of us. We jumped into the ditch that ran alongside the road and lay still till the lights were gone, then we got up and kept walkin again.

I couldn't feel my nose after some hours. The sun started to rise. Then again Jonny screamed:

"TRUCK!!!!"

Ugh, jeez. So I jumped into another fuckin ditch and— NOOOOO!!!!! I looked up and Jonny, all six-foot-three of him, was hurdling through the air about to land right on top of my face.

"FUCK!!!!"

"OH SHITTT!!!!!"

Rafal screamed "SHUT THE FUCK--"

But Teddy hushed him "Shhhhhhhh!!"

BOOM! Jonny landed right on top of me and nearly squashed my face.

"Sorry dude."

"All good." I was not all good.

So the truck passed and we got to the end of Camp Wahsega Road by 5 or 6AM, although I had no idea what time it really was. I never knew what time it really was. There were never any clocks when I needed them.

We just kept sprinting then walking then sprinting then jumping in ditches then running then sprinting but finally, we got there. We had made it. Well, we had made it to another road at least, which still left us in the middle of nowhere, but one road further from Hidden Lake was progress I suppose. There was still nothing in sight except for a broken-down auto repair shop. Then Teddy screamed:

"CAR!!!!"

But now there were no ditches to hide in. Shit. We were on flat farmland. But there *was* a tin storage-lookin building that we saw so we ran behind *that*.

We hid ourselves nice and tight but then I looked around and asked "Where's Jonny?"

Jonny was walking in the middle of the street.

Rafal was *furious* "WHAT THE FUCK YOU DOING JONNY!? YOU'RE GONNA GET US ALL CAUGHT!"

"Fuck it man. I'm hungry and tired and fucking cold."

Teddy pleaded:

"JONNY!"

"Oh no." I said to the group. "That's the... is that a... is that the sheriff?" But before I could process my sentence a loud siren came on and a blinding white spotlight blinded our sight.

Now we were *fucked*. We had been caught. They'd probably make an example outa us when we got back. Shit. A loudspeaker came on:

"You boys bout ready to go back to school?" It was the Lumpkin County Sheriff. The jig was up. We were *really* fucked.

They shackled our legs and handcuffed our wrists and put us in the sheriff's car and took us a mile down the street to the police station and offered us fruit as we sat, shackled in a room, staring at a display case full of drug paraphernalia.

The sheriff went to a computer and said "Tewe a yew er court ordered. Ya'll go to juvie if ya'll wawnt."

It was a weird statement and I wondered who was court ordered and whether whoever it was, maybe Teddy and Jonny? I wasn't sure who the second was. I knew Teddy was there for being arrested for something, don't remember what. But anyway, I wondered if whoever it was would opt for juvie insteada Hidden Lake. After all, at least they fed you in juvie. I think. I mean I'd never been to juvie or anything... But then the sheriff said:

"CAY-YAY-Uh? KAH-AY-A?"

I looked at him, "Cayea." I said. "Like Kay-Uh." And I did the pronunciation for him.

"And Rafal Lvvett?? Lah-vett??" The sheriff asked.

"Yeah?" Rafal said.

"Ya'll tewe court ordered."

"What?"

And Teddy said, "What about me?" Like he felt left out or some shit.

"What's yer name?" The sheriff asked.

"Teddy. Moskowitz." Oh right, he was adopted by Jewish parents, forgot to tell you that... But I bet he kept that one a secret from the rest of his gang of Bloods back in the wealthy suburbs of Baltimore...

"Teddy Teddy Teddy Teddy…" The sheriff said as he looked at his computer screen or maybe it was a sheet of paper, I can't remember, but he said, "Nope. Don't see ya here Teddy. Good news fer yew ah guess."

But Teddy wouldn't give up, "I'm pretty sure I'm court-ordered."

And Rafal said, "And I'm pretty sure I'm not."

And I said, "Wait. I'm court-ordered? How? I wasn't arrested anywhere. Right? Yeah. No. I haven't been arrested ever." I was thinkin real hard… like, did I miss a courtroom appearance or somethin? What the fuck?

"Well that's what I got. School or Juvie?" The sheriff asked Rafal and I.

I asked "How long would juvie be?"

But the Sheriff said, "I ain't know."

I couldn't leave my friends and separate and start all over at another place. I had to go back with them, plus juvie sounded scary. We were all in this together and the last thing I wanted was *another* separation. Everyone is always goin away. I was sick of it. Or maybe it was *me* that was always goin away? I dunno but then I heard the sound of a tire scraping the pebbles of the dirt parking lot outside. Headlights shone through the cop station blinds.

There was the sound of a truck door opening and in came Scary Gary, head of Hidden Lake night security. He had a huge beard, trucker hat, thick flannel shirt, wrangler jeans, bloodshot eyes, and was angry as all hell about life.

They unshackled us and took the handcuffs off as we got in the back of Scary Gary's truck. I was court-ordered? Scary Gary didn't utter a word the whole drive back down Camp Wahsega road. That road was so much shorted in a car.

The Colonel waited for us in front of the admin when we pulled up the steep Hidden Lake road. He took us all into a large empty room and made us each sit cross-legged on the floor, each of us facing a different corner of the room.

My eyes kept closing with fatigue but my heart was pounding. I wonder what they're gonna do to us?

Then the door opened. Somebody quietly walked in but I don't know who it was cause I was starin at the corner of the room.

"DON'T YOU DARE MOVE YOUR HEADS! YOU KEEP STARING AT THE WALL!"

I heard the sound of footsteps pacing around. The voice exploded again:

"GET THE FUCK UP!"

It was Bear.

His face was so red it was on the verge of popping like a water balloon. And boy was he mad...

"DO YOU KNOW WHAT IT'S LIKE CALLING YOUR PARENTS ON CHRISTMAS EVE TELLING THEM THEIR KIDS ARE GONE?!"

But I'm Jewish... maybe he meant Chanukah?

"FORMATION! NOOOOWWWWW!!!"

We formed a line. That's what 'formation' meant.

"WALK!"

He led us outside the building down to Lower Left Field, some field drenched in goose shit that sat right next to the lake, to a pile of firewood and he got on his walkie-talkie.

"I think the kiddies are ready for some *discipline.*"

His eyes were still fixed on us.

"SHUT UP!!!!"

But we hadn't said anything you crazy fuck.

Then through the walkie-talkie there was demonic laughter, "Oh I got it from here Bear. Don't you worry. Over." Fuck. I knew that laugh from a crowd of people laughing. It was Harris.

My heart dropped as he laughed a bit more before taking his thumb off the 'talk' button of his walkie-talkie. He was happy. Happy we'd been caught. Bear said:

"Now ya'll are in for a real treat. SHUT UP!"

But nobody had said anything... psycho-hick.

It was probably about 8AM judging by the sun and we hadn't slept one bit when Harris came into view. He walked through the grass and over the goose shit toward us. I watched him put his walkie-talkie to his mouth as he walked closer.

"You can take off Bear, I'll handle it from here." Then he laughed again.

"Have fun with them Harris." Bear said as he smiled and said: "Bye kiddies." And walked away.

Then Harris stopped in front of us.

"Welcome back boys!"

CHAPTER 23

S.O.S. KIDDIES IN TROUBLE

"TURN BIG STICKS INTO LITTLE STICKS" Harris shouted again as the sun started to go down. My arms felt like rubber. I couldn't break one more branch.

"YA'LL AIN'T EATEN TILL YA'LL BREAK MO' BRANCHES. C'MON, BIG STICKS INTA LITTLE STICKS LEZGO!"

"Harris I need water", I said.

"STOP! YA'LL THIRSTY HUH? FOLLOW ME!" And he took us to some creek that ran right next to Lower Left Field. There was goose shit everywhere. "DRINK!"

"I'm not drinkin that water Harris, fuck!" Jonny cried.

Harris laughed.

"YA'LL WANNA QUENCH THAT THIRST YA'LL BETTA DRINK UP! YA'LL GOT 10, 9, 8, 7, 6—"

And we put our heads into the creek and started slurpin up as much water as we could. I was so damn thirsty and hungry and tired and hurting and it was only the first day…

"GET UP! BACK TO WORK YA'LL! BIG STICKS INTA LITTLE STICKS, BIG STICKS INTA LITTLE STICKS!"

The sun was almost *completely* gone and my memory was fading in and out as I searched in the dark for a branch that was brittle enough that I could still break it with what little strength I had. It was gettin real dark in those woods and I wasn't sure where Harris took us that night to sleep cause I couldn't see where we were, but when I woke up, I was on a damp carpet in the middle of a flooded basement floor in a sweaty sleeping bag.

The carpet reeked of mildew. Jonny, Rafal and Teddy were asleep next to me, also in sweaty sleeping bags, and through my sleep-crudded eyes an unfamiliar woman in army attire sat in a chair reading a magazine in front of the only door that led outa the basement. Her walkie-talkie kept goin in and out.

I had no idea where Harris was. I don't remember the night ever ending. I don't remember gettin to this basement. I don't know what time it was. But all I could think about was how I could rush this bitch and drag her ass to the floor. Rafal could bloody up her face while Teddy smashed her walkie-talkie into the side of her temples until he knocked her unconscious, or maybe even dead. Then Jonny could pee all over her dead body and we could make her hair into a wig and sneak out, but not before I kicked her in the ribs and robbed her money from her pockets... but fuck, where would we go after *that*? Where would we go *then*?

There was no way out. Next to me I had this big camping backpack stuffed with long underwear and rain gear and wool socks and a buncha other shit. I don't even remember anyone giving it to me, but there it was, right next to my sleeping bag.

It musta been five in the morning, but there was no way for me to really know. But I was sure that I'd only gone to bed like a few hours ago. No way that was a full night's sleep. Actually, I don't really remember anything, we mighta been sleeping for longer than that. My body was sore all over and I hadn't eaten anything except grass and paper in the last forty-eight hours and that piece of fruit the sheriff offered us at the station when we got caught. Forgot about that. I felt delirious. I'm so fucking hungry.

Then the door opened.

ENTER MORT.

Finally, we meet Mort. Remember Mort? The dude that Thea always threatened to radio during Realizations when shit got outa hand? Well he was a short stocky man wearing a well-fitted uniform and had this fresh military haircut. He only worked morning shifts. I never really met him… and now here he was. Short as fuck. And probably real mad about it.

The cunty-lookin woman sittin in the chair in front of the basement door stood up. I looked at her. She caught my eye and we made brief eye contact but I looked away quick and pretended to fall back asleep. She rolled up her magazine like she was all tough-like and grabbed her backpack like she earned it or somethin then left the basement. So it was us alone with Mort, whose arms were crossed as he sipped water from his water pack thingy. Man was I thirsty. He was starin at his waterproof-lookin watch for about a minute before he lunged into action:

"GET UP!"

Rafal and Jonny and Teddy opened their eyes. Mine were already open.

"TWO MINUTES! GET THE HECK UP!"

None of those dudes ever cursed, I noticed. At least Gary and this idiot didn't. Harris cursed all the time, or at least sometimes he did. Must be some kinda religious military thing. Anyway we stumbled outa our sleeping bags.

"THREE, TWO" he counted more slowly on one, **"ONE… POST!"**

Post meant we had to form a line, so we formed a fuckin line. Jeez, this goddam place and all their fuckin words.

"TOO SLOW!!!! BACK BACK BACK!!!"

"Back where?"

"STOP! EVERYONE DOWN DOWN DOWN!!!"

He kept sayin everything in threes. What a moron. I got in a pushup position cause that's what 'down' meant. My arms were all wobbly from yesterday, but whatever… I can take it. I was feeling strong. I had these moments where I felt strong and tough.

"RAFAL GET UP UP UP!!!"

Hmm… He knew Rafal's name. Does he know my name? He should. Anyway, Rafal got up.

"CALL CADENCE! FIFTY-FOUR-COUNT PUSHUPS. GO GO GO!!"

Cadence meant call out the 'up downs'. All these dumb words. So I put my knees to the ground cause my arms gave out. I was too tired. I was too sore. I couldn't do this right now, I wasn't in the mood. I didn't feel strong anymore. I hadn't even slept or eaten, man… I was a mess. But then Mort singled me out:

"YOU! WHO TOLD YOU TO GET OUT OF FRONT LEAN AND REST?! BACK UP NOW NOW NOW!"

He *didn't* know my name. What a cockdrip. Anyway, I picked my knees off the ground to keep myself up. I kept thinkin of the best way to kill him. Maybe I beat him to death with his coffee thermos, cause he had this coffee thermos and it was like, metal or some shit. I could steal the coffee thermos, dump the scorching coffee on his face and then pound the thermos into his skull till he started crying.

I snapped out of it.

"Rafal GO GO GO!"

So Rafal started 'callin cadence' "One, Two Three"

"ONE!" We said.

"STOP! GET UP!"

This idiot can't make up his mind. So we stood up.

"FRONT LEAN AND REST! DOWN DOWN DOWN!!!"

Soooo…. We got back down. What a fuckin surprise. I was so damn mad at my parents. I'ma kill them too. I wonder what my brother is doin? I wonder if the BOPS know about this… I wonder where Delson is? Is he home yet? Does *he* talk about me? Okay, don't think right now, stay focused.

"Rafal you better be louder than that!!!! CALL CADENCE! LOUDER LOUDER LOUDER!!!"

So Rafal started callin cadence louder "ONE TWO THREE"

"TWO!"

"STOP!" So we stopped. Jeez, this idiot was pissin me the fuck off. You want us to do these pushups or what dickface? **"Did I just hear a TWO? That looked like the first push-up to me! I told you to START OVER! Now GO GO GO!!!"**

I'll be home in thirty days, huh? How the hell did this happen again? Where am I? When will this end? I couldn't do one more stupid pushup. My arms kept shakin and I kept fallin on my face.

One day I'ma write a book about this and kill Mort and that'll be in the book too. Shit, but then I'd go to prison for murder. I can't *tell* everyone about it in a book. Well, I'll figure that out later.

So somehow I did those dumb fifty pushups. I mean, they were all sloppy and I was slurrin my movements but Mort didn't say anything about it, he let me do the shitty pushups cause I mean, what the fuck was he gonna do? Make me stronger?

"GET UP UP UP!! GET THOSE SLEEPING BAGS IN THOSE PACKS AND MOVE MOVE MOVE!!! YA'LL GOT TWO MINUTES! GO!!!"

I got up and shoved my sleeping bag in my pack and put it on my back and then—Whoa, now my whole body was wobbly. I couldn't really see cause my eyes were droopy and I couldn't really keep my walk straight cause my pack was swinging my legs in whatever direction gravity took me.

"POST POST POST!!"

So we got in a line again.

Then Mort took two small Corn Flakes cereals, the size you find at a shitty motel continental breakfast, and one carton of milk and an apple from his backpack then he walked us outa the basement door and took us outside. The sun was up and it pierced my eyes. It was too bright. Someone shut the sun off.

"YA'LL HUNGRY?!"

"YES!"

Boy did that make him mad when we didn't say 'sir'.

"YES WHAT?!?!?!?"

"YESSIR!"

"YOU!" And he pointed at me. He *really* didn't know my name. **"GIVE OUT CHOW!"** And he handed me the cereal and the apples and the milk. One apple slipped my grip and fell to the ground onto the dirt. **"DON'T YOU PICK THAT APPLE UP YOU! EVERYONE SIT DOWN DOWN DOWN!"**

So then we all sat down. Happy now Morty-boy?

"NOT A WORD! DON'T YOU DARE TOUCH THAT FOOD TILL I SAY SO!" Then again… **"YOU!"** He was talkin to me. Man, he's never gonna ask my name. **"PICK UP THAT APPLE UP AND TAKE A BITE! DON'T YOU WIPE IT OFF EITHER!"**

Okay psycho…

But I was so hungry that it didn't even matter. So I took a bite. I guess that satisfied him cause then he looked at his army waterproof watch and said: **"TWO MINUTES! EAT! I'M TIMING YOU! GO GO GO!!"**

"We need spoons." Teddy said.

"STOP!! EVERYONE UP UP UP!!!"

Mort stared at his watch as we stood up.

"SEE THAT TREE?" And he pointed down this cliff by where we were standing to a tree. **"THE CLOCK IS STILL TICKING! BETTER GO GIVE THAT TREE A HUG AND GET YER BUTT BACK UP HERE 'FORE YOUR CHOW TIME IS UP! GO GO GO!!!"**

That's it. I'm gonna sue this place. But I'll do that later. I'm so damn hungry, FUCK! So we all side-stepped down this fuckin cliff to some fuckin tree and gave the fuckin thing a fuckin hug.

"MAKE SURE YOU HUG IT!!!" He screamed from the top of the cliff thingy.

I just did you moron. But I didn't actually say that. By the time we got back up I thought I was gonna faint. I can do this. Yes, I can do this! Or I can just kill him. Nah, that'll just make shit worse, I thought.

"TWENTY SECONDS LEFT! EAT EAT EAT!!!"

He still didn't give us a spoon. Whatever, I ripped the milk open and poured it in my mouth then ripped the Corn Flakes open and poured them in my mouth too then swished them both around together and chewed as best as I could with my cheeks filled to the brim with milk and corn flakes then swallowed. Then I took some bites of my dirty apple while the cereal was still kinda in my mouth. Before I'd even eaten half of the small ass shitty meal, Mort was already screamin:

"STAND UP UP UP!"

I wasn't done eating. Fuck. I stood up anyway, cause I had to. Damn it's cold. Think of heat. It's hot. Not cold, hot. Anyway then he marched us back into the woods in a straight line behind the lake, kinda close to where we were yesterday, then he stopped us mid-walk. Then I heard crunchy leaves. Mort looked at his watch. Then a familiar voice.

It was Gary. He was in a winter military uniform, crunchin the leaves beneath his boots as his brick-like jaw cast a crooked shadow through the branches of the trees onto the shitty dirt ground as he approached.

Did the school know what they were doin to me?

We stood there shivering as Mort and Gary stared at each other, and then at us. I wonder if they're friends with each other. Nah, Gary probably gets laid. Mort definitely does not.

"POST!" Gary shouted… these guys are all the same. White bible belt army meathead cockheads. Anyway, we formed a line in front of he and Mort.

"FASTER!" He was overly mad, Gary was, for some reason. **"What's wrong boys, you tired? GET BACK TO WHERE YOU**

WERE! I DON'T EVER WANT TO SEE YOU WALK AGAIN!
WHEN I SAY POST, YOU RUN!"

So we ran back to the tree we were at to make him happy.

"POST!"

Then we ran back to Gary, faster and formed a straight line.

"NOT FAST ENOUGH! GO BACK AND DO IT AGAIN!"

Ugh. And again… we did it. Then he just looked at us for a while.

"GOOD. FOLLOW ME. NOT A SINGLE WORD!"

Where the hell we goin now? Mort hung out at the back of the line
and we walked for about fifteen minutes past dead trees and fallen leaves
and creeks and up and down hills and then stopped at a tree stoop. Gary
sat down and took out his food. Mort sipped his coffee. I really should
smash that thermos into his face. Our mouths watered. Then Gary
yelled with a mouth full of food:

"DOWN!"

Oh that's a fuckin surprise. So we got into pushup position.

"CALL CADENCE SOMEONE!"

So Rafal started: "ONE, TWO, THREE"

"ONE!"

"ONE, TWO, THREE"

"TWO!"

"ONE, TWO, THREE"

"THREE!"

"UP!" He finally said.

So we walked again, Mort at the back to make sure nobody ran away
I guess, and Gary at the front cause he was cooler than Mort, and we

walked over dead leaves and pine needles through the endless woods and kept goin and goin and goin until STOP.

We were at some creepy lookin cabin. It wasn't that cabin I saw when I was in that pickup truck with those private investigators either, but it was this *other* cabin, some cabin I never seen before... some cabin probably nobody had ever seen before. Where the *fuck* are we?

"Boys, welcome to Isolation Cabin."

CHAPTER 24

ISOLATION CABIN

My heart stopped as I realized where we were.

Isolation Cabin.

I had *heard* about Isolation Cabin, but I didn't know it really existed.
I thought it mighta just been some dumb rumor the kids started around
here. This really *is* Hells Little Acre. It really *does* exist. After all the
rumors about Isolation Cabin, here I was. With Jonny and Teddy and
Rafal and two meathead lunatics. Nobody would hear us scream.

I saw an old, weathered axe propped up against the side of the old,
weathered cabin wall.

**"I'M COLD! SOMEONE MAKE ME SOME FIREWOOD
FOR MY FIRE!!"**

Now is my chance I thought. An axe, KILL EM! KILL EM BOTH! I could kill them right here and end this.

So I grabbed the axe and cut Gary's head off, it was a hard chop, but it cracked through his bones and left some spare vertebrae on the ground, so I picked up the vertebrae and shoved it down Mort's throat. Then he choked and begged for forgiveness and then he died.

Snap out of it Greg! Okay so yeah, that didn't happen. What happened was I picked up the axe but couldn't feel it through my numb fingers. All I had on was long underwear thermals.

"YOU BETTER BE MUCH FURTHER 'WAY FROM ME WITH THAT AXE! THE REST OF YOU GATHER ME SOME WOOD!"

Okay fine, I'll kill him later. Both of them. Then I'm outa this bitch.

I went off into the forest to look for fallen down trees to chop as Rafal and Jonny and Teddy picked up big sticks one by one and brought them to Gary. We were all just walkin around in our dirty long underwear gathering wood. It was a sad sight.

I was delirious from hunger and no sleep and the cold. The hours went by, or minutes, or decades, who knows. I took one step. Then another. I fell over my numb foot this one time but I got back up.

Find trees Greg, find fallen down trees and just chop them sons a bitches. I couldn't feel my legs. I think I mighta sprained my ankle just now. Stay focused, then kill them. But for now just turn trees into logs, turn trees into logs, turn logs into logs, careful with axe, logs into logs, logs into—I mean trees, turn logs into trees, from trees—Fuck. What?

My hands were blocks of icy flesh and I couldn't feel em for shit. I stared at Gary's fire. His fire was already kickin up flames. He was toasty warm. I could push him into the fire at least... nah, then he'd just get out and be all mad. Fuck, I felt sick. Then a voice came in through his radio, Gary's radio...

"Gary, come in. Over."

"Go 'head Harris. Over."

Oh no, not Harris again. He was the fuckin *worst*. Jeez, no Harris please. No Harris.

"What's your location? Over." Harris said through the radio.

"We're out by Isolation Cabin. Over."

"Copy."

It was like... twenty or so minutes maybe when I heard that fuckrag's voice:

"You punk ass kids—"

I could see him through the trees. He showed up and I grabbed the axe. I flung it through the trees and it landed deep in his skull, and now his skull was all cracked and he was screaming for help as blood poured over the dead pine needles. He was whispering before he died for good. I laughed. GOT YOU BITCH!

Snap outa it. He was almost here. Harris was the worst, fuck. He seemed like he was angry all over again as he trudged toward us.

"Gettin' MY ASS written up??! Oh HELL nah. Nah uh!"

Yeah... so apparently he had gotten written up when we ran. I guess he just found that out cause he was a whole new level of mad... I wonder if Gary got written up too? Focus Greg, Harris might kill you.

"Oh hell nah! Nah uh. Mort get on outa here, I got this, oh boy do I *got* this!" Gary smiled, Mort left. **"BRING YO ASSES HERE! POST!"**

So sick of that fuckin word *post*, but we posted anyway. We *really* had to when Harris said so cause I wasn't so sure he wouldn't just kick the living shit outa all us at the same time and not even feel bad about it. I mean, he was a giant, an angry giant with a small penis probably.

"Now, ya'll being run-risks and what not, I don't know if it safe you wearin them shoes. Git em off!! Give em here!"

It was like fuckin twenty degrees outside. No way am I doin that. But everyone else did. So I just did it too.

"Socks too. Don't want em gettin all dirty."

So then we threw our socks to him cause by that point, what good was fightin back anyway. Shit was just bad. Then the dipshit bent down, tied each pair of laces together and threw them toward Gary.

"They eat chow yet Gary?"

"Nope. Got it right here." Gary held up a loaf of cheese sandwiches. Then Harris said:

"See that creek right there?" And he pointed to a creek ten feet away. **"Ya'll ain't eaten nothing till that creek empty!"**

Empty the creek? How? It's a fuckin creek. What's this guy even mean? But he nudged us all toward the water.

"GET IN!"

GET IN THE WATER? WITH BARE FEET? IN THE FREEZING FUCKIN—HA! Well I've had JUST about enough of this crap—

"GET THE FUCK IN MUTHAFUCKKAH!!"

He was getting kinda scary though, so I got in, so did Teddy and Jonny and Rafal.

"EMPTY THAT MUTHAFUKKIN CREEK!" and he kicked the water with his boots as he said that like he might kick our heads off next.

My feet were completely numb. My face felt raw from the icy air. We cupped the water with our hands but it all trickled out by the time we tried to dump it out.

"Faster!"

It was impossible. The water kept re-filling. But that wasn't the point. The point was he was mad and he was gonna try and get us to the point where we were nearly dead. Which wasn't too far away.

"Guess ya'll don't wanna eat." And Harris grabbed the loaf of cheese sandwiches from Gary. **"Ya'll know what? I'm hungry."** He opened the bag and shoved some bread in his mouth. **"Mmm! That good!"**

Jonny got out of the creek all mad like he was gonna do somethin. I got a bit worried for him.

"WHAT THE HELL YOU DOIN?"

"Fuck this shit!"

"BOY DON'T MAKE ME WHOOP YOU!"

Harris grabbed Jonny's shirt and threw him against a tree.

"HUG THAT DAMN TREE BOY!"

Then Harris pushed him even harder against the tree and got all up in his face till Jonny hugged the tree in this defiant typa hug.

"UPSIDE DOWN! LIKE A KOALA!"

And he made Jonny put his hands in the dirt and push his legs up against the tree so that he was kinda in this headstand position. Then Harris put his knee against Jonny's back and made him hug the tree upside down.

"HANG! Get your hands off the ground!"

So Jonny gripped the tree with his face pressed against the bark so hard it looked like it was gonna bleed. But uhh… didn't look like Harris gave too much of a shit.

"YOU BETTA STAY THERE TILL I TELL YOU TO MOVE!"

Then Harris went back to the cheese sandwiches and dropped them on the dirt and looked at us. Gary was still by the fire, watching with amusement.

"FRONT LEAN AND REST OVA THE FOOD, NOW!!"

Ay yay yay… okay okay okay… So I wandered outa the creek all wobbly-like.

"GET DOWN!"

I thought of something happy. But all I saw was that cabin. What's gonna happen in *there*? Don't think about it. I got down in the pushup position facing the food. I looked at the sandwich in front of my face. Jonny was still hanging upside down from the tree holding on for dear life.

"When I say down, you take ONE bite, and ONLY one bite. DOWN!"

My arms were shaking. I took a bite of the sandwich quickly. My teeth kinda scraped the ground but I couldn't feel it, I could just hear it.

"UP! DOWN!"

"UP! DOWN!"

"UP! DOWN!"

Gary was laughing by the fire like a jarhead maniac and chimed in as if this were all a game:

"NOW GIT UP AN DIG ME A FIVE-FOOT HOLE! GO!"

"But we don't have a shovel." I said as if to enlighten the brainless hick... but it came out more like 'buh-wee-dun-hav-uh-shovLL' cause I was nearly dead.

"*NOW* YOU BETT'R FIGURE IT OUT AND DIG ME A *TEN*-FOOT HOLE OR YOU AIN'T EATING THAT OTHER SANDWICH!"

We didn't move cause I wasn't sure if he was serious or just fuckin with us and Harris was still standin there and he was more scary than Gary, but only by a little, and then the sun started to set. That's when Jonny finally came crashing down onto his neck. He was *really* in bad shape.

Saliva dripped from my mouth and I kept swallowing it to quench my thirst. Then Harris pointed to a fallen down tree.

"YA'LL FORGET THAT HOLE AND GO HEAD AN GRAB THAT TREE! AND *YOU,* GET BACK IN FORMATION!!"

He was talkin to Jonny, so Jonny came back to us with his face all scratched up and red and terrible lookin. He looked like he might crack at any moment as we walked over to this tree, but I didn't have the strength to fight back anymore... not that I was fightin back anyway, but I didn't even have the strength to talk shit in my head about it anymore. We bent down to pick up that tree but it was dark and couldn't find a grip.

"PICK IT UP!" Harris yelled.

We finally got it up in the air. Now Gary started talkin...

"REPEAT AFTER ME" He said... and with a melodic tune he sang:

WE LIKE THIS PLACE WE LOVE THIS PLACE WE FINALLY FOUND A HOME."

Uhhh... okay... So we sang his tune.

"WE LIKE THIS PLACE, WE LOVE THIS PLACE, WE FINALLY FOUND A HOME.

Then Gary said **"A WHAT?"**

We didn't know what that meant.

"YA'LL SAY 'A HOME, A HOME, A HOME AWAY FROM HOME!'"

Then Gary said again **"A WHAT?"**

Oh I get it:

"A HOME, A HOME, A HOME AWAY FROM HOME."

AGAIN! SING IT!

"WE LIKE THIS PLACE WE LOVE THIS PLACE WE FINALLY FOUND A HOME."

Gary smiled as he said **"A WHAT?!?!?!"**

"A HOME. A HOME. A HOME AWAY FROM HOME."

"AGAIN!"

Then Jonny let go and started throwin up all over the leaves—FUCKKK—and the tree dropped. It almost crushed my feet. The sound of Harris laughing came outa the darkness.

"GET BACK ON THAT TREE BOY!!" He shouted at Jonny... but Jonny was still pukin all over.

"LETS GO! KEEP SINGING BOYS!!!!" Gary said.

"WE LIKE THIS PLACE… [gasping for breath] *WE LOVE THIS PLACE…* [about to die] *WE FINALLY FOUND A HOME!"*

"A WHAT?!"

[with all our might] *"A HOME! A HOME! A HOME AWAY FROM HOME!"*

"LIFT THAT TREE OVER YOUR HEAD!"

But my vision started to go blurry. My eyes stung from the salt as sweat dripped down to my mouth.

"KEEP SINGING!!!!!"

Just get through this… just, keep on, Greg, come back, Greg! I was fallen asleep.

"WE LIKE THIS PLACE… WE LOVE THIS PLACE… WE FINALLY FOUND A HOME!

A HOME!

A HOME!

A HOME AWAY FROM HOME!"

And I collapsed.

CHAPTER 25

COMING BACK TO LIFE

I woke up in the cabin.

It was an empty cabin that started to get built but was never finished. There were holes where the windows woulda been and there was a fireplace that had a fire in it, yeah, they finally let us warm up by a fire…. and there were bugs and spiders all over the wood-planked floor.

I was in my sleeping bag. The sun was kinda up. There was a guy with curly hair sitting by the fire. Then I remembered, oh yeah! He was the guy that let us build the fire! He was nice! Thank GOD! I wonder where Harris and Gary went? Where'd they go?

There was a blood stain right next to me. Was it my blood? I couldn't remember. The curly haired dude said, "Keep sleeping and get some rest before they get back." But he was only talkin to me cause Jonny and Teddy and Rafal were still asleep. They were always sleepin. I was always up. Wait—before they get back?

Oh no, he must be talkin about Gary and Harris or Mort or whoever. Who was this guy anyway? Whatever, he was lettin us sleep by a fire. But the bugs were all over and I couldn't fall back asleep. I was too scared I'd get bit and die or something cause they were all over my sleeping bag. But Teddy and Jonny and Rafal were asleep with the bugs. They didn't seem to care.

Then I heard Mort's voice... Time to do this all over again, I thought. Man I was so hungry and tired and thirsty and weak-feeling, I couldn't imagine doin it all over again today. But I had to. It was horrible.

And it lasted for eight days, eight really *fucked* up days, the worst eight days of my life.

But alas, it ended. They took us off Isolation and put us on Restrictions, as a way to transition us back to reality. Finally, I made it out, back to General Population. It was the most grueling eight days of my life, but now it was over. I was even happy to be back in my dormitory my first night back. Man, gettin outa here ain't gonna be so easy... So I just wrote a buncha poems and read a buncha books about religion and meditated and tried to keep myself calm for as many days and weeks as I could.

It was now the beginning of summer. I was trapped. That much I'd come to realize. I'd been there months and months now, longer than four months, maybe six or seven, and I had not yet spoken to my parents. I hadn't talked to them since I saw them in Minnesota. But since I arrived here at this shithole pile of illegal activity, I had absolutely no communication with the outside world. But rest assured I would tell them *everything* that they had put me through as soon as I could.

But that never happened, you see, cause when I finally walked into that phone call room, a small room with five phones, each phone in its own cubicle area and each cubicle area in use by a kid, there was a big guard with a notepad taking notes on everything that was being said. He was only a foot or so away from me when I sat at the empty cubicle phone area and picked up that phone.

"PUT THE PHONE DOWN"

Okay, so I guess they had to dial the number for me…

The guard sat with a little box with some switches that allowed him to cut the line if any one of us started sayin something 'Out Of Agreement', another one of their dumb fuckin phrases. Basically if we said the truth—CLIP—no more phone call for you and off to Restrictions you went. They really had some kinda racket goin on here. Point is I wasn't able to say anything truthful so I just hung up the phone after one minute, even though I had a full five minutes to talk to them… What a prize that was. Besides, the second I heard my mom's voice I got furious and thought I might lose my shit.

The next day I went into Realizations and Thea's cunty ass was all like:

"Greg"

Oh right, she got up for the 'three seat rule' and sat directly across from me.

"Greg, would you like to discuss what happened on your phone call last night?"

"Uh no Thea, no I would not like to discuss what happened on my phone call last night."

"Greg, drop the attitude."

"This is just how I talk, Thea."

Anyway, you get the picture… I got all mad and she radioed to a guard and POOF! I was back on Restrictions, which didn't bother me mind you, Restrictions gave me time to read. I got all into reading and writing poems and shit, like I told you. But all I was always thinkin was damn, I'ma be stuck here for *two years*. TWO YEARS I'd be stuck here.

I really didn't know what to do. Then I came to a decision:

I would cause more chaos than even Hidden Lake could handle. Nothing would stop me. Nothing. I would be exactly what I wanted to be, and live exactly how I wanted to live. It was time for me to live on *my* terms.

But all that thinkin got interrupted this one day when I was in The Lodge.

So I was in The Lodge reading *On The Road* by Kerouac, whom had become my newest idol, and I was envisioning how I could live a better version of Kerouac's life. His life seemed about right to me. I think I'll live just like he lived when I break outa this place for good. Anyway, I was really diggin his shit. I had found his books at the Hidden Lake library, somebody musta snuck em in cause we were only allowed to read about religion and shit, or boring shit with no curse words or subject matter about drugs or whatever. I couldn't even read Fight Club when it came out… So yeah, someone had gotten his books in somehow and by now I had read all of them I think, like ten or so books, maybe more, and I was reading *On The Road* for a second time.

So I was just chillin out in the FNK section… you believe that? After seven or so months I was *still* an FNK! Apparently I *still* hadn't graduated to another section of couches. And anyway, you had to be invited by the couch section leader to sit in one of the other sections of couches and I hadn't really made a name for myself at this place yet like I did in Louisiana. I wasn't the notorious *Juden* here at Hidden Lake. Nobody really knew who I was in fact. Here at Hidden Lake I was just *Greg*. But like I said, everything changed this one day in The Lodge when some girl that I'd never seen before walked in.

Enter Poe.

She walked into The Lodge barefoot and sat Indian-styled on the floor in the FNK section with utter confidence and I totally forgot about Isolation and my anger and I forgot about everything that wasn't her.

She had long knotty light brown hair and a freckly nose and she looked like a country hippie chick from like, I dunno, maybe Idaho? And she had these tits that you could see even through the dumb uniform we all had to wear, which meant they musta been *real* nice cause those uniforms made all of us ugly as fuck. Even her ass nearly popped the seams of the dumb uniform khaki pants that we had to wear… so that was pretty impressive too. Anyway, she was hot. She had these freckles all over—wait, I said that. Well anyway, those freckles, I loved those freckles and—well, it was love at first sight.

What could *she* possibly have done to land herself in here? I thought.

Then I saw the sign.

ARE YOU FUCKIN KIDDING ME?! SHE WAS HOLDING *ON THE ROAD* BY KEROUAC! THAT'S WHAT I WAS HOLDING TOO!!

I couldn't believe that shit! What the *fuck* are the chances of *that*? She was holdin the book with both her hands, like it might slip and run away. Man, this was crazy. I decided right then and there that we would live together on the road and never come back. I hadn't even introduced myself yet. I was just observing her in the damn FNK section. She looked like she didn't give a fuck that she was even here.

She looked peaceful, in fact, and she was all by herself in the corner of the room, swaying back and forth, giggling at the book, which isn't even a funny book really, and having the time of her life. She never looked up once as I stared at her. Well, that had to change. Lemme tell her all about our new lives together. So I got up and walked over.

"Hey!" I said to her.

"Hiiiii!"

"Are you new? What's your name?"

"Yeah. I'm Poe."

"Poe? I've never heard that name before."

"Yeah it's short for Elizabeth."

That didn't make sense, but, whatever... "So how'd you end up here?"

"Oh my. I don't even know. I stole this car and then they sent me to juvie and—"

"Wait, you stole a car?"

"Yeahhhh haha!"

This chick stole a car? "Where are you from?"

"Virginia!"

"I'm from New York." I was still a bit confused by her 'I stole a car' answer so I asked her again, "Wait—tell me again how you got here?"

"Well I had this boyfriend... Alex. He called me in the middle of the night and told me we had to go cause the police were after him."

"For what?" But she didn't listen to me, she just kept going...

"Then we drove to Florida... But the cops found us back in Virginia and we got arrested."

Huh? "Wait, why were they after him? The cops?" It seemed like she was thinkin real hard before she said:

"Ohh I don't really know." But she kept goin... "Oh my... there were cops everywhere, a lot of 'em... It was all very dramatic..."

"Then they sent you here?"

"No, no then I ran away with this girl, we hitched a ride with some guy in a truck who brought us back to his trailer...Oh my gosh... there were helicopters and cops and all sorts of fun stuff!"

"Wait so that's when you were sent here?"

"No then they sent me to Clearview Horizons and I loved it, I could express myself ya know? I didn't wanna be there though cause I never wanna be where I am, I just wanted to go! And Jenny wanted to go!"

"Who's Jenny—"

"And we just wanted to be free. I saw these car keys on the table so we just left. But… we didn't get too far…Turns out we stole the Program Director's car and her son was in the NFL and had just like… won the super bowl!"

"WHAT?" What in the fuck was this chick talkin about?!

"Oh my gosh… yes! How funny right? So we were caught and Jenny went to jail and I went to Juvie. Then Alex overdosed on pills and died. Oh my…then a friend of mine AJ came to juvie to keep me company!!!!"

She was all over the place…

"What do you mean, he came to keep you company?"

"Yeah dude! But then two men came and picked me up and I don't remember why really…but they said something about grand theft auto. And now I am here… with you!!!!!!"

"Umm— Well, Welcome."

"Gee thanks. What about you? Why you here? You steal a car too?"

"I actually got kicked out of a bunch of rehabs." By a bunch I meant two.

"Whoaaaa are you like some sorta drug addict?"

"Umm… No, not really, well—yeah, I'ma- well, yeah. I suppose so."

"Like heroin?"

"Nah, not heroin."

"Coke?"

"Nah."

"Meth? Are you like a crazy meth-head?"

"No, why are you?"

"Oh my gosh, no I've never done drugs."

"You've never done drugs?"

"Well I tripped on mushrooms once, or maybe twice! Or maybe three times! I don't really remember!"

"Maybe it was four times." I tried to make a joke but it wasn't *that* funny, but she laughed *really* hard anyway:

"Haha! Maybe! You're so funny!!"

This chick was NUTS. "You're nuts. How you liking that book?"

And then... THEN I showed her what made us so special together... I showed her *my On The Road* book that *I* was reading. I'd been holdin that back as a surprise, cause I knew that would prove to her that I was her soulmate and that we were destined to live a happy life as teenage runaways together. But she just said:

"Wowwee!"

Wowwee? Never heard anyone say that before... thought people only said that in movies an shit. Whatever...

"Oh my gosh! It's my favorite!" She said.

She didn't even seem to think it was a coincidence... hmmm... weird, anyway, I said "Me too!!" Then she said:

"You love Kerouac too? Did you know the Beatniks all used to have sex with each other and stuff?"

"The guys did??" I asked.

"Yeah dude like Cassady, Kerouac, and Burroughs they all used to sleep with each other and stuff on like morphine!"

"WHAT? Is that true?"

"Yah I know!!"

Then I tried to one up her by saying, "Did you know Kerouac wrote *On The Road* in thirty-six hours on one scroll of paper, without stopping?" But I wasn't even sure if that was a hundred percent true...

"Oh my I didn't know that!"

"Crazy, right?"

"I love him! He's so handsome!"

She thinks he's handsome... Is he? I never thought about that. Do I look like him? Does she think *I'm* handsome? She must. But I just said "I have his whole collection. Have you read Dharma Bums?"

"No! Do you have it? Oh my gosh!!! I'd love to read it! I'll be done with this one by tomorrow."

She kept sayin 'Oh my gosh'. That was also only from the movies I thought... But whatever, I told her:

"I can bring it to The Lodge tomorrow if you want."

"What's The Lodge?"

"Where we are now."

"You will? You'll bring it here tomorrow?!"

"Yup!"

"Yayyyy!!"

I decided at that point to let her in on that fact that I had already started planning my life with her.

"Sooo..."

But then she went on this rant "Oh my! I wish we could travel all over and go everywhere! Just like the beatniks!"

And it was EXACTLY what I was gonna say! "Me too! I want to give away everything I own and just take my journal and write poems about it!"

"Let's runaway together! And be free!" She said that!!! *TO ME!!!!* But I played it cool…

"Are you sure you wanna play it cool?" Oh shit… it was my soul! It was my soul talkin to me again! I said hi then responded…

"Yeah, of course. Should I? I should, right?"

"You don't sound too sure about this. You never are."

"Never are what?"

"You're never sure about anything. You don't know what the fuck you're doing."

"Fuck you soul."

Back to Poe.

"Okay. Where should we go first?" I asked.

"We should go toooo… ummmmm—Kansas!"

"Kansas? Why Kansas?"

"I don't know! It's so wide and open and free and windy! I love the Midwest!"

"But Kansas?" Kansas sounded so foreign to me. I mean I was from Long Island… She kept going…

"Can we hop freight trains? Oh can we pleeease?"

"Is it dangerous?"

"Yeaaah! I don't know! Probably but we can just be careful and—"

"Okay I'll go with you."

"Yayyy!!!… Can you learn how to play some kinda instrument?"

Wait… she wanted me to learn an instrument? Well I guess I could do that.

"YOU TWO! SEPARATE! NOW!" It was Bear.

Fuck you Bear. I already been through the worst you got, go fuck yourself hickboy. So I ignored him and continued with Poe.

"Yeah. Okay. What should I play?"

"You should playyy ummm…. Banjo!!!"

"Banjo?" I asked.

"Yeah! I'll play guitar and you'll play banjo! We'll make music, and then hop off the train while it's still goin real fast."

"And just get off anywhere?"

"Uh huh!! We'll just show up in any town we want just to say hi!!"

This girl was perfect. "That sounds great." I said.

"Then we can wait tables! Play music for money! Leave and go somewhere different!"

"Just like that?" She was so inspirational.

"Yeah! Cassady did it! And we can be just like him!"

"And we have to write about it too." I said.

"Yay! Yes! We can write a book together too!"

"Are we gonna switch off pages?" I asked.

"You want to?"

"Yes!" I said with certainty.

"Okayyy!! I'm sooo excited! I cannot wait!"

"And we can plan everything out while we're here." I was already thinkin of breaking out again.

"Let's start writing the book here too!" She said.

That's such a great fuckin idea. Why didn't I thinka that? So I said "Yeah, ok! I'll bring my notebook for us tomorrow! I want to show you the pictures I drew of the VW bus you can live in with me. I already designed it!" And I was tellin the truth! I had drawn a pic of this VW bus that I was certain I would live in, and now I was inviting Poe to come with me!

"I LOVE VW BUSES! We're gonna have one?" She said with more excitement than any of her other sentences.

"Yeah, I can't wait to show you what it looks like! I drew it!"

"So we can sleep in it an stuff?"

"Of course! It's a hippie bus! I planned out everything!"

"Oh! We should have like a portable greenhouse where we can grow our own vegetables!" She said.

"Of course we will."

"And we have to eat vegetarian, are you a meat-eater?"

That's the day I became a vegetarian... "I can stop! I'll stop! I'll just eat vegetables with you!" And I did... for three years I was a vegetarian from that day forward. Until 9/11. But I'll tell you bout that later...

"Well we can eat other things too, ya know? Like tofu an stuff?"

I had never eaten tofu. But she told me:

"Oh my it's so yummy! You'll love it!"

I had an idea, so I said it: "We can buy our own pots and pans from an antique shop and just use chopsticks as silverware."

"Oh I know one! It's in West Virginia! Can we stop there?" She told me.

"We'll definitely stop there." I said... but then I also started thinkin to myself, what color is the sky in this fuckin idiot's world? But she was beautiful. And I was being mean. So I stopped thinkin those thoughts.

"Yay this is all so amazing." She said.

"MAYBE YOU DIDN'T HEAR ME!" Bear grabbed my arm and pulled me to my feet. What a hillbilly moron. I bet he doesn't even know how to add.

"Oh nooo. Are you in trouble?" Poe said with innocence.

"SHUT UP YOU!" Bear shouted to Poe. But Poe didn't really get it. She only seemed to comprehend joy. She was a moron. STOP TALKING ABOUT HER LIKE THAT!

But it's in my head!

Fucking soul...

Anyway she asked me if I was in trouble and so I said:

"Yeah, but don't worry, I'm always in trouble.

"SHUT THE HELL UP!" Bear said.

But I continued anyway, "I'll see you tomorrow. I'll bring the book and we'll keep talking."

"Be nice to him!" She yelled at Bear as if that would work. Bear snarled at her like the ugly beast that he was as she said that. I looked back and shouted:

"I'm Greg by the way!"

"Bye Greggyyy."

And that was how I met Poe. I knew she might be bad for me... I knew this was not right, that she was just another girl I was gonna pretend fall in love with and use to get my mind off being where I was... I knew it was wrong. But I loved wrong. I hated right. I mean, how bad could she *possibly* be anyway?

Let's find out.

CHAPTER 26

FUCK YOU THEA

Thea got up and walked across the room and switched seats with someone, I don't remember who, and then sat across from me and stared. JUST FUCKING STARED. GOD I WANTED TO KILL THAT BITCH. Benjamin, my other counselor who I *never* talk about... He was just all fat and sweaty in his seat, just watchin the whole thing go down. But this bitch, Thea, she's *still* lookin at me!

WHAT THE FUCK YOU LOOKIN AT BITCH?!?!?

But I didn't say that, what I said was "What?"

"Is there something you'd like to share with us?" She asked.

"Uhh... No, as a mattera fact, there is absolutely nothing I would like to share with you."

The group laughed. Yes! I'm funny!

"Who's Poe?" Thea asked, "Besides a dark and gothic 19ᵗʰ century American poet and novelist who believed in the virtuous concept of incest…"

"Huh?"

"Poe. Who is she?" She said with a sly stupid cunty grin like she had found out my little secret.

"Why?"

"I've heard that you two really like each other."

Then Thea gave a stupid smile as if nothing could get by her.

"We're friends, why?" I told her, as I grit my teeth and held back my temper. "Friends? I heard it's a little more than that." She said with her condescending cunt voice.

"Okay Thea."

"I'm placing you two on Bans."

"WHY?"

"Well, if you're just friends it shouldn't be a big deal."

"I LIKE TALKING TO MY FUCKING FRIENDS TOO, *THEA*!"

"Okay. I don't think you're ready to do the work right now Greg." And she took out a blue folder. "I'm placing you on a Table-Restriction, hopefully you'll be off before the weekend." But she didn't mean that. She hoped I'd be on FOREVER **YOU DAMN WITCH!** So I just said:

"What a fucking surprise. You're puttin me on Restrictions. How creative of you."

Then she switched the blue folder to a black folder and said "Make that a *Fall-in Restriction.* I can extend it even longer if you'd like Greg, is that what you want? More? Would you like to go back on Isolation?"

What a fuckin skank she was. Finally I shut up and let the wicked witch of the South get what she wanted... which was me on Restrictions. Sure, whatever.

Anyway after the four-hour interrogation room—I mean Realizations—I went to chow and sat across from Poe in The Lodge and I mouthed the words:

"I GOT PUT ON RESTRICTIONS"

"You got put on Prescriptions?"

"No." I mouthed the words again. "I GOT PUT ON RE-STRIC-TIONS". But she
still didn't understand me.

"What prescription? Like medication?"

"NO NO!" So I shouted to her: "RESTRICTIONS!"

"Re-wha?"

"Never mind". I mouthed to her. Dense bitch. STOP SAYING MEAN THINGS GREG! "Just come sit with me during lunch."

So I surprised her with *Dharma Bums,* that book I told her I would bring, and I presented it to her the second she sat down.

"Oh yay Greggy!!! YAY!"

"So I gotta go to Restriction Village after this but you should write me notes and just give em to one of the girls on Restrictions while you're in the dorm and they'll pass them to me, okay?"

"Okay... if you say so Greggy!"

"I do say so!" I'm not even sure she understood what I was talkin about, but she was convinced she knew exactly what I meant. I think. Or maybe she just didn't care? I got no idea. I wanted to fuck her, and run away with her, but man was she *dumb*.

"So tell me more fun stuff! Where's your family from?"

"My real family?"

"Ummm— Do you have a fake family?"

"Well I was adopted. I can tell you bout them?"

"Okay! Tell me!"

"Um… Maybe I'll just tell you bout my birth family! My adopted family's kinda boring."

"Cool. Entertain me." I was addicted to her laugh and her stories and her smile and I had only known her a day. Plus I wanted to fuck her.

"Well I have four cousins. They're brothers and sisters but they're also cousins."

"That's interesting." Damn this girl is trashy. I gotta jerk off. But I held it in. So yeah, I said "That's interesting."

She broke out in laughter, "Oh nooo is that bad?"

"No! I wanna hear more!" I told her.

"Hmmm… A great Aunt of mine is in the nut house in Texarkana for chopping her son up and putting him in a bottle."

Blank stare.

"Are you kidding me?"

"No dude. I know right? My whole family should be in the Looney Bin."

"What about you, are you crazy?" I asked her flirtingly trying not to make a big deal outa her last insane comment. I mean, it wasn't a big deal. Nothing she said coulda been *that* bigga deal. It's not like we were gonna spend the rest of our lives together. We'll run away and live in a VW bus and be like the beatniks and we'll have sex and then part ways and that'll be that. So, I guess I had to be cool with whatever for now. Ya know? I even started sayin 'ya know'… cause that's what she said. Ya know? Anyway she went on…

"Oh my… *I'm* the craziest. Wait till you get to know me…"

"Do you ever talk to your real mom?"

"Well, my birth mom… she was a lady of the night."

"Like she went out to parties?" But I knew what the hell she meant.

"Um, kinda. She was kinda like, uh—well, she was like a—a prostitute?"

"Oh. Okay." HAHAHA this chick is NUTS.

"Yeah dude I know. Her and my sister used to work the corners together in Detroit."

"Your mom and your sister? Were hookers? Together? In Detroit?!"

"Is that bad?"

"No no. I'm listening."

"Hmm… Well, she had three other children too, with three different fathers."

"So wait do you still talk to her?"

"No she disappeared in 2004. I've only met her once as an adult."

"Oh, what happened to her?"

"I don't know but the detectives promised me they're still looking for her."

I tried to not make a big deal outa that last thing she said either. "What about your dad?"

"My daddy? His name was…Allen! He loved me very much. He died of

Cirrhosis…when he was… thirty I think? I was a little girl. I remember him having a cooler of beer wherever he went, but that's about it."

"That's all you remember?"

"Well I know his favorite movie was *Eddie and The Cruisers.*"

"Where was he from?"

"My daddy? I can't answer that. I have no one to answer that for me. No one knew where he came from, but my mom remembered his body being flown to Connecticut to be buried. I love my mom but her brain is mush! She wasn't even sure if he had any other kids." Confusion must run in the family, I thought.

"UH, SEÑOR CAYEA, BREAKING BANS ALREADY? FALL OUT!! GET TO RESTRICTIONS!" It was the Colonel. The Colonel said that. Remember? The Colonel? Well, he'd been watchin me from afar. I just then noticed it.

"Poe I gotta go but remember to write me notes! DON'T FORGET."

"Oh nooo. Wait—When will I be able to give them to you again?"

"Give them to your friends on Restrictions, they'll give them to me and—gotta go."

"Bye Greggy!"

"Bye!!!"

I got up and walked out of The Lodge to the line of Restrictions kids all standing still in complete silence. Everyone's eyes followed me as I tried to blend into the line without being noticed. I was late... I knew I was. See, you're supposed to go to Restrictions when they call out 'Restrictions', but I musta not even heard them call it. Fuck, I hadn't realized how late I really was. So I said sorry with my eyes to the group and hoped there'd be no consequence. I was wrong.

"**DOWN!**" It was fuckin Gary. "**CAYEA YOU LIKE MAKIN YER BUDDIES WAIT??**"

He knew my name! GOOD bitch, bout time... All it took was an Isolation.

"No sir!" I said in the pushup position.

"**GET UP! JUST YOU CAYEA! UP!**"

I got up as everyone stayed in position.

"**YOU WERE FIVE MINUTES LATE! THAT'S FIVE MINUTES OF P.T. FOR YER BUDDIES!**"

Grunts and groans from the kids on the ground as I stood up comfortably.

"**I'LL EVEN LET YOU PICK WHAT EXERCISE THEY DO!**"

I stayed silent as everyone struggled to keep their pushup position without falling. I didn't wanna pick an exercise. I was sorry, shit, isn't that enough?

"**CAYEA! YOU WANNA MAKE IT TEN MINUTES!?**"

Everyone got pissed off.

"Just say fuckin pushups man! Shit!" Some kid shouted at me. What a dickhead that kid was. Whatever...

"Okay, sorry… Sir. Sorry sir. Pushups."

"LEAD THE GROUP!" He told me.

"Down", I said feeling guilty. "Up!" I said feeling even more guilty. I had to keep going until I reached fifty pushups. Fuckin fifty. I hate that number. By the time we were done, I was the most hated person on Restrictions, at least for that hour of that day.

"Fuckin asshole! Try bein on fuckin time!" Some other kid shouted.

Yeah yeah yeah, you're mad, I get it, put it in your diary loser.

OH WAIT! Did I tell you we weren't allowed to have diaries??? YEAH! I mean you could have one, but they would search the dorm every couple of weeks and steal our diaries or journals or whatever and they'd read them and laugh at our poems and if we wrote anything that scared them, like suicidal notes or pictures of shrooms or weed leaves or if we even cursed for that matter THEY THREW US ON RESTRICTIONS AND TRIED TO GET US TO TALK ABOUT IT DURING REALIZATIONS!

Like this one day… I got back to the dormitory to get ready for evening chores, but when I got back, I noticed there were ripped pages from my journal all scattered and torn and laying all over the ground. They were crumpled up like someone had read the pages then threw em away. I was devastated. Who the fuck had found my poetry? Why were all my poems all torn outa my notebook and now on the ground? What the fuck is goin on?

I bent down and picked one of the poems up, then another, then another, most of them were from when I first started writing, the ones that *really* sucked. THEN I saw all the guards were huddled around something laughing and joking and nearly on the brink of crying of laughter. And as I got closer, I saw what they were laughing at. IT WAS MY JOURNAL!! They were reading my poems then ripping the pages out and throwin em all over the ground! WHAT THE FUCK IS WRONG WITH THIS PLACE? How embarrassing. I hid everything I wrote from that day forward as best I could... but there was no way to keep them totally safe, I mean, they were always goin through our shit! Jeez, what a fuckin buncha bullshit. Anyway, just had to tell you about that. So much for nurturing our insecurities, right?

Back to Restrictions:

So Gary took us to Restriction Village and gave me a shovel and told us all to make the fire pit two feet wider, cause remember I told you there was a fire pit at Restriction Village? So we shoveled for hours until dark came. Sweat soaked through my mud-covered shirt, BUT the fire pit *was* wider and looked prettier than ever when we were finished. Funny how you can feel good about that typa shit after all is said an done.

So we stacked our shovels in a neat pile outside of the shack and Gary told us to sit along the edge of the floorboards in silence, like always, and so we did, like always.

Then Harris came on shift that night. He was in a *terrible* mood. We were supposed to eat dinner at the start of his shift at like seven or whatever time it was when he got on, but because he got into a fight with his girlfriend earlier that day, we didn't eat till like nine, or whatever time it was. And I knew about the fight he had with his girlfriend cause he told us all about it. Then he told us about the sex they had. Then he got mad again.

When he finally decided to give us dinner he passed out our cheese sandwiches and told us to eat only the bread. When we finished, he told us to eat only the cheese. After that he gave us hot soup without spoons. When we were all done he passed out the spoons as a joke and asked if we were still hungry.

"WHO HERE STILL HUHNGRY?"

We all raised our hands cause of course we were still fuckin hungry. He pulled out another round of cheese sandwiches and passed them around. I couldn't believe my eyes. MORE FOOD! YES!!!! He told us to shove the food down our throat before he changed his mind. THEN, when we were done, *again* he asked if we were still hungry!

"WHO WANTS MORE??"

For the third time, he passed out *another* round of cheese sandwiches. We all ate until we were stuffed. It was the first time I felt full since I had gotten there.

Then Harris stood up with a crooked smile and looked at us till he started laughing.

"YA'LL FULL?"

He said between his crooked laughter.

"NOW YA'LL GET UP!"

He didn't even give us a moment to rest. We stood up all lethargic from the bread and cheese and shit. I got cramps immediately just from standing up too quickly. Then he took us to Lower Left Field, that wide field covered in goose shit, and he made us all take off our shoes and said:

"RUN!!"

Run where? I thought.

"YA'LL RUN IN A CIRCLE, AND KEEP YA'LL FORMATION!"

And so we started runnin barefoot in circles. I could feel the soft fresh goose shit press between my toes as I ran. I had to just accept the fact that my feet were pressed in goose shit and move on, I mean, I couldn't keep getting upset about it every time I landed in goose shit, it was everywhere! I had to keep my mind right. Plus, it was dark as fuck and I couldn't see shit.

"BETTA BE RUNNIN FAST YOU CAN!"

One kid had to stop because he was cramping up so bad, so Harris radioed to Bear to have all his clothes confiscated from the dormitory. Then the kid started cursin up a storm and walked off furious. That typa thing happened all the time... and it never ended well.

Harris took out his walkie-talkie with a smile.

"GOT A REFUSAL WALKIN UP THE ROAD TO THE LODGE FO YOU BEAR." Then Bear replied with a chuckle:

"Copy."

And that was it. I never saw that kid ever again.

Sharp pains shot across my chest and back but I kept runnin. I wasn't about to let him win. But I could barely breathe.

"THIS WHAT HAPPENS WHEN YA'LL GREEDY WITH YA'LL FOOD!!"

FUCKIN NIGGER! Oh man. I shouldn'ta said that. Wait, I didn't. I just thought it. Is that okay? Am I racist? Or am I just lookin for hurtful words? I'm losing it. And this was just what was happening with the *dudes*... I can only *imagine* what it must be like to give the guards blow jobs in exchange for food... Cause, well, that was something that happened every now and then with the girls… At least that's what we all heard from some trusted sources… But yeah, anyway, at least I wasn't at the brink of sucking dick like some of the others, but I *was* at the brink of insanity.

CHAPTER 27

ON THE BRINK OF INSANITY

Something had to happen. Poe was a nice distraction an all, but if she wanted to do this shit with me, she'd have to pop into reality and figure out where the fuck we were. It was time to leave, and leave for good. There's gotta be some way out.

I got off Restrictions a month later cause I kept breaking Bans to talk to Poe, and kept gettin caught passin her notes and shit so they kept extending my Restrictions sentence. Anyway, I got off Restrictions a month later and got to The Lodge this one day and sat next to Poe, breaking Bans again, as per usual, and then was waved over to one of the couch sections by this kid named Chris that I had become somewhat friendly with on Restrictions. He made the BIG move of inviting me to join his couch section.

"Ey man, come have a seat."

Oh cool, I'm allowed to be a part of your pseudo gang couch section? Great. Go fuck yourself. I mean, liked Chris, but I didn't wanna be a part of his fuckin gang, especially with Alejandro in the middle seat of the couch section on the middle couch. He was the leader and I fuckin *hated* that kid. Anyway, I wasn't about to leave Poe just sittin all hippie-like on the ground in the FNK section alone. You think I'm a FNK yesterday and cool today Chris? Well fuck your invite, I ain't leavin Poe. So I just said:

"Nah man, I'm all good." And I walked away, declining his invitation and sat back down next to Poe. Fuck our Bans, I thought. No one's tellin me where I can and can't sit and who I can and can't like. So sick of this shit. I'm sittin with Poe and everyone can fuck themselves. I was really gettin all riled up. Then Chris shouted over to me:

"You know, everyone used to think you were cool, when you ran away and all, and now the only person that thinks your cool is *that* hippie."

He was talkin about Poe. You believe this fuckin kid? Then Alejandro laughed. Damn, I *hated* Alejandro.

"What'd he say Greggie?" Poe asked.

"He's just talkin—hold on…" And I nearly lost my shit when I stood up and said, "You go ahead and keep suckin Alejandro's dick. I bet it tastes *real* good in the morning." Fuckin prick.

"Fuck he say?" Alejandro asked in broken stupid English. He was this rich kid from Mexico City who grew up with like ten kahzillion dollars and he was already the 'big man on bootcamp campus' even though he was only in like... Peer Group 36. Peer Group 36... and he already had a couch section? *And* he sat at the center couch? Fuck this kid. I already thought he was a piece of shit before, but now thinkin about it again I hated him all over on a much deeper level.

"CAYEA! SIT YOUR BUTT DOWN! AND GET AWAY FROM POE YOU TWO, SEPARATE!!!" Bear said that. He was at the front of The Lodge about to give his 'kiddie' speech.

Later that night I was in the bathroom waiting for my shower, after all, I had seniority now. I could finally fuckin shower. But then Alejandro walked in and jumped the line and got in the shower that *I* was waitin for and turned the water on immediately. So I pushed his towel that was hangin over the side of the shower door into the shower and it got all wet, which musta sucked cause we only got one towel per day.

"WHAT FUCK IS YOUR PROBLEM!?" He said to me in his best impression of a US citizen.

"Get the fuck outa the shower FNK." Yeah that's right, *he* was the FNK.

But he didn't move, he just kept showering without even pickin up the towel.

That made me get all burning inside with temper, but I just held it in. What was there to do? Another shower opened up and I got in, but I was boiling with rage. Just as I got the water the temperature I wanted and got the anger a bit outa my system *my* towel came crashin down on the shower floor and it got all wet. Was that fuckin Alejandro who just did that?

So I opened the shower door butt-ass naked.

YEAH. IT *WAS* ALEJANDRO.

So I went after him and pushed him into the wall as he was walkin outa the bathroom. A bit of a sucker push I'll admit, but I was just so damn mad.

So he turned around and was like "Look at fuckin faggot pushing from back."

So I pushed him again, this time against his chest… bear in mind my dick is all out and floppin around. Well that got him all mad so he pushed me back. But before we really got into it a guard came in and broke us up. I was still naked as fuck.

The next day in The Lodge I sat down next to Poe again.

"UHH… SEÑOR GREG, PLEASE REMOVE YOUR BOTTOM FROM THE FLOOR OF THE ROOM AND MOVE YOUR LEGS TO ANOTHER PART OF THE UNIVERSE WITHOUT LEAVING THE PARAMETERS OF THIS BUILDING, AND MAKE SURE THAT SPOT YOU MOVE TO IS FAR AWAY FROM POE… DOES THAT MAKE SENSE TO YOU YANKEE-BOY DOODLE?" The Colonel said that. He always talked like a weirdo. So I got up and moved away from Poe… again.

"Oh no Greggy! We got in trouble again!"

"Don't worry, they won't do shit, it's all good." I assured her. "I'll pass you a note later." And then I sat next to some other kid named Billy Hutto, but we all called him Slutto.

So I started listenin in on his conversation when I heard the name 'Alejandro'. So I listened in a bit closer about some shit that went down in the dorm last night in this new kid's room.

So yeah, apparently after our shower incident, Alejandro and his pseudo gang walked into this *really* new kid's room, like this FNK in Peer Group 39 that had *just* gotten there, and while the kid was asleep, Alejandro and his crew held his sheets down on the kid so that he couldn't move and couldn't get outa his bed and couldn't fight back and Alejandro beat the shit outa him with a sock full of dirt and red clay and some other shit he found from outside. So I asked Slutto:

"Why'd he do *that* shit?"

"Ah dunno man, cuz I think it wuz cuz he wuz gay." He was from Alabama so he spoke with a twang. Nothin new there, I mean, I was the one with the accent in Georgia... but yeah, so when I found out they did it cause he was gay, that *really* set me off.

"WHY THE FUCK IS EVERYONE SAYIN WHAT A PIECE OF SHIT HE IS AND NOBODY IS DOIN ANYTHING ABOUT IT?!"

Poe started laughin cause I guess she heard me and saw me get all angry.

"Maybe you should beat him up Greggy! Hahah!"

Why did she think that was funny? Did she not think I could do the job? No, she was probably just kidding cause she was a pacifist that wouldn't even slap a blood-thirsty mosquito off her eyelids if it were the last pint of blood left in her body. She couldn't *imagine* me fighting. But I was REALLY fuckin mad!

She opened up the Shakespeare book that we usually read together and she started reading it without me… so that made me mad too, so I got up and sat back down next to her and she played Titania and I played Puck in A Midsummers Night's Dream. Yeah, we used to act the plays out, even though I barely understood what the damn dude, Shakespeare that is, even though I barely understand what in the world he was writin about half the time. But whatever, I needed something to calm me down and Poe always got me cool. So we read Shakespeare in the FNK section till they called us in for chow and till the Colonel yelled at us for breaking Bans again.

"MOVE THAT GLUTEUS MAXIMUS OF YOURS CAYEA! HOW MANY TIMES SHALL I REPHRASE THAT SIMPLE DIRECTION FOR YOU?

So I got up again and moved, but man, that new kid… the gay kid that Alejandro beat up… I couldn't stop thinkin about that. Why didn't I hear about it till today? Then I noticed he wasn't even in The Lodge, the new kid. He was missing.

"Where is he anyway?" I asked Slutto.

"Infirmary." He said.

Oh man, that *really* twisted my soul up inside. THE INFIRMARY? PIECE OF FUCKIN SHIT—I'LL FUCKING… But then:

"PEER GROUP 34, EAT!!!"

So I got up and went to the chow hall, but I *knew* I had to do something…

CHAPTER 28

THE BITCH SLAP

So later on that night when lights out was called I was in my room and I was angry and I was waiting, waiting for the right idea to come to my mind. I couldn't just think about this all night and not do anything, I mean, what the fuck was wrong with all these pussies? Was I the only one feelin like this?

Then I heard night security's flashlight clank against the cement wall, sending ricocheting echoes into my room and through my eardrums, so I popped my head out the room. When night security wasn't lookin, I made a run for the bathroom. But he saw me and said:

"Yew think yer some kinda special?" He was like some toothless hick from Dahlonega. So I just played the game.

"Oh, sorry. May I please use the restroom?"

"Git back on in yer room!"

So I retreated.

"ALL THE WAY!"

So I got back in my room all the way. Then he turned his head when he was satisfied with the way I got back in my room and then I had to wait a moment until he looked back over in my direction. Then I raised my hand... like I always did... like we always had to, and I asked again... this time the 'correct' way.

"Excuse me Warren? May I please use the bathroom?"

"Two minutes. Go!" The fat redneck said to me.

So I turned down the hall and headed for the bathroom, only I didn't stop when I got to the bathroom. I walked fast as I could past the bathroom and down to room seventeen, by the end of the hallway... Alejandro's room. I wasn't sure what I was gonna do, my legs just brought me there. I couldn't help it.

I walked in and surprised everyone in the room. He had his whole crew still in there, chillin out, even though everyone's supposed to be back in their rooms after lights out, and they were all just hangin out with the lights on and everything. They all looked at me like, what the *fuck* do *you* want? Why the FUCK is this kid gettin treated like a king?!?! HE'S A PIECE OF SHIT!

He looked right at me.

"You gon fight with me?"

"You're a fuckin faggot, you know that?"

He laughed a weird nervous laugh.

"I don't want fight weeth you."

But it was too late. I wound up and slapped him in the face with all my might, as hard as I could. Then I immediately saw the look on his face. That's right bitch. You're not even worth a punch. I cunt-slapped you, whattaya gonna do bout it huh? But then I thought, fuck, I shoulda punched him. Shit. He was still standing, just the left side of his face was all red now. His friends all started oo'ing and ah-ing as if this was gonna be a good show.

He charged me and threw me on the ground and I wrestled with him until we were against the corner of his room. Everyone was standing around us. We were makin a lotta noise. Then he put me in a submission that I couldn't get out of. I couldn't move. DAMMIT GOD! I'M SUPPOSED TO WIN THIS FIGHT! But I couldn't get out! What the FUCK?! He just kept yellin:

"I don't want fight weeth you! I don wan"—gripping me harder— "fight weeth you!"

Then I heard a noise. It was the redneck security fat hillbilly hick, Warren. He ripped us apart and sent me back to my room. I had lost the fight. FUCK! I shoulda PUNCHED him! WHY DID I SLAP HIM LIKE A BITCH?!

I laid awake all night that night, feelin like shit. What if Poe finds out I lost the fight? *Did* I even lose that fight? Yeah… I totally lost that fight. But did I? I mean, I wanted to keep goin, he was all keepin me stuck on the ground. If only I had more time, maybe he woulda gotten up so I coulda lunged at him and grabbed his socks off his feet and shoved them in his mouth until he gagged and puked all over his stomach and then I woulda put his vomit-covered sock back in his mouth and suffocated him then while he was unconscious I'da taken his tongue from out his mouth and made him lick his own vomit up until he puked again when he came to. Then I woulda wedged the big chunks of his dumb vomit into his eyes until he was blind. Yeah... Everyone is gonna find out that didn't happen. Everyone is gonna know I tried to be the hero and got my ass pinned to the ground. Maybe it won't be so bad.

But I couldn't get to sleep. I could hear them all laughing from down the hall. Dumb Mexican doesn't even know when he lost a fight. That's right. I won that shit. But still, everyone in the dorm had their head out their rooms. Everyone already knew.

I was a failure.

FUCK.

I couldn't sleep all night even though I wasn't a failure, I was the man. I won. Or lost. FUCK MY BRAIN HURTS.

The next morning, I walked into The Lodge and no one said a thing to me. Nobody looked at me either. Well, actually, I wouldn't look up from the floor so I'm not sure if anyone was lookin at me. Maybe it was all in my head? Whatever, at least I was the only one who did somethin about it. Fuck these people. I went in and found Poe and sat next to her, breaking Bans again. But something weird happened. Bear saw us, but he didn't even make us move apart. Hmm... odd. Anyway, back to Poe:

"Heyyyyy whattaya up to?" She asked me as if there was something to be doin other than sittin in the FNK section of The Lodge. Whatever, she could say anything. It all sounded cute... or moronic, I dunno, I just wanted to fuck this girl and get it over with. No that's not true. I loved her. In a I-wanna-fuck-your-ass-in-the-back-of-a-beater-VW-bus-on-our-way-to-Oklahoma typa way. But boy oh boy do I hope she didn't hear anything about last night. I still wasn't sure who had won that fight. I gotta find out. But I had to respond to her question, so I said:

"Oh just being stuck in the middle of the woods. We readin anything today?"

But I was really just tryin to see if she'd say anything about Alejandro, if word had gotten back to the girls' dorm yet.

"Yay! Yes! What should we read?" She said in her normal ditzy way.

"Hmmm... I got these Buddhist scriptures with me... there's this one story about a disciple who feeds himself to a lion... want me to read you that?"

"Oh yay Greggy that sounds wonderful!"

Okay great, she didn't know shit. So I read her that story then buried my head under one of the couches in the FNK section then I snuck my way into Realizations after chow, tryin desperately not to make eye contact with Alejandro.

Goddammit I wanted to beat that kid's ass so fuckin bad. But why? Why'd I hate him so much? Maybe it's cause that girl Sam gave him a blow job in the gym, I mean, why the FUCK would anyone suck this asshole's dick? Why does he get to be such a flying dickwad and STILL get a blowjob and get to sit in the middle of a couch section when *I* got here like seven months before him? WHAT THE FUCK DOES THIS KID HAVE THAT I DON'T FUCKING HAVE? I'm gonna slit his throat. No... maybe I should wait to do that.

I walked into Realizations and sat down in the circle and waited for Thea to deliver my death sentence, or say somethin to me at least. I waited for Benjamin to actually say somethin other than quotin some bible verse. He *never* talked. Like, twice I heard him open his fat mouth... usually I just stared at him profusely sweating all through his shirt while Thea acted like the cunt that she was.

Well, when's it comin? What the fuck is goin on? I mean, I *know* I got written up... I *know* she knows what happened... so what the fuck is goin on?

But the Realizations went by and she didn't say ONE word to me.

Something was off. Then after Realizations was officially over and as my Peer Group was leavin the room to go back to The Chow Hall, Thea said:

"Oh Greg..."

"Yes Thea?"

"Can you hang back for a second?"

"For what?"

"I didn't know I needed a reason for wanting to talk to one of my favorite Peer Group members."

"Uhh... Okay."

So I hung back.

"Come, let's walk."

So we walked outside of the academic building, where Realizations was held, where we had school two-and-a-half days a week with unaccredited teachers that made us do pushups if we didn't do our homework, which nobody ever did. Let's just say the head chef taught the Spanish class, the only thing was, he didn't speak Spanish. And he was a chef in the Vietnam war, so he was better versed in physical training (even though he was only a damn chef) than he was in knowing how to pronounce even the most BASIC of Spanish words, like "ella" which is like, one of the most basic words in the world. It means 'she'. It's a fuckin pronoun. It's like an English teacher saying the word "of" as "uhff". He said it like "el-ya", not "ey-yah", which is the correct pronunciation you idiot cook. Anyway, school was a fuckin joke is the point.

So I'm following Thea and she's walkin toward my dorm, even though I'm supposed to go to The Lodge for chow, when she says:

"You're going to be sleeping in dorm one tonight."

I lived in dorm two. Why the fuck would I be in dorm one? "Why?"

"Just so you can think."

"Think? Think about what?"

"You'll be given a sleeping bag and will spend the night next to night security."

"Wait... Why?"

Something was REALLY off... she didn't even say anything about the fight.

"I thought I was pretty clear Gregory, you need time to think."

Then she stopped walking and sat on the clean white wall that surrounded the garden that surrounded the academic building that we were forced to lay mulch in front of and clean and sweep and rake every afternoon. She sat down and looked at me.

"That's all. You can go to The Lodge now. You're late."

"But wait, is something gonna happen?"

"Why would something happen Gregory?"

What the fuck is she callin me Gregory for?

"Uhh... cause you just told me I'm sleepin on the ground of dorm one in a sleeping bag tonight... that's why."

"No Gregory, this is just time for you to think, that's all. Time for you to go. I'll be heading home now."

Fuckin bitch... she just *had* to throw in the fact that she was able to go home, didn't she? What a whore. I left her ugly sight and went to The Lodge to try and catch a meal at chow before they ran outa food... but I wasn't hungry really.

Later that night, as I lay in my sleeping bag on the floor staring up at night security with his flashlight bangin against his wedding ring... someone married this dude? Anyway I was starin at his ugly face and the surveillance cameras all over the ceiling and I noticed the breeze from the door bein open a bit and it felt especially cold. I was a bit sweaty though. Clammy is a better word I guess. My heart skipped a beat. Am I dying?

No, I wasn't dying, it was something worse. And it all came about in the middle of the night...

CHAPTER 29

GET THE FUCK IN THE CAR

"Greg. Wake up. Can you hear me?"

His voice was stern and curt and cut right through my sleep. My eyes opened but my sight was blurry. There was a man.

"I want you to listen very carefully."

Grant-Lindsey, the headmaster kneeled over me, clenching his bible.

"If you think it doesn't get worse than Hidden Lake Academy, you're wrong." His silver hair parted to the side and fresh shaven face stared at me with an eerie calmness. "We're not backing down Greg." The door was wide open and it was pitch black outside. "This will get harder and harder."

The cold didn't seem to bother him. The smell of his cheap aftershave hit my face.

"What's going on?" I finally said.

"We're not afraid to make your life miserable Greg." I had no room to speak. "The more you fight us, the harder we'll make it."

"Wait—"

"No more waiting Greg. We've contacted your parents. They're fine with this."

"Fine with what?"

"Get out of your sleeping bag."

"Where am I going?"

Grant-Lindsey stood up and took a few steps backwards. Two large men guarded the door waiting for my reaction. One of them spoke:

"Do we need to pull you to your feet?"

All I could think of was Poe.

"Am I coming back?" I asked.

Grant-Lindsey crossed his arms and lowered his voice:

"Frankly, I don't give a shit if I ever see you again."

He turned his back. The large men grabbed me by my shoulders. They threw me in a car and locked the doors. My heart was about to cry.

"Where are you taking me?"

But they didn't answer.

"Hello???"

Nothing. ANSWER ME MOTHERFUCKER!

"WHERE ARE WE GOING?! YOU CAN'T JUST DO THIS!
YOU CAN'T JUST THROW ME IN A CAR AND DRIVE ME
SOMEWHERE! WHERE THE FUCK ARE WE GOING?!"

The car stopped. The large man looked back at me.

"Do you need some help calming down?"

"No sir."

Oh man oh man oh man... I'm fucked. I'm FUCKED. SHIT
SHIT SHIT. Neither of them said a damn thing to me on our way to
Atlanta. We parked outside the airport and I was handcuffed and walked
through security... again. We arrived at a gate. We boarded a plane. I
sat in the middle seat for four hours. We landed in Salt Lake City.
Everyone in the airport looked at me like the badass criminal that I was
as I was taken to a different car that was parked outside of that airport. I
was thrown in the middle seat. It was a truck... if only the kids from
middle school could see me now. I'd be a damn legend already.

We drove past Park City. I saw the big ski jump. That reminded me
that they were holding the winter Olympics there that year. How fun it
would be to be free and be able to watch that on TV. We drove through
the mountains for another two hours or so. I had NO fuckin idea where
the HELL we were goin.

We got to a building. It read "BASE CAMP".

The two large men told me to 'GET OUT' and then they left. I was
then taken into custody by some other large man with a handlebar

mustache and cowboy hat at the base camp and strip-searched. Great, another fuckin cowboy lookin at my balls.

"Where am I? How long is this place?"

"Utah. You're in Utah and that's all you need to know."

He gave me a backpack. I picked it up and it literally weighed like sixty pounds. I wobbled and almost fell over.

"Better get used to that." He told me.

He took me to another car, this car had a young guy in it. His name was Curtis. Curtis was a dick. I knew his name was Curtis cause he told me:

"I'm Curtis".

I probably coulda knocked him out with a stick, but I got in the car in the backseat and the doors were locked and I had this giant backpack and we just started driving. It was the afternoon. We drove until night.

Not a word was said the entire trip. Animal skeletons and cacti were on the side of the road. When the sun went down completely, we were still driving and the road had turned to dirt.

A little speck of orange in the distance grew bigger and bigger as we drove toward it. There were a million bumps as the dirt road came to an end and we drove directly on the desert, powering over sage and dips in the sand. The orange speck got brighter until I realized it was a fire. It blazed as we pulled up. I was nauseous from the car ride.

I saw seven or so kids building tents from tarps and tending to fire. Curtis kicked me out of the car and drove back off into the desert. Then a man, who appeared like he had been born and raised in the wild, walked over to greet me.

"Welcome. My name is Running Oak"

"Where am I? How long am I here for?"

He spoke slowly and calmly, "For the first three days, we don't give you any information about the program. We ask that you stay a hundred-feet away from the rest of the group at all times, and that you not speak to anyone other than staff. This will give you the time you need to reflect."

"How long am I here for? Where do I sleep? I need to get in touch with someone and let her know where I am. It's serious. She might think I left her." I was talkin about Poe. I didn't want her to think I just left her. What if she leaves me? Fuck what if I never see her ever again? Do my parents know about this? Do they care? Do they know where I am???? Do I know where I am? Of course I do. I'm here. SUCK IT UP GREG.

"Am I ever going back to Hidden Lake?"

"I'm not sure what you mean, what is Hidden Lake?"

"It's where I just came from. Am I ever going back?"

"That's F.I."

"F.I.?" I asked him.

"Future Information."

Great, another place with their own secret acronym vocabulary. Goddammit, how the fuck did I end up *here*?

"I don't have any idea where you *will* be going, but what I *do* know is that you are here, right now."

"Well what is this place? How long am I here for? What's this place called?"

"That's F.I."

"JUST TELL ME!! FUCK!!"

No answer.

GODDAMMIT!!! FUCK YOU RUNNING OAK!! YOU AND THAT STUPID FUCKING NAME THAT'S NOT EVEN A REAL NAME YOU FUCKIN WANNABE INDIAN—SHIT!!!! I was so damn mad.

But he just ignored me and said "I'll show you where you should set camp."

The sound of wind blowing was all I heard and Poe's face was all I could see and my parents... I couldn't even remember what they looked like. And oh yeah, Delson. And Marks. And Robby. And Sargon. And Lisa. And Lacey. And... hmmm, who else do I know again? Where the hell am I? My head was interrupted by Running Oak.

"Follow me" he instructed in a calm voice.

I walked and walked. We walked so far I could barely see the fire. Then he stopped.

"Here???"

"Yes. Here."

"Are you kidding? Are there bears? Am I safe here?"

"Have faith in Running Oak. You are safe. We'll talk more in three days."

CHAPTER 30

ARE WE TRIPPING?

I woke up the next day in my sleeping bag on the dirt of some sage-filled forest with my tarp draped sloppily over me in case it started raining. I hadn't seen where I was till then, cause it had been dark out. But now it was light. I dunno what time it was but it was bright. All the six or seven kids in my group were makin breakfast and joking around and talkin to each other.

I watched silently cause I had to. I couldn't even ask anyone what I was supposed to do. Whatever, peace and quiet sounded nice to me. I just copied what everyone was doin as best I could, cause I couldn't really see what they were doin all that well from where I was. I was real far away. I stuffed my sleeping bag back in my pack when everyone else stuffed *their* sleeping bags back in *their* packs and I got up when they got up and sat down when they sat down.

An hour or so later we started walkin on this trail. Running Oak told me to stay a hundred meters behind everyone. Meters? What's this dripping dick using the metric system for? I bet he thinks it makes him more Indian... are Indians on the metric system? Anyway I was walkin behind everyone sweatin my ass off. We hiked and hiked and hiked and then when the sun went down we stopped and I lay my sleeping bag on the dirt and went to sleep. Then we woke up again and did the same shit.

It was the third day and we were hiking in some valley full of pine trees when the group of kids I was with, that I had to hike a hundred feet behind and not talk to, they found this football.

So they all dropped their packs and started playin this game of tackle, but all I could think about was Poe and getting back to her and I didn't wanna do anything to fuck that up. Plus I'm not a football dude. I'm just a dude.

So when they looked at me to join their silly football game, I hate football, did I say that? So when they looked at me like 'cmon new kid, don't be a pussy!' I was thinkin to myself, *PUSSY?! YOU DON'T KNOW WHAT THE **FUCK** I'VE BEEN GOIN THROUGH HERE, DON'T YOU CALL ME A GODDAM PUSSY! GO DO WHATEVER IN THE **FUCK** YOU WANT BUT I'M STAYIN RIGHT THE FUCK HERE AND I'M **NO NEW KID EITHER, YOU HEAR ME? I'M AN O.G.!** AND I'M NOT GETTIN MY ASS IN TROUBLE FOR YOUR STRANGER ASS CAUSE YOU*

WANNA FUCKIN PLAY GODDAM FOOTBALL. **SO DON'T FUCKIN CALL ME A PUSSY, BITCH!**

But I didn't say any of that. In fact, nobody called me a pussy. It was all in my head. Where the fuck was that soul when I needed him?

I was so mad. I just stood there and said nothing and stared at them like I didn't speak English. Maybe none of any of this really happened? Maybe I wasn't a loser in middle school and this whole life, all this time, it was *all…* just in my head. Hmmm.   Nah, I was definitely a loser in middle school, UNTIL I BECAME A LEGEND— Anyway it certainly *seemed* like the dudes in my group, it *seemed* like they were lookin at me like 'Greg, c'mon. We got a football here. And you're a pussy.' That's sure how it felt anyhow. It felt like the way it felt when Gavin Wick looked at me, when JD looked at me, when Robby and Marks and everyone at New Beginnings and everyone in *life* always looked at me and you know what?

I was FUCKIN SICK OF IT. GO PLAY YOUR DAMN FOOTBALL!

If anyone *woulda* called me a pussy, that's what I woulda said though, that whole 'I'm not a pussy speech' I just gave before. But like I said, it was all in my head. No one said shit. So I just stood there in the middle of this trail in the middle of the mountains somewhere in Utah and watched in silence as these kids had the first bit of fun they seemed to have had in a long time. It was actually kinda nice. Maybe these kids aren't so bad.

Then Running Oak called his people, what people? I don't know, *his people,* and all these REALLY scary lookin cowboys with cowboy hats and thick coats of skin and heavy sets of weight and strong-carved grins showed up and separated everyone and brought us each to a desolate part of the forest and questioned us alone about what happened. But hey, at least the cowboys and Indians were getting along, bet that musta made Running Oak real happy... even though he was a ginger white dude from Lubbock, Texas.

Then after they questioned us all about what happened with the football, the cowboys put us in these white vans—MORE WHITE VANS?! WHERE THE FUCK DO THEY MANUFACTURE ALL THESE DAMN VANS AND PAINT EM WHITE!?!

Anyway, we drove for four hours to the center of a desert with no shade and no trees and no nothin but animal skeletons and sage. It smelled really nice though, the sage did. I should pick some for Poe. I bet she'd like it. So I did.

Running Oak told us we couldn't use a fire to cook our food and nobody was allowed to find any shade, not that there *was* any shade to begin with, but I guess if someone found a sage bush high enough to shelter them from the sun, they couldn't even use it. Everyone but me. That was my reward for not joining in on the football game and for once, following the rules.

I was given a candy bar and as much shade as could be found and was given a fire at mealtime so I could finally warm up my food. I hadn't eaten hot since I got there cause I didn't know how to make a fire, and you were only allowed to eat hot if you could figure out how to make a fire by rubbing two sticks together, which I hadn't yet learned, so I was eatin these cold and crunchy rehydrated beans and rice for days. They were goddam disgusting. So finally, I had some good food. Well, cooked food at least.

Anyway, we were out in that desert for like two or three weeks, but I lost count. I had to just remember how many sunrises we went through. When they brought us back to the forest, it was like walking into an illustrated page of some wonderful fairy tale. If only Poe were here. What if she forgets about me? Don't think that. Stay focused.

I made a friend while I was there. His name was Schmitty. He was this surfer dude with dyed blonde hair from somewhere in California. And I'm tellin you this story about wilderness because it's where my life changed overnight, but I'ma tell you about that soon. Right now I wanna tell you about the day Schmitty and I roamed around these cow patties.

So one day Schmitty and I, we strayed away from the group and stumbled upon a large meadow. The group was settin up camp, you know, diggin the latrine and hangin the food in a high up tree so the bears wouldn't find us and puttin up their tarps and what not. So we found this meadow, it was a surreal meadow, a flat piece of grassy field in the middle of these sharp mountains. It felt like a really bizarre find, so we *had* to explore it.

The grass was high and cows meandered around aimlessly hanging out in the sun, and all over this meadow was cow shit with mushrooms growing from out the manure. My life as a drug addict had taught me one thing, well maybe two or ten things, but it taught me this: These are the mushrooms that make you trip. Well, at least I knew that that's where the mushrooms that make you trip grow from, from cow shit. So what if *these* mushrooms would make *us* trip? Well, that's what we were thinkin… So we picked thirty of them and ran off in excitement. I said:

"You go first."

"*You* go first. I'm the one that saw em!" he said.

"Yeah but you have more experience."

Schmitty looked at me confused. "Experience?" He said… "What the hell does that mean?"

I wasn't quite sure what I meant. "Well I just thought—Man I don't know! Just take them!"

"FINE!" he finally agreed, "Give them to me."

Schmitty stuffed ten mushrooms in his mouth and swallowed.

"Holy shit dude! Why'd you eat so many, what if they're poisonous?"

I think I freaked him out when I said that cause he was like "Are you serious…why didn't you think of that before!?"

"How was I supposed to know you were going to eat so many?"

Now he's all freaked the fuck out: "GREAT! Now what if I die?"

"You won't die." But I wasn't sure… he might.

"Should I make myself throw up???"

I didn't know. "I don't know."

"I'm gonna make myself throw up!"

"But what if they aren't poisonous and do work then you wasted them!"

"But what if I die???"

"Shit. You're right."

"Great."

I had to make him feel more comfortable. I wasn't bein a good friend I felt. So I said:

"Actually, don't worry…If they were poisonous you'd be dead by now."

"Is that true?"

I had no idea if that was true, but I didn't say that. I just said "Yeah, that's definitely true."

"Are you positive?"

"No, not really."

"WAIT!!!!!"

"What?"

"I think I feel something."

"Are you tripping?"

"Maybe."

"Okay give me one. I want to try."

I ate one mushroom.

"I ATE TEN! THAT'S ALL YOU'RE GOING TO EAT? ONE MUSHROOM????"

"I know I have no idea why you did that! I never told you to eat ten!"

"SCHMITTY, GREG, COME JOIN US"

It was Running Oak. He was calling us to come over for "Group".

"GROUP?!" Now Schmitty was *really* freakin. "I can't do group right now! They're going to know I'm tripping!"

"But you're not tripping."

Schmitty thought for a second… "I have to say something."

"No!! You can't tell them! Talk about your feelings. You'll be fine."

"GUYS! WE'RE WAITING FOR YOU!" Running Oak screamed again.

So we ran over and joined the circle, sat on the ground, and waited for group to start. We had to start each sentence with: "I feel [INSERT FEELING] when this or that happens." It was pretty cheesy and phony.

Schmitty sat paralyzed with fear the entire time. He looked like he may throw up at any moment. It was hysterical. We never ended up tripping though.

So a buncha weeks had passed, maybe months, I don't know. I was startin to get used to it. But then this one day...

This one day, Running Oak blindfolded me and told me to follow him.

CHAPTER 31

SOLO TIME

It wasn't a punishment or anything when Running Oak came up to me after a long hike through the mountains and blindfolded me.

"Greg, it's your Solo Time." And he tightened the blindfolds over my eyes.

I knew at some point I'd have to do Solo Time, and after bein there for like forty sunsets or so, I had pieced together enough 'F.I.' to know what to expect. Ya see, while I was there, the eight or so kids in my groups, they kept rotating out cause everyone got there at different times throughout the year and it was only like a four-to-eight-week program. So I kept meetin new kids and some of the kids that were leavin had already done their Solo Time and they'd tell me all about it.

It was mid-afternoon that day when Running Oak came up to me after that hike and blindfolded me with a bandana and I don't know where he was takin me, but all I could think about was Poe. I think I'm in love with her. I mean, she enamored me before with her hippie ways and granola spirit, but bein away from her for so long, yeah… I definitely love her. So I started writin her a million letters about nature. Cause I was around nature and I write about what I'm lookin at, or remembering.

"Stop." Running Oak told me.

So I stopped. I hadn't even realized how far we'd been walkin.

"Okay. You may take your blindfolds off."

But I had been peeking through the bottom of the bandana the entire time. I took it off and was between two large hills and a million trees. None of the seven or so kids in my group could be seen or heard. All I could feel was the start of a fuzzy beard building on my chin. I kept touching it wondering what I might look like. I hadn't seen myself in so long I forgot what my face looked like. I wonder if my beard looks cool? Well, it wasn't really a beard. It was fuzzy strands of random hairs pokin out awkwardly all over random spots of my chin and cheeks. But it felt cool.

"This is where you will be living from now on." Running Oak told me.

"Alone? Here? For how long?"

"That's F.I."

Whenever I asked what day it was or what time it was or where they were hiking us to that day, it was *always* 'F.I.' Life was F.I.

"This is where I'm living? What about the group? Is Schmitty doin this too?"

I knew the general gist of what this was supposed to be all about, but when it actually happened, it all seemed pretty weird. I knew the answer Running Oak was gonna give me, but I asked anyway.

"Is Schmitty doin this too?"

"That's F.I."

Then he gave me instructions.

"You have to be up by the time the sun is two fists above the horizon. Make a fist, extend your arm and hold it over the mountaintop. Once the sun is two fists over that mountain, you MUST be out of your sleeping bag. You cannot go to sleep until three visible stars are out."

He told me how far I could and couldn't stray off. It was weird. And he assured me he would bring me food every day. Then he showed me what to do if I saw a bear.

"A BEAR?!?!"

"Relax." Running Oak told me.

A black bear meant I should lift my hands over my head and scream while running downhill, since their hind legs are longer than their front legs so runnin downhill is tough for them. For a grizzly, I was supposed to play dead. None of that made me feel safer. Confusing the two bears would be fatal.

Running Oak suggested I meditate and reflect to occupy my time before he said:

"Goodbye, and enjoy the nature."

Enjoy the nature? Running Oak was gettin on my nerves. Whatever, at least now I had some time to think.

I looked around after he left. I had no idea what to do first. I started digging a hole to use as my bathroom, that much I knew. Gotta build the latrine. That's the first thing we always did everywhere we went. So that's what I did, I built myself a nice little dirt hole toilet. That kept me busy for a buncha seconds before Poe crept back in my mind. FOCUS GREG! So I took out my tarp and tied it up against some trees and made a tent and put my sleeping bag and stuff under it... so that took me some time I guess. Uhhh.... I mounded a bunch of dirt together and made a seat for myself in fronta this tree. Then I sat down and looked at that tree. Hmmm... What now? I had only been alone for a little bit and my heart was racing. I checked the food spot, the place where Running Oak told me he'd leave my food three times per day... but it was empty. I guess it had only been fifteen minutes, maybe I just had to be patient.

I felt alone, but that was normal, so I guess I didn't really feel alone, I guess I just felt normal. But normal is weird, and this place is weird. But that wasn't so weird either, cause I was always in weird places. My life really didn't add up in my head. It made no sense. Where was I? How did this all happen? I kept thinkin tryin to figure it all out. Maybe

I've been too mean when I shoulda been nice? I don't know, too much shit goin on in my head. Just chill out Greg.

Sometime later it calmed down, my head. Running Oak dropped off a tortilla and some peanut butter and left it in the food spot, but I hadn't seen him drop it off. I just checked at one point, and it was there, the food, in the food spot. So I ate it and sat still in my dirt-mounded chair. I looked at that tree. A bit later I was still lookin at that tree. I tried meditating and tried to keep still but I opened my eyes every time I heard the rustling of leaves to make sure it wasn't a bear. But so what if it was a bear? It's the bear's home, not mine. Why am I even here?

Then a deer ran in front of me. I said hi. Then it hopped away.

What the fuck was that all about deer? Even the deer didn't wanna hang out with me.

Some stupid ass mosquito bit me and I got real mad. I told him to fuck off.

Then I stared back at the tree. "HEY TREE!" I knew it could hear me and was sure it would respond.

"HeLLLOOO??????"

Nope. Nothing.

"Fuck you tree."

The sun fell. The sun rose. Was it two fists and three stars, or three fists and two stars, or four suns and two fists? Whatever... Plus, who was keepin track of all this shit, God? Food was delivered, but I never saw it being dropped off. Running Oak was like a ninja.

Then one day I was sittin in my dirt-mounded chair and lookin at that tree with a paper and a pen, oh right—we got a pen and paper, anyway, I was sittin lookin at that tree with my pen and paper when a lightning bolt of realization hit me. I thought about everything I had done. Callin my mom a *kike,* ugh, the thought of that made me shiver. Robbin Conner's sweaters, stealin those girls' money, callin my dad a faggot, scarin my brother, stabbing my pillow with my knife that I stole from the Roosevelt Field Mall, pickin fights at New Beginnings, lyin about everything in the world, the drugs and girls and all those angry actions of hatred. Then it just hit me:

All I gotta do in life is be nice and say sorry to everyone I was mean to.

I made the decision that I would never again be mean to my parents. I will never again be mean to anyone. Then I wrote my parents a letter and told them I was cured. I could write them anything I wanted cause it wasn't censored, so I wrote it all down. Running Oak sent out mail like every two weeks or so, so I'd have to wait till it went out and that made me frustrated cause I wanted to tell them right away that I was cured. I'm not very patient. But I had no way to send it out anyway, so I had to wait. Then I wrote Poe a ten-page letter. Our life together will be perfect.

That damn mosquito bit me again, so I just asked him politely to please leave me alone. I told the tree I was going to make some chopsticks out of him, and asked his permission. I think he said yes. So I did. I made some chopsticks. I broke off some branches and whittled them down all day with this knife that Running Oak left for me as well.

Night.

Morning.

Four fists, six stars, I was goin a bit nuts by now.

I looked at that tree and gave him a hug. He was my favorite tree. It felt good givin my favorite tree a hug. See? Bein nice was workin already. I let the mosquitoes bite me, at least I tried. I think I only made it to like three of em before I whacked the shit outa the fourth and killed that motherfucker. But the ones I didn't kill, I waved them off gently and bid them farewell, careful to not hurt any of them, except for the ones I killed. I called for my deer to come back, but the deer never came back. I fucked that relationship up. Just like I did with everyone else. That wouldn't stop me, so I kept screaming for that fuckin deer to come back so I could apologize for scaring her away.

"DEEEERRRRRRR??????"

But she didn't come. She was gone. It made me real sad.

A bird flew down and landed right in front of me. How nice, I thought. She wants to be my friend.

"Hi bird."

"Hi Greg."

Wow! A response! She knows my name!

"So what's it like flying through the air?"

Oh no. She left me. I must have been too aggressive.

The sun beamed. Marty kept me company. Marty was the name of my favorite tree.

And then:

"Solo Time is over. Follow me."

It was Running Oak. He scared the livin shit outa me, damn ninja...

"Solo Time is over. Grab your stuff and follow me."

Solo time? Oh, that's right. I was on solo time. I packed up my gear and followed him back to group. Everything I thought about in life was different. I was now officially nice. I would be nice.

Then I saw Schmitty sitting in a circle with the others. He looked like a Native American warrior. He had painted thick red lines under his eyes with these rocks that if you got wet made this red paint like shit, and anyway he had rubbed it all across his face. He looked like a fucking lunatic outa Deer Hunter or some shit, although at the time I had never seen that movie.

Schmitty explained to me what each line represented. I tried my best not to laugh, cause I was nice now. Plus I liked Schmitty.

Then there was this white van. SO MANY WHITE VANS, I thought. I was becomin an expert on white vans. They're everywhere. So yeah, I watched as the rear tires kicked up a trail of dust all up over the place. I hadn't showered or brushed my teeth in over a month, at least it felt like a month, I had lost track of the sunsets, it was a buncha fists and stars. I still kept feeling my face to imagine what I might look like with the frilly beard I could feel on my cheeks. I gotta beard thingy goin. Right on. But wait, what's this van all about? I was a bit delirious feeling...

Oh shit! The van was for me! I was leaving. I had made it through. I was still alive and still relatively sane. Where in the fuck was I goin *now*? Where am I again?

Right. Utah. I prayed they would take me back to Hidden Lake, back to Poe.

"Where am I going?"

"Back to where you were before", Running Oak told me.

"Hidden Lake?"

"The place in Georgia." He told me. I guess he didn't know about Hidden Lake.

But yes, thank God. I had never heard words so sweet. Wait... Oh no. Back to Hidden Lake??? NO!!!!! At least they fed us food here! But I had my stack of letters I'd written Poe and I couldn't WAIT to see the expression on her face when I gave them to her. How was I gonna sneak them past the naked frog jump strip-search? Not sure yet, but it'll come to me.

Anyway, she was my life, or distraction. I was her life, I think. But together we would hitchhike the country and never come back ever again, that's what mattered most. She and I, we're gonna be FREE one day. It was only a matter of time. And FINALLY, I had figured out life. Be nice. That's all I gotta do. I felt like I was finally on track. Maybe all this was happening for a reason.

I couldn't wait to get back and tell Poe all I had learned in the wilderness. But then something terrible happened.

CHAPTER 32

THE TERRIBLE THING

But before that terrible thing happened, I was in a really good mood. I knew everyone would be waiting for my arrival when I got back to Hidden Lake, which is why I was so pumped up about gettin back to the worst place on Earth. It started to feel like home. I had no home. But this was at least consistently shitty and I could consistently break the rules and consistently get about the same punishment and now that I'd been sent away, which is one step worse than Isolation, I'd been through it all. I'd graduated the school of fuckups. I was officially awesome and had enough stories to keep me happy for a few years at least.

So anyway, the *same* two escorts picked me up from base camp and drove me to Salt Lake City to the airport and took me through security and boarded a plane with me back to Atlanta, where there was another truck waitin for me in the parkin lot. We drove the two or so hours back up to Dahlonega, past all the cruddy towns and finally pulled up the Hidden Lake Road after the ten-mile stretch on Camp Wahsega Road.

I was taken outa the truck and strip-searched. I had stashed my letters to Poe by my cock thinkin they wouldn't see em cause I had this way of cupping my balls that I thought might conceal em, also cause I thought my elephant trunk cock might hide them from view, but obviously they saw the thousands of letters and took em away from me and I was pissed the fuck off but then remembered I had to be nice and so I calmed down. Then they sent me off to General Population to The Lodge.

Ahhh… a fresh start. Lemme find Poe.

"Eyo Jen, where's Poe?" Jen was this southern chick in Poe's Peer Group, Peer Group 36.

"Poe? She ain't… uhhh… yew juhst git back?"

"Yeah! I was in Utah! Where she at?!"

She kept silent for like, a minute or so. Why she doin that? Finally she was like:

"She gawn."

"Huh?"

"She gawn off."

"What do you mean she gawn off?"

"Quit it!" She was talkin bout how I always made fun of her accent.

"No but for real, where she at? I gotta tell her about this deer."

"Ah'm sorry. I thaut yu knew…"

Why she still playin with me? I didn't quite understand what she was tryin to say or get across.

"Why do you look so sad?" I asked her.

"Wayell, Ah just thaut yu maight be sad an all, an so ah told yu."

"Told me what?" I was real stooped. Jen looked at me like I was dumb as fuck.

"That she's gawn."

"Who's gone?"

"Poe."

"Wait, what?

"Ah'm sorry,"

"GET AWAY FROM HIM DARLIN SWEET COUNTRY BELL!" The Colonel had been watchin us... I didn't even see him.

"I hafta go."

"WAIT! Are you serious?"

"Ah'm sorry."

Maybe I just didn't understand what she was tryin to say to me cause of her retarded southern accent.

Anyway, I was supposed to keep away from everyone that day cause it was my transitional day back to civilization in the woods. But every time I saw the girls' line walkin anywhere, cause they all had to walk in lines everywhere they went too, I stared until Poe smiled at me and saw me and ran to me and hugged me and loved me and asked where I had been. I had so many stories to tell her.

Then this girl ran up to me while some guard was turned around and slipped me this note. I put the note in my pocket, not even wondering what it was for. She ran back to the line and got in formation. I kept lookin everywhere!

Where the fuck is Poe!? Where the *fuck* is she? Maybe she's on Restrictions… But no. She wasn't on Restrictions. She wasn't on anything. She wasn't here. She was gone. I looked everywhere. But I couldn't find her.

I don't remember the rest of that day, but I remember the feelings. It was the worst I had ever felt. I couldn't swallow. I didn't shower for a week. I didn't eat for two. I spoke to no one, except Slutto. Remember him? The kid who told me about Alejandro beatin that gay kid up? Yeah, he and I became good friends real fast, so I only talked to him and this girl named KC. She was friends with Slutto, so I talked to her too. But that was it.

I opened the letter that girl slipped to me and there was a phone number on it with the name Kiki above it. A moment of hope. Who the fuck is Kiki? I had no idea. Below the number it said 'ask for Poe'.

Wait… this number will get me to Poe?!

I got excited all over again, but then after a few weeks, it faded. My hope dissipated. She was gone. I mean, I didn't throw the letter away or anything, in fact I took better care of it than I did myself, but how in the FUCK was I supposed to get to a phone? KC and Slutto didn't have any ideas. The whole situation fuckin sucked.

Assimilating back to Hidden Lake was a blur. Weeks went by, Realizations happened. Manual labor happened. Pushups, cheese sandwiches, work assignments, they were all still here, but Poe was gone. So life was blank. Thea kept punishing me cause I wouldn't talk to anyone, but I could care less about any form of punishment. I had tasted the worst of it and my taste buds were immune.

At night I stared at that phone number trying to figure out how to get to a phone, wondering if it was even a real number. It started with a '401' area code, but I had no idea what city or state that was. I couldn't ask anyone except for KC and Slutto cause I didn't wanna lose the letter and I couldn't trust a soul other than them, but they didn't know where the hell that area code was either. I was destroyed. It was like they couldn't think of anything else to do to me, so they took away Poe. My only friend. Man, it really fucked me in the head. I was distraught. I mean, I was *really* fucked in the head.

And then on my worst of days, a day when the thought of never seeing Poe again plagued my thoughts on repeat, constantly, all day, at the worst possible moment, Thea asked me if I could 'hang back for a second' again. The last time this happened I was woken up by Hitler and handed off to ex-FBI agents and ended up counting fists and stars and tryin to recognize bear types… Whatever, take me to another goddam airport. Who gives a shit. What now? What this time?

"Greg, I'm just going to need you to hang back for a moment"

"Why? Just tell me. What is it? I did nothing wrong."

She told me to follow her. So I did. Who cares. All I kept thinking was this was never gonna end… I didn't even give a shit about my legacy anymore. No one would ever be able to comprehend it anyhow by now. This was all for nothin. I just followed Thea in silence cause I hated her. She really was the wicked witch of the dirty South.

I followed her to the Gym, but then she started walkin behind the gym, where all the offices were of the head honchos. We got to an office and stopped.

Oh my God.

Grant-Lindsey. It was Grant-Lindsey's office. That piece of fuckin bible shit. I bet *he*'s the reason Poe was gone. That son of a fucking bitch. I'll kill that cocksucker fuckbag. That motherFUCK—Wait. I gotta be nice. And then—

Oh man.

Yeah, I totally spaced there. My thoughts of homicide were completely interrupted when I saw em.

There they were.

In the flesh.

My mom and dad.

I hadn't seen em in so long it looked like they had more wrinkles than the last time I saw em. They looked older. They *were* older. Was I missing my family gettin older? Were they gettin older too quick? Was it cause of me? Did they get the letters I sent em in Utah?

Wait a hot dang moment...

WHAT THE FUCK ARE MY PARENTS DOING HERE?!

Then Thea was like:

"It there anything you'd like to say to your family, Greg?" Cause I was just starin at em, all blank-like. Like all the shit I had ever wanted to say to them just escaped my head and I was totally mindfucked. It had been almost three years since I'd seen em. They definitely looked older. And they definitely had more wrinkles. I hated them. I hated them more than I hated... I don't know. But I hated them. Wait, be nice, remember? Right, nice. Okay, got it. I hope they read my letters.

But I looked harder at my family and realized I had no family. SO I DON'T *KNOW* WHAT TO SAY TO THEM THEA YOU BULIMIC WHOREBAG. BE NICE GREG!

"Sit down, Greg." Grant-Lindsey's corrupt ass said to me.

So I sat down. Then I started to think, fuck! In a few months I'd be seventeen—WAIT, I didn't even tell you about the day I turned *sixteen*! My *second* institutionalized birthday! And you know why I didn't tell you about it? CAUSE IT SUCKED. But you know what *was* special about it? NOTHING. ABSOLUTELY FUCKING NOTHING.

Anyway, in a few months I'd be now *seventeen,* and that musta made my so-called parents kinda nervous, cause in Georgia, it was the legal age to leave Hidden Lake. In most states it was eighteen, but in Georgia the legal age was seventeen... I think. At least that was what everyone around here said. We were all just tryin to make it to seventeen... then we were free. Unless the court ordered you there. Oh wait—

I *was* court-ordered. That's what the sheriff said at least... Remember? But how would I be court-ordered? Did I get arrested and go to court and forget about it or somethin? Focus Greg. Your ex-parents are right in front of you.

It had been nearly three years and I *knew* that all *they knew* was I was *still* fuckin up. After all this time, I was *still* fuckin up. And they had tried everything they could think of to fix me. But I was unfixable. Cause I wasn't broken. I was just different. They didn't even know about Poe or my nickname in Louisiana, or Lisa or Lacey or Alejandro or Schmitty or Sargon or anything. They knew NOTHING about me! And these were my parents?

All they knew was that I was never allowed to call them cause I was *always* on Restrictions and when you're on Restrictions you're not allowed your ten-minute supervised phone call (where you're not allowed to say shit anyway). All it was, that phone call room, it was nothin but aggravating when all I got was a guard listening in on me waitin for me to start tellin the truth so that he could cut the line... so I just started gettin myself thrown on Restrictions so I wouldn't have to deal with the phone call, it was just too annoying. I mean, they *really* didn't understand. They knew nothing.

"We love you Greg"

I wonder if she meant that... so-called mom.

"How have you been?"

I wonder if he was *really* asking me that, so-called dad.

"Greg, your parents are trying to communicate with you."

I wonder if he honestly expected me to respond cordially to that, Mr. fucked up Christian asshole evangelical anti-Semitic bible thumping crackpot, Grant-Lindsey. Wait, be nice Greg. FUCK NICE.

"So, we *have* made a lot of progress here, Mr. and Mrs. Cayea."

"It's doctor." My so-called dad said in a jovial typa way.

She obviously didn't know my dad was a doctor. IDIOT.

"My apologies Dr. Cayea,"—haha! She looked angry about that!—"but like we talked about, we do believe there is still *a lot* of work to be done." Then Thea looked at me like she was askin for my approval.

Was I hearing all this right? Cause it sounded like Thea was tellin my parents that I hadn't done my time yet.

"Greg? Do you want to say anything?"

"Uh yeah. I think you're a hundred percent right Thea. I'm still broken."

"So you can see what we mean, Mr. and Mrs. Cayea."

She definitely forgot he was a doctor, or maybe that was her bulimic whore way of regaining control. Ehh, what the fuck do I know about what my dad wants to be called anyway…

"Greg, they said you'd be able to have a CD player." My mom said.

I was crackin up on the inside… A CD PLAYER?! WHO GIVES A FUCK ABOUT A FUCKIN CD PLAYER!?

"Oh wow," I said. "That's a major step forward. I thought you said we weren't makin progress, Thea?" So much for bein nice…

"No Greg, that's your selective hearing. What I said was we *have* made progress, but we still have a lot to work on."

"Oh right. That's what I meant. Are we done?"

And I got up.

My dad stood up, "Gregory."

He was the only person that ever called me Gregory. Him and that twat Thea.

"Gregory, we just don't know what to do. We can't have you back at our house yet." He was about to cry. "We just want this to all go away. I want my son back!"

Shit… now I was about to cry. Don't cry. Just, I dunno, leave maybe. Yeah, leave. But I couldn't, cause, well, I wanted my family back too. I wanted my dad too. Even though I hated them. I just stood still.

"Greg." Grant-Lindsey said, "We don't think August is a good release date for you. We're extending your stay until May"

You gotta be fuckin kidding me. Did I just hear him right? This was about as bad as it could get.

"EVERYONE IN MY PEER GROUP IS GONNA GRADUATE IN AUGUST BUT I'M GONNA BE STUCK HERE?! THE ONLY ONE?!"

"Yes, Greg. That's right."

"Oh thanks Thea, for your fucking clarification." Yeah, I *really* wasn't ready to be nice to *her*.

"Greg, you need to calm down."

"Oh shut the fuck up. Everyone. Everyone here shut the fuck up. Or keep talking. Yeah, just keep fucking talking. No one shut up, talk your lips off."

Then I was unsure how to react after that little episode, so I didn't. I didn't do anything. I just went silent. My parents couldn't even look me in the eyes. Then, after a moment that felt like an hour, I got up and walked out of the room.

"GREG YOU DON'T WANNA DO THAT!" Thea yelled.

But that was it. I was gone. I had nothing left to lose.

Thea ran after me.

"Where exactly are you going?"

"I'm placing myself on Restrictions Thea." And I walked behind the lake. I had to figure out my life.

CHAPTER 33

SODA POP

I wrote in my journal that entire night; poems, short stories, thoughts, everything. I wrote and wrote and wrote trying to figure out my life. But here's the thing, I had to be careful, cause at Hidden Lake, the only way for them to *truly* know how you felt was to know your deepest, darkest secrets and expose them during Realizations, which is why they stole all our journals and diaries at some point or another and made us talk about what was *really* on our minds. You just never knew when they'd do a dorm search so I had to keep those pages I wrote hidden, especially cause I had figured it all out. I had come up with a plan. So I tore the pages out of my journal and wrapped em up together with that note that had Kiki's number on it, I still didn't know who the hell that was, but any chance to one day get back to Poe was as precious of life as I had at the moment, so I guarded it like gold.

I shoved all the loose papers in my pocket and slept with my pants on… I think I had come up with a plan that would finally work… So I had to REALLY make sure those pages were never found.

The next day in Realizations, Thea didn't even start by talkin to me, she sat right across from Inky, my friend in my Peer Group from Tennessee and also my roommate at the time, cause they were always shuffling us around from room to room, *sometimes* even dorm to dorm, but that woulda been a pretty big deal to be transported to another dorm. Anyhow, Inky was like a genius, one of those kids who's far too smart for his own good.

So Thea sat across from him and she did that stare thing that she did until Inky nearly blew up. He was pretty funny like that, when he got mad, it looked like he had no idea what to do other than start throwing things and he got all flustered and always got this hysterical look on his face. Thea could pretty much drive anyone insane.

"Steven, we're concerned."

"Because you stole my journal and read my feelings?"

See? I told you… they stole our journals and read them front to finish! I caressed my pants pocket to make sure none of the papers had fallen out. Thea went on…

"Steven, you know that's not the case. You know what I mean."

"No actually I don't Thea because when I got back to the dorm and looked for my journal I realized that it was gone, so uhhh… I'm pretty sure that's exactly the case." He was gettin a bit loud and funny. Thea stared still. "SO WHAT THE HELL DID YOU WANT ME TO

WRITE ABOUT THEA? MY HAPPY FEELINGS ABOUT THIS
HAPPY PLACE I'M IN?!?"

"Steven, if you're not ready to—"

"Steven if you're not ready to do the work then we can move on,
and that's absolutely okay Steven, it's your choice, we have all the time in
the world, I'm from Harvard. I'm smart. I'm so smart. Is that what you
were going to say Thea?"

HOLY SHIT THAT WAS SO ON POINT!
HAHAHAHAHAHAHA!!!!! We all started laughing like mad then
Thea's skinny, boney and wicked demonic spirit took a deep but
empowering sounding sigh and just said "Okay…" Then she smirked…
"We're done." Then the witch smiled as if to say 'I still win'.

She got up and moved onto me. She switched seats with Jaime, this
girl in my peer group with blonde hair and librarian glasses from South
Carolina that I've never talked about, and she sat across from me ready
to move one, but Inky was still talkin. Oh, and Inky, if you haven't
figured out by now, is Steven's nickname…

"Is that it Thea? Steal my journal then move on? GIVE IT
BACK!"

And he got up from his chair.

"Steven, sit down. Now you're threatening me and I will not have
that." And she picked up her radio.

"GIVE ME MY FUCKING JOURNAL BACK!"

And he took a step toward her.

"Mort, come in" She said into her radio. "Peer Group 34, please,
now."

"YOU THINK YOU'RE WALKIE-TALKIE MAKES YOU TOUGH? DID THEY TEACH YOU HOW TO USE THAT AT HARVARD? HOW TO PRESS THAT BUTTON AND GET OTHER PEOPLE TO DO YOUR JOB?!"

The door flung open.

Mort saw Inky like a foot away from Thea. He was a small kid, but even I thought he might hit her.

PLAOW!

Mort pummeled Inky to the ground and put his knee on the back of his neck and smushed his face into the carpet and grabbed his wrist."

"Real impressive *Morty.*" Inky said while he was in a pretzel.

Man did Mort *hate* being called Morty. So he twisted Inky's wrist even harder. But I wasn't freakin out, that typa shit happened all the time...

But the day that was the *greatest* day of my life was when we showed up to Realizations two days later and Inky sat at his chair with a Pepsi and his journal right next to him. I hadn't seen a soda in years. It looked so good compared to the water fountains. Inky just sat there with this hilarious smirk, slurpin his Pepsi loud as hell.

"Steven, where'd you get that?"

"Your office Thea." And he threw this little tool kit thingy he made from paperclips on the floor in the middle of the circle by Thea's feet. "Yeah, it was right next to my journal, and I was thirsty. So, you know, I just... took it. From your desk."

The kid was a genius. He had picked a DEADBOLT. WITH PAPERCLIPS. Genius. I always admired him for that.

"Steven, that's fine. I hope the soda pop was worth a Fall-In Restriction."

But it wasn't Restrictions he was put on. I never saw him ever again. That was the last day I ever saw Inky. They actually *kicked him out.* Which mind you is *impossible* to get kicked outa Hidden Lake. We *all* tried to get kicked out at one point or another… Inky was just too smart. They couldn't take him.

FUCK YEAH INKY.

Rest In Peace.

He passed away one year later from a drug overdose.

Anyway, sorry for the sad tale, but that damn Pepsi. Just sittin there and watchin him sip away with his journal right in fronta Thea's face was pure joy.

Benjamin, my other fat counselor, that literally had said ten words up until now, it even got a response from *him* when he said in his fat voice "Now Steven, thayt's steeElin and that's nawt raight. Yer gon hafta give that back."

"No thank you Benji." Inky said to him without even lookin in his direction.

HA! I can't get over that story.

Anyway, later that Realizations when Thea asked me to tell the group about the ambush my parents and Thea and Grant-Lindsey surprise attacked me with, and what had been decided for me, I was almost embarrassed to tell the group that I wouldn't be leaving with them.

"Greg? Would you like to tell the group about the visit with your parents?"

"Huh?? He got a visit with his fffu—with his freakin parents?!" Jonny said.

Yeah, wait till you hear what it was about...

"Well, ummm..." I had no idea how to say this. Jeez, it was so embarrassing. "I'm not gonna be graduating."

"Greg, why don't you go ahead and tell the truth, you *will* be graduating, will you not?"

But I was so depressed I just said, "Yeah I just won't be going home. I gotta come back after one night in Dahlonega."

"Well, that's something you can certainly *earn*, Greg."

Right, so they were holding this one-night visit with my parents over my head. They said that if I was 'well-behaved' I could leave on graduation night and spend one night in a hotel, in Dahlonega, under this weird contract that I had to sign that I would come back... as if a piece of fuckin paper would mean anything.

The whole group looked at me in this 'we don't care as long as *we're* goin home, but that *really really really sucks* for you' kinda look. Yeah, after one month in Minnesota and six months in Louisiana and one month in Utah and twenty-two months in Georgia... I had to come *back* for another TEN months in Georgia? Jeez. I was so depressed. So when Thea asked me:

"How do you feel about the decision Greg?"

I was honest. "I feel horrible."

"Why is that?"

"Cause my parents don't want me."

"Now that's not true Greg, there's just some work that still needs to be done."

"Well I feel unloved. That's how I feel."

After Realizations, Thea called me over.

"That was really great work today Greg, keep it up and you'll get that visit."

So I went back to my papers later that night and solidified my plan. Yeah, it was a pretty solid plan. Here's what I would do: I would talk about my feelings for the remainder of my time here, and I would get that visit, and I would GET THE FUCK OUT.

But I just had to fix *one* small thing. I needed some things from home.

So I added an integral step to my escape plan:

I finally stayed off Restrictions for long enough to get my supervised phone call with my parents, it had been so long since I actually showed up for one of those things, and I walked into the phone room and looked at the guard as he picked up the phone and dialed my parent's number. He sat back down as the phone started ringing.

"Hello?"

"Hi mom." My so-called mom was so excited that it was me. "I have a favor to ask you." The guard immediately looked at me real hard, ready to cut the line at any moment. But I continued…

"So… um, I was wondering if, on our hotel visit, if you could just bring me some real clothes. Just for one night I wanna wear some *real* clothes."

Tread carefully Greg…

"Well, is that allowed?"

But the guard couldn't hear her ask that.

"It is. I asked. It's totally cool."

My mom sounded worried, but she always sounds worried.

"So how's Eric?" I asked.

Only nine more minutes of phone call to go, but I think my plan had worked. Normal clothes, need normal clothes. I could only pray that it actually happened, and I did, every night before I went to sleep. I prayed and talked about my feelings during Realizations so I could get that damn visit… Cause on that visit, I would make my final escape.

Then came graduation day, the day I was supposed to leave with the rest of my Peer Group. It was the happiest moment in everyone's life… except for me. I still had a whole lot more to do before I was *really* free.

CHAPTER 34

TRASHLEY

It was graduation day. The Gym had been transformed into this room that semi-resembled a normal school, with chairs and shit, and I had officially earned my one-night visit with my parents later that night. Peer Groups 34 and 35 were on this stage at the far end of The Gym and Grant-Lindsey was at this podium givin a speech that you might find at a normal school, not that I know what a normal school was, but you know, he was givin this typa graduation speech.

I looked at KC and Slutto. We had become so close that I told em all about my runaway plan and how I intended to leave in the middle of that night while my parents were sleeping. I even promised to come down and visit KC for her graduation in December, not like I was gonna come *back* on school property, but see, the night before you graduated, you were given a night off campus to celebrate with your Peer Group before showing up the next day for graduation. Of course I wasn't given that privilege, my night off campus was *after* graduation and I was only allowed to hang out at the Econo Lodge with my parents... But anyway, I promised KC that I would be there for her at the Econo Lodge on the night before she graduated, and I promised that no matter what, I wouldn't miss it. Later on, that 'privilege' of going off campus the night before graduation would be taken away... cause of me. But umm... I'll tell you about that later, for now just know I promised KC I'd be there, and that Slutto, well, he and I would re-unite on the road since he had *just* turned *eighteen.*

Slutto was gonna leave tomorrow. Oh, and if you're wondering why the hell he didn't leave when he was seventeen, it was cause no one *really* *knew* if seventeen was *actually* the legal age, so he didn't wanna take any chances... I don't blame him after what happened to me. So he wanted to wait till he was *sure* they couldn't do shit. And now he was finally eighteen and he had been waiting for my graduation before he left, and now it was here, and so he would be walking down that road first thing tomorrow morning. The plan was to meet Slutto in Birmingham, where he was from, right after I ran... but that all got a bit messed up as you'll see in a second.

But anyway, I promised KC I would be there for her in December and that I wouldn't forget her. But they looked kinda blurry from where I sat cause I was all fucked up on the painkillers that Ashely gave me, you know, the girl that tried to give me my first blow job?—OH WAIT!

I NEVER TOLD YOU THAT STORY! Sorry! I was bit distracted with all my master-planning and all...

Okay... It was before I even ran away on Christmas. It was *right* when I got to Hidden Lake after I was kicked outa Louisiana, and it was also right when *she* got there. I remember it so clearly even though it was two years ago when she walked outa the administration building after having just gotten there and after just having been strip-searched... I remember perfectly how broken she looked.

I could relate. I knew that pain.

I looked at her through The Lodge during breakfast as she was being escorted to her new home for the next two years, to the girls' dormitory. I couldn't imagine goin through that first day again. Jeez, that first day was terrible.

At lunch later that day I went up to her in the FNK section of The Lodge before and said:

"Hey."

She was *real* Southern from this small town in Mississippi.

"Hayyy" She said all seductive, probably itching for some male validation, which I was more than happy to give her.

"Let's make out later." That's what I said. It's just what came outa my mouth. Not the most charming dude sometimes, I know.

"Migh migh migh" she said all southern-like, "Where we gon do thaight? Hmm?"

I had it all worked out in my head. I always had everything all worked out in my head. So I told her exactly what to do:

"Okay so the girls do dishes after chow tonight. And the guys go to The Gym. So, you just meet me at The Dumpster when you gotta take the trash out, cause you'll have to do that somewhere around 9ish. I'll ask to go to the bathroom and I'll slip out the door and we'll meet there. Okay?"

You see, the dumpster was right in between the kitchen and The Gym, so it was perfect. A perfect plan, for once.

So we met at like 9PMish. At the dumpster.

What's up with me and dumpsters?

Anyway, I met her at the dumpster but the allure was already gone and she was all frazzled and nervous and barkin at me like:

"H'rry up!"

So I unzipped my pants and took out my not-erect dick. I had to move fast. My first blow job. I was gonna cum in this hot trashy Mississippi chick's mouth and I was so excited.

She got on her knees but kept lookin back at the kitchen to make sure no one was comin, it was givin me tons of anxiety. Especially the way she kept sayin:

"C'mowhn! H'rry up!"

So I hurried up as best I could, flingin my dick back and forth tryin to get it hard enough but by the time I was ready to go, I nearly came. I didn't, but I felt the cum about to come out way too fast, so I thought about nasty shit to not fuck this up, but then she said:

"I gotta go Graig!" And she turned around for a moment to look at the kitchen again to make sure no one was comin, and during that SPLIT SECOND that she turned around, I came. By accident. But I didn't see where the cum went.

Where the fuck did I cum?

Where'd it go?

I tried to play it off like nothin happened but I was all outa breath.
It was pitch black outside so I kept my body still and tried to slow my
breathing so I could pretend that nothin happened. But when she
turned back around, still on her knees, and finally stood up, she was like:

"Graig Ah'm sorry, but I gotta—did yew cum?"

Shit.

"Ahh... a little."

"Did it git on me?"

"Uhh.... I don't think so, no. Of course not."

"Are yew shur?"

"Yeah, I just, you know, wanted to finish myself off so I didn't get
blue balls or anything. I thought you were leavin anyway, I woulda
waited! You shoulda told me!"

Yeah, that was what I said before we both took off, me back to The
Gym, her back to the kitchen. But when she walked back into the
kitchen, one of the girls was like:

"What's that?"

Annnndddddddd, yeah. It was my cum. A lot of it. All over her
shirt. Her name became Trashley. We both went to Restrictions.

Anyway... *THAT* was why I was on painkillers. Cause Trashley's
mom snuck it to her before we went up on stage and she gave me two of
em... I guess we still had that special bond. But yeah, even the parents
were fucked up like that, which is great I guess to a certain extent, I
mean, I *needed* those painkillers, *especially* right then, when all this shit was
goin on in my head..

So I was on stage with Trashley, I mean Ashley, and I was listenin to
Grant-Lindsey say some nonsense about how much we had all grown

and all I kept thinkin in my slurred state of mine was that I was the *only* *one* on this stage that had to come back after the graduation. Or did I?

For the rest of the kids, it was the greatest day of their lives.

For me, it was the greatest anxiety and rush of adrenaline in my life… thus far. Also a permanent reminder of how broken the world still thought I was. I was SO angry, but the painkillers helped that go away, that and the painting of freedom I could see on the horizon. I had to be ready tonight. It was now or never.

So when my mom and dad and I got to the hotel, it was all quiet. None of us had any idea what to say. My mom said:

"Look what I brought for you, I don't know if you'll be able to keep it, but, I just wanted you to know we still had it. I know how much you love this bag."

IT WAS MY ORANGE BACKPACK FROM NEW BEGINNINGS!!!! YES!!!!!!!!!!

"THANK YOU MOM!" I'm about to FUCK your world up, but THANK YOU! Not only that, but she brought me this black-knit hoodie and a brand new Banana Republic tee-shirt and a pair of Mavi jeans. I guess she didn't get the memo that I was a hippie now… but anyway, the expensive clothes'll do… I mean, they'll have to.

So I put them on, since I was only allowed to 'wear them till I went back to HLA', to make it seem like I had nothing up my sleeve. But of course, this was my big moment.

When the clock struck dark outside, I knew my time was slipping away. I had to do this *now*, but I was so goddam nervous. So I said,

"Gonna go get some ice." And I grabbed the bucket and my backpack. Oh fuck, I need money, and why would I need ice? Shit.

"Ice? Why are you bringing your backpack?" So-called mom said.

"For the ice" I said. Jeez... I was fuckin this up.

"You need your backpack for ice?"

"Yeah! I mean, I just like it."

"Well, what do you need ice for?" My mom said.

I was flustered. I was already fucking this up.

"Huh? Oh, I'm uhh... I'm thirsty!" I said that without thinkin. OH SHIT! I STILL NEED MONEY! GODDAMMIT! WHY THE FUCK DID I FORGET... Snap out of it Greg, there's *no* time to fuck anything up. You're a winner. Fix this.

"You're thirsty?" My mom said a bit skeptical. My dad was watching TV trying to avoid the family disaster. Maybe he could feel it... I mean, he *was* a doctor.

"Yeah, I don't want warm water." I said. Jeez, warm water? What the fuck was I talkin about? Then my mom was like:

"But we have—"

"—Can I actually have a dollar for some soda?" Good save Greg.

Whenever money was brought up, my dad came to the rescue. So he was the one who gave me a dollar. But I needed more than a dollar. So I kinda stood there by the door searching for the right thing to do. My dad went to the bathroom while my mom stared at me like I was up to something. I walked over to where her purse was, then I said:

"Look! Even the wall is cracked." I said as I pointed to the wall behind my mom.

She turned around and I grabbed her wallet from her purse and then turned around so that when she turned back around all she saw was my back... and my backpack.

"Greg? What's going on?"

Thank God. She didn't see it. Thank you God. Thank you. I carefully snuck the wallet down my pants and pretended like I was adjusting my dick… I mean, better than my mom knowing I took her wallet, right? And it was a big wallet, like a purse-wallet typa thing, so I had to keep bent over after it was in between the waist of my pants and my stomach so she wouldn't see it poking through that dumb tight Banana Republic tee-shirt she bought me that I was still wearing. By the way, the wall wasn't cracked at all, so when she said:

"Greg, are you okay?"

It was kinda funny cause my mom thought I was nuts. But I was right on point.

"Oh, it looked broken or something, I mean cracked, the wall did, okay I'll be right back. Gonna go get a soda."

I didn't even drink soda. I only drank seltzer. My mom knew that, but she didn't say anything. After all, three years institutionalized can change a dude's taste buds, can't it?

I dunno but I left the room and walked by the ice machine and then off the motel's weed-filled lawn and over to this payphone to catch my breath cause I was like hyperventilating. I picked up this yellow phone book that looked like it had blood and spit and vomit all over it and the pages were all wiggly and puffy from the rain and decades of not being touched and I found this one taxi company a few towns over. So I jiggled the wallet outa my pants looking for some quarters… I had no idea how much money was even in there. I counted it, a little over two-hundred bucks.

Then I got real paranoid. I looked up at the motel room my parents were in and saw the door was open. FUCK! Did I not close it? Or were they already lookin for me??? They were onto me. I was gonna get caught.

Fuck.

They're callin the front desk right now I bet. I'm never gonna make it. I gotta go, I gotta start running. I was sweaty and I had to pee. I whipped out my dick and peed on the pole that the phone was on like a dog but I crouched at the same time to hide myself and got pee all over my beat-up sneakers. I put my dick back in my pants before I finished peeing and my boxers got all soaked and I ran and ran and ran and ran and THUMP!

I tripped.

What the hell do I do?

Some guy in a truck drove past me. I dove onto his hood and his truck punched me in the stomach and I fell onto the cement. The truck stopped. I threw up. I teared up a bit and started hyperventilating again. I reached into my mom's wallet and found a twenty-dollar bill.

"Yew ahriight?" This dude ran outa his truck like he thought he mighta killed me. He was wearing a baseball hat and had a dip in his mouth. He was like twenty. He musta been some redneck hick in the marines. I handed him the twenty.

"Please take me to Atlanta, please."

"You aright?" Then he saw my mom's wallet. "You steal women's wallets a lot?"

"Oh shit, no sir, this is my mom's wallet. Plus, you just hit me man! PLEASE! I need a ride!"

He paused, a bit confused. I don't blame him, what I said made no sense. It was actually quite alarming I imagine. He looked at the twenty-dollar bill after he realized I was not hurt at all and grabbed it. "Git in" and he spit on the ground, "Yew fuhk me ah'ma rip yer head off." And he shoved the bill in his pocket. But then I realized it wasn't a twenty, it was a hundred. Fuck it who cares.

And so I left again, but this time, it would be the last.

CHAPTER 35

THAT 401 NUMBER

I showed up at the Greyhound station in downtown Atlanta and I think I paid this guy's whole salary when I gave em that hundred bucks… he was pretty happy about it. I walked up the handicap wheelchair access walkway past these homeless dudes and it was about 1AM and so it was pretty sketch.

I got inside and it was no better than the outside. I went to the food counter thingy and ordered a seltzer water and a calling card with forty minutes on it. Okay, it was time to make my move.

I walked to the payphone and carefully unfolded that piece of paper that was in my pocket, in fact, it had been in my pocket ever since I got it. Okay. Kiki. A '401' number. I dialed the number… but then I hung up immediately cause I looked at the clock and it was now actually closer to like 2AM. Then I realized I wasted a minute of my calling card on nothing! And now I only had like eighty-five bucks left!

Fuck...

I saw this atlas on the shelf by where you order the bus tickets and from where you can get pizza and shitty hot dogs, and in the back of that atlas there was a directory of area codes. I found 401. Rhode Island. Then I went to the Rhode Island section of the atlas and saw in bold print Providence. There were only a few other cities but they were in lighter black and I felt eyes on me.

I was being watched.

I had to make up my mind now. I had to get on a bus NOW. I had to get the fuck outa Georgia. So I walked up to the ticket counter and bought a ticket to Providence. It was like eighty-nine bucks or somethin, so I had to use nickels and quarters and shit since it was more than I had in dollar bills. I *just* made it! PHEW. That coulda ruined *everything*.

So I bought the ticket and waited in those movie seat type chairs and watched the clock till 5:15AM. The bus to Providence left at 5:45AM but I could board the bus a half-hour before it left so I sat there for three fuckin hours like a nervous runaway wreck until it was 5:15AM.

Then a cop walked in. Fuck. The cops found me ALREADY?! I ran to the bathroom and into a stall. I waited for twenty-minutes until it was like 5:40AM. SHIT! THE BUS IS GONNA LEAVE! I had to get to the bus without the cops seeing me. I poked my head outa the bathroom.

FUCK! THEY WERE STILL THERE! THEY WERE SITTING DOWN! Were they looking for me? Or were they looking for someone else?? Wait, how do I even know they're lookin for someone? Maybe they're just, uhh, I dunno. FUCK!

Please God get me outa here. I bent down and unzipped my backpack to make it look like I was searching for something in my backpack. I looked at the line outside my bus terminal gate thingy. The door was about to close, there were only three people left in line. FUCKING MOVE GREG! Now the cops were walkin around, lookin at shit. Lookin for me. HOW DID THEY FIND ME? Are they looking for me?

Shit, now there was only one person in line. Oh no. She's boarding the bus. They are gonna close the gate! YOU ARE GONNA MISS THE BUS!!!! RUNNN!!!!!!

So **BOOOOOM!!!!!**

I ran and pretended that I was only running cause I was in the bathroom and hadn't noticed my bus was about to leave. I got to the door and flashed the bus guy my ticket and didn't turn around once. I hopped on the bus and every seat was nearly taken except this one and so I asked this fat black dude with cornrows with the empty seat next to him if he could save my seat.

"Can you save this seat??"

"Aiight."

"Thanks!"

And I ran to the bathroom in the back of the bus and peed again. I always gotta pee when I'm nervous. I stayed in there till I jolted forward. The bus was moving.

I DID IT! I MADE IT!!!

I'M FREE!!!!!!!

PART III

THAYER STREET

CHAPTER 36

MIDNIGHT IN PROVIDENCE

The bus pulled onto a dark street but The Greyhound station was closed. The city was desolate. It was now midnight of the next day. Nobody was around. I sat on the street corner and took a deep breath.

Ahhh... real life. It was my first night of liberation, my first night I wouldn't have to ask to go to the bathroom, speaking of bathroom... I gotta pee again. So I did, on the street. I was already feeling homeless. It was the greatest night of my life. I had never felt so free even though I wasn't sure where I'd sleep, or how I'd eat or what I'd do. I had absolutely no agenda, well, except one. One very important goal that nothing would keep me from:

Find Poe.

I took out that paper in my pocket again and unfolded it and stared at Kiki's '401' phone number. Dammit I hope this shit is right, cause uhh... if not, I'm stuck in fuckin Rhode Island with no goddam money.

I walked over to the payphone that was outside the closed up Greyhound station and took out my calling card with thirty-nine minutes on it, and even though it was midnight, I dialed her number anyway. I had to. What choice was there? Well, I suppose I finally *had* choices for the first time since I was fourteen, so the choice I made was to call Kiki and use the minutes and find out who in the FUCK she was. And how to find Poe.

Some thug-sounding dude picked up

"hehLO?"

"uhh..." I thought I had dialed the wrong number or some shit. But I went on anyway... "Hi, I'ma, I'm sorry for calling so late. Is Kiki there please?"

"Who?"

"Uh... Kiki?"

"EYO CORINNE! SOMEONE ON THE PHONE!"

Then

"Hello?"

"Kiki?"

"Yeah?"

"Oh shit I thought I dialed the wrong number cause someone screamed for Corinne and—"

"That was my half-brother. Corinne's my real name, but I don't go by it. What's up?"

Why does everyone have weird names? Anyway...

"Hey, uhh... My name is Greg, and I think I'm supposed to ask for Poe. Do you know Poe?"

"Yeah I know Poe, of course I do. Is this... uhh, Greg?"

YES YES YES! IT'S ME! "Yeah! It is! Do you know me?"

"That's a weird thing to ask." She told me.

Fuck.

"I don't know you because I've never met you. But I know you know Poe."

"Right, that's what I meant." Good save stupid.

"Ugh... and she just left. She's going to be so upsept. Ummm, where are you? Are you still at that place?"

Yeah right would I be able to make a call like this from that place... but I guess she didn't know that.

"No, I'm here! In Providence! Wait, that is where you are, right?"

"Are you serious? You're here?"

"Yeah!"

"Oh wow, Poe's gonna flip. Yeah I live in South Providence but Poe might already be back on Thayer, I would just go there if I were you, you'll find her." She said to me.

I didn't know what the fuck that meant. So I just said "Well, I really don't know what to do or where to go… can you maybe—"

"—Where are you?"

"The Greyhound station on… ummm…" I looked for a street sign. "Somewhere in Providence—Is that close to you?"

"—Okay stay there."

"What?"

"Stay there."

Click.

And that was that. Thank God! I WAS IN THE RIGHT PLACE! YES!!! But what if she doesn't come get me? Wait, that *is* what she meant, right? Yeah, of course it is. Fuck, what if I'm here all night. Should I call back? Just to make sure? How long was I on the phone for? Damn I gotta be careful with my minutes. I probably only got like thirty-five left or whatever. All good. I'll figure this out. This is my Kerouac moment. I'm livin on the road! Fuck yeah! AND SHE KNOWS POE! YES! Who the fuck *was* this girl anyway?

I turned around and stared at my reflection through the dark storefront windows of the Greyhound station cast by a nearby streetlamp to make sure I looked the part. Yup. Black-knit hoodie, Mavi jeans… ugh, I *gotta* make these look *way* more raggedy if I wanna do this right, whatever, at least I had jeans AND I had my *ORANGE BACKPACK! YES!* Then I looked at my hair. I looked so dumb the way my hair was cut. This'll never work. All I wanted was long hair, but they made this shitty barber buzz our heads every two weeks at Hidden Lake to this stupid *Dumb And Dumber* length, but now that was all over. I'd never cut my hair ever again.

I sat on the ground to think and I was also kinda sleepy, so I covered my head with my hoodie and buried my ears between my knees and sat against my backpack and closed my eyes and thought real hard about what life would be like from here on out. But I was so damn sleepy… I fell asleep right there on the street.

"GREG!"

I looked up. There was some beautiful girl with dreadlocks, maybe fifteen-years old, with each dreadlock dyed a different shade of red.

"Kiki?"

"GET IN!" She screamed.

So I got into her beater of a car and she took off like we were on the run and ran a red light and drove over the curb and waddled the steering wheel all over the place like she had never driven a car before and said to me:

"Sorry I just gotta get this car back before my Uncle realizes I'm gone."

"No, I mean", holding onto my seat, "It's totally cool, thank you so much for getting me! So how do you know Poe?"

"We went to Switzerland together." And she ran another red light. "Oops?"

"Jeez, are you like, a fugitive or something?" I said that just kidding, but she was like:

"Well I've stolen his car before and—"

"You stole his car?"

"Well you didn't wanna stay there all night did ya?"

This girl was incredible. "Thank you thank you thank you… wait, did you say Switzerland? You met Poe in Switzerland? Why was she in Switzerland? What's in fuckin Switzerland?"

But she wasn't listening to me.

"Sorry I'm just trying to concentrate and I don't have my license or anything so, sorry."

She was *really* holding that steering wheel like it was the first time she had ever held a steering wheel. I couldn't believe how bad she was.

"Where you taking me? Do you know where Poe is?"

"Thayer street. We'll find her… she's always just walking around with, whoever, she's usually not too hard to find. And if not you can just come back with me but you gotta be out by 5AM, that's when my Aunt goes to work."

"Oh, okay, sweet, thank you!"

We drove up a hill. That's when I saw her. Poe. On the side of the road. I couldn't believe it. She was frolicking down the street with bare feet and a chipper skip, and she had on this long flowery dress that was draggin on the road behind her, and she had these beads and hemp woven into her knotty hair and she was with some skinny dude with a scraggly beard right behind her.

"Told you we'd find her!"

"HOW'D YOU KNOW SHE'D BE HERE?!"

"She's always here, or around here."

Kiki pulled over.

It felt like I was in a dream. It was too good to be true. I couldn't believe how perfectly this was all working out! I got out of Kiki's car and ran to Poe.

"GREGGY!!!!! YOU MADE IT!!!! I KNEW YOU WOULD COME!!!!"

And she ran to me just as I had always imagined. It was JUST how I envision it would be. My dreams were coming true. Our hug lasted ten minutes and by ten minutes I mean like twenty seconds.

But something already felt very off, like maybe she didn't wanna hug for longer than twenty seconds? Hmm… I figured our hug woulda lasted a bit longer, I mean, I'M HERE! SHE'S HERE! I GOT HER NOTE!! I ESCAPED! THIS WAS ALL A MIRACLE!! But maybe I was just still a little jumpy, it mighta all been in my head.

Kiki leaned over and rolled the passenger side window down and said:

"Hey Poe… Nice to see you too! And you're welcome!"

"Kiki!!" Poe said with her signature tone of flightiness. I had forgotten about that. Her flightiness.

"Gotta get the car back." Kiki told Poe.

"Noooo you're leavin us already??" Poe said.

"Oh stop it, you'd be gone with some rando by 1AM anyway."

Hmmm…. What'd she mean by that, I wondered.

"Have fun with your lovers." Kiki said and she drove away.

Lovers? Whatever, who cares, I'M FREE! WITH POE! LET'S GO BE BEATNIKS!

Poe grabbed my hand and introduced me to the uncomfortable dude she was with named Mike, who I hadn't even really noticed, ANOTHER GODDAM MIKE?! WHY IS THE WORLD ONLY COMPOSED OF WHITE VANS AND DUDES NAMED MIKE?!

Anyway, Poe started pullin me up the hill. She told me we were going to Thayer Street.

"What the FUCK is Thayer Street??"

Mike laughed. Poe smiled.

"You'll see!" She said. "It's the greatest place on Earth!"

CHAPTER 37

THE GREATEST PLACE ON EARTH

    The Greatest Place On Earth, Thayer Street was a short gravel strip about a mile long, full of colorful mayhem and shady deals. There was nonstop energy and risky adventure and teenage runaways mixed with

Ivy League prep students. There were drug-dealers and pimps and gypsies and hippies roaming around and there were random kids kicking a hacky sack by this dumpster in some parking lot of this store called Store 24. No one seemed to have an agenda, but it still seemed very fast-paced as Poe dragged me further into her world. We walked past the hippie kids kicking hacky sack and over to the dumpster of Store 24.

We sat on these milk-crates and then Poe was like:

"Watch this!" And she got up and rummaged through the dumpster and pulled out these empty boxes with trash stains all over them and ripped apart the cardboard. Then grabbed this marker from her hippie-knit purse thingy she had with her and wrote 'RAISING MONEY TO KEEP SOBRIETY OFF THE STREETS'. She laughed. "Look Greggy! This is how we make money, ya know? This is our sign!! This is how ya spange!"

"Spange?"

"Yeah Greggy look! Watch! You hold this", and she handed me the sign, "and I'll work the street! Watch!"

And she ran up to some random dude and said somethin all chipper-like and then the dude took out his wallet and handed her a dollar or somethin and she jumped for joy in front of him but he was already walkin away and then she ran back to me and threw the dollar on the part of the remnants of the cardboard box.

"Yay! Look!", and she pointed to the dollar, "That's how we eat an stuff ya know? Tomorrow we'll get up early ya know cause we hafta and you can do that side of the street and I'll do that corner over there and we'll make double!—Oh! I hafta introduce you to so many people! Come!" And she got up from the milk crate and grabbed the dollar and grabbed my hand and I grabbed my backpack and she pulled me down the street.

Then these dudes from the corner that were chillin out on this dark cement stoop outside of this Tarot Card shop that was closed for the night, one of them grabbed Poe. I was ready to fight. But then I heard her say:

"No I can't tonight! This is my friend from New York I was tellin you bout!" And she looked over at me, "Remember?"

But he didn't seem to remember. Did she not tell them about me??? Do these dudes know who the fuck I am? Where the fuck I've been these past three years? I felt like I had just done a decade in prison... even though it was three years in two rehabs, one boot camp and a wilderness program. I dunno, maybe I should just go back to Long Island and make my appearance. You know, solidify my legacy. But then I started thinkin that the longer I was gone, the more of a legend I'd become. So I better live on the streets for a while before I go back. Besides, it would be more impactful if I waited till the end of the school year... Holy shit, I hadn't even realized that they were in their senior year already! Man, they're in their *senior year* of high school. Wow, they're almost *done* with high school! I wonder what happens after *that?* College? Then I started wondering if they went to prom and got a driver's license and did all that shit that normal kids do. They must have, right? Hmmm.... I wonder if they're not virgins anymore? Man I've been gone a while! I *really* need to get laid. Okay, stop your mind Greg, back to Thayer.

Anyway, this guy didn't know who the fuck I was. He had all these tattoos and piercings and looked like he'd been smoking weed and shoving heroin down his veins for the last century while I was battling for survival and NOW they were tryin to take Poe away from *me?* Do they know who I am? I'm an institutionally-hardened criminal. Man I was gettin all pissed off. Finally, she shook him off, like he wouldn't let go of her, which made me a bit scared and mad and made me wonder if I should be protecting her or something, but after she got away she looked at me without missing a beat and said:

"Come! I'll introduce you to the Shocker Dude!"

I followed her down the crazy ass street past all these other homeless kids with no supervision and then it struck me. I WAS FREE! Then all I kept thinkin was man, this was true freedom. It was the most freedom I'd ever experienced, at least since I was fourteen… no, even *before* that. I don't *ever* remember a time when there were no adults tellin me what to do or where to go, and especially no adults and guards tellin me how to count stars and stack my fists above mountaintops and do pushups and no one tellin me when to go to the bathroom or when I could shower or how I should walk or when I could eat. There were no skinny whorebags from Harvard. No obese bible belt pastors posing like psychologists. No angry jarheads. JUST ME. Finally! FUCK YOU WORLD! I WON!! And just as I was *really* feelin my stride, *again*, some *other* guy pulled Poe away from me mid-walk and this time the dude started, like, gropin her an shit. Like all rapey-style. And she didn't even seem to mind it. What the fuck? But she loosened his grip and said:

"I gotta go! This is Greggy! Remember?"

But he didn't remember who the hell I was either, nobody fuckin remembered me. What in the fuck? She didn't tell anyone about our past? All we had been through? I mean, what had she been talkin about then? Whatever, I'm a legend back home. And I'm free. Maybe this'll all pass. All these dudes grabbin Poe.

So we walked over to this big ass black dude in a dashiki sitting at a table with a tapestry cloaked over the table and he was wearing dark sunglasses, even though it was past midnight, and he had this sign over his table that said 'PSYCHIC'. That's all it said. Just 'Psychic'. Then Poe was like:

"This is the Shocker Dude!"

I looked at him and said nothing, actually I stared for a bit. Poe was excited about this guy? He didn't seem to see me, or anything for that matter. Was he blind? Or was I thinkin of Ray Charles? Am I racist? Too much thinkin Greg, just enjoy the freedom and the weird psychic. Say hi to him for God's sake.

"Hi." I said to him. But he didn't even turn his head. Then without warning he BLURTED OUT:

"SHOCKED!!!"

And he said it with this voice that sounded like his vocal chords were flingin back and forth. Poe broke down hysterically laughing:

"See? Isn't he great!?"

Hmmm…. *Is* he great? I dunno. Maybe, I suppose. The whole transition to freedom was a bit unsettling cause I couldn't really remember what was normal and what was weird, or if *I* was normal or if *I* was weird. But weird was cool so I wanted to be weird, but weird in a cool way, not in this dude's way. He was a fuckin lunatic I decided. Dammit, too much thinkin again. This freedom thing is kinda gettin to me.

Anyway, so this nutcase that Poe called the 'Shocker Dude', he hadn't even moved an inch except for his mouth. Only his mouth moved when he blurted 'SHOCKED' but now his mouth was back in place. Wow, I was *really* missin out on people like this in Long Island. Is that bad? Or good? Damn I was confused. Life was confusing.

Then the Shocker Dude took out a bag of pot, shitty ass pot, and loaded his shitty ass pipe. There were cops goin up and down the street, but he just loaded it up anyway.

"Aren't the cops gonna say somethin?" I asked Poe.

"Drugs are legal here! See? It's the greatest place on Earth!"

Wait, what? Drugs are legal here? Nah, that can't be true. Did they legalize drugs for the millennium maybe? In any case, the cops didn't give a flying fuck about us so the Shocker Dude handed the bowl to Poe, but Poe immediately handed it to me and said to the Shocker:

"I don't do drugs! Remember?"

But he didn't remember. Then without giving a fuck about what Poe had *just said*, about her not doing drugs, he handed her the lighter anyway. So she handed *that* to me too, and for the first time since I was fourteen, I got high. Well... there *was* this one time at Hidden Lake when this girl I was passin notes with after Poe left snuck in some pot by shoving it up her pussy and got it past the strip-search and she gave me half of it and Slutto and I smoked it out of an apple we stole from the kitchen. Yeah, but then we got caught cause someone ratted us out during 'Fall-Out'... which was when the guards took all of us, everyone at HLA, they took us all down to Lower Left Field and tortured us with labor until we ratted out our friends. So someone ratted us out and Thea made me tell my parents on this phone call in her office that I had 'relapsed' even though I wasn't trying to stay sober anyway. Then I went to Restrictions for like a month. But whatever, that's neither here nor now, so when I hit that pipe… I got *real* high.

Very high.

So high I started freakin out.

"Where are we gonna sleep?" I asked Poe. I guess I wasn't totally ready to embrace this homeless freedom stuff.

"We'll find a place!" She told me. "Come on! Let's keep walkin!"

So we kept walkin and *AGAIN*, MORE GUYS! THEY KEPT PULLIN HER AWAY FROM ME! I swear if this bitch does this shit ONE more time I'm outa here. But where? I guess I could go to Birmingham and stay with Slutto. Fuck, I need to call him. I was supposed to call him tonight actually to see if he made it back home and to let him know where I was. Okay, I'll call him when I get to a phone. I looked around and re-diagnosed Thayer Street as being absolutely fuckin awesome and decided to just go with it. If she wants to bounce around like a whore, go for it. I could take care of myself… and plus:

I'M FINALLY FREE!

But I *was* startin to feel like maybe she had better things to do than take care of me. That was *not* in our plans. We were supposed to do this *together*. She musta totally forgotten about our VW bus. It almost felt like I was her charity case cause I kept askin her what we were gonna do and how we were gonna live and where we were gonna go.

But whatever, so we wandered off of Thayer Street to some neighborhood where all the frat houses and shit were. Yeah, Brown University and RISD were right around the corner so all the sororities and fraternities were scattered all over.

We stopped in fronta some broken down lookin house.

"We can sleep here for a bit, ya know? Cause they're all asleep an they don't check the porch and there's these couches an stuff here so we can try an catch a few z's ya know? Till we gotta keep goin! We're free Greggy!"

She was right. We were free as fuck. We were also broke as fuck. I wasn't so sure about this house. I wonder if they are all looking for me? The cops. I gotta be safe till I turn eighteen cause no way am I gonna get caught and have to go back to that place, no way. I gotta be careful. I gotta stay hidden. But what if I wasn't free? What if they were after me? STOP YOUR HEAD GREG.

It mighta been like 2AM or so, I'm not sure. But the lights in the house were all off, if the house even had electricity, and there *was* a nice shitty dumpy couch on the porch, which started lookin more comfy the later it got. So we lied down together and for the first time ever, I held her in my arms. Time stopped. It was paradise. It was a beautiful thing. It was bum love.

And then…

SIRENS!

I LEAPT OFF THE COUCH AND JUMPED INTO THE BUSHES!

Poe started crackin up.

"Whattaya doin dude?"

"Oh man. I thought that was them. They might be after me." I told her. "The cops. I got spooked."

I was so terrified the cops would find me. But are they even lookin for me? Doesn't even matter, I mean, they'll never find me. I'm in

Rhode Island. I wonder how my mom and dad and brother are… Are they sad? I was so fuckin scatterbrained and paranoid and happy and weird feeling. It was the first time I could do *whatever* I wanted in such a long time that I was so overwhelmed with possibilities that it made me sick a bit.

Anyway yeah, so I heard those cop sirens and woke up in a sweat and plunged into the bushes and waited till the sirens died down while Poe was laughin at me. I still had to cover my tracks, so I *really* waited till those sirens went away. Then you know what happened?

Mike, that emo dude from earlier, the guy that was with Poe when Kiki and I found her, he just showed up! It was like fuckin 3AM maybe and he was just wandering around the neighborhood. What the fuck is this dude doin?

"There you guys are! I was looking for you." And he smiled and sat down next to us. Doesn't this dude have sleep to get? Don't I? I guess no to both questions. Well, he sat down and we all chatted till like 4AM. Turns out he went to Brown University, so his name immediately became College Mike to me, and I guess he just wanted some other shit to do than Ivy League nonsense, so he came to hang out with us, or Poe at least… I hadn't built my name up around these parts just yet. Don't worry, I will. Finally he said:

"Okay. I gotta get some sleep."

And since the sun was startin to come up, we had to leave the porch anyway before anyone got up, so Poe brought took me to this tree on the Brown University main green and said:

"We can sleep here for a bit too!!"

Hmm... okay, I guess this was cool. So I lay down on the dirt next to the tree trunk of this big fuckin tree with Poe and we went to sleep.

I woke up like an hour later with dirt plastered to my cheek and she was gone. Not only that, but there was this big ass black dude's feet all up in my face when I opened my eyes. Then I realized it was the Shocker Dude. He was sleeping right next to me with his big toe all up in my nose and shit. *And* Poe was gone.

Nowhere to be seen. What the FUCK? Is she dead? Did someone steal her and rape her and kill her? I got real worried.

I grabbed my backpack and jumped up and went roaming the vacant street to find her. It was all foggy and I couldn't see shit and I was starving. I saw there was a Dunkin Donuts on the block. It opened soon. Awesome. But I had no money.

So I sat down by the front door of Dunkin Donuts. Then someone walked by, it was the first person I had seen on the street that morning. I had to give it a shot so I got up as the dude walked by and was like:

"Hey hey!" I think I spooked him. Hmm... Am I scary? Anyway, I said "So super sorry to ask so early in the morning, totally feel bad about this but can I just borrow a dollar real quick? Is that cool? Just a quick buck, that's it, so sorry, and thank you man, really, thank you."

And before the dude could even grasp what I was sayin, he mighta been goin to class or maybe his job or I dunno, he was like twenty-five maybe, he took out his wallet and GAVE ME A DOLLAR! YES! SPANGING WORKS!

Then Dunkin Donuts opened and I got a motherfuckin donut! WITH MY OWN MONEY! THAT I HAD EARNED! This homeless thing was really workin out!

Then I thought of Poe and I lost the rest of my appetite. Oh man, someone probably murdered her. Where the fuck do I look? Who should I ask?

Oh shit.

And I looked down the street and there she was! Poe! She was walkin toward me from down the street, so instead of runnin to her, I just waited in my spot like I didn't give a fuck. Like it didn't bother me. I waited till she got to me but then I couldn't hold it back.

"WHAT THE FUCK!?"

But she just started laughing and said:

"Sorry Greggy I was climbing a tree with Ari—"

"WHO THE FUCK IS ARI?!"

And she started describing his hair as if that helped me figure out who he was or what she was talking about or why she just randomly left in the middle of the morning. I wanted to fuckin kill her. For the first time ever, I was truly feelin like I might kill her. So I told her that.

"I'm gonna fuckin kill you."

But I needed her, at least for now I did, so I didn't kill her… not yet at least…

CHAPTER 38

ANOTHER MIKE

That night I went into this Tarot Card shop. It sold nothing but
Tarot Cards and some weird hippie Indian-lookin blankets and incense
and hacky sacks and shit like that and I wanted everything. But I wasn't

about to spend the only money I had managed to spange on a blanket, cause I had made some more money since morning, maybe like five bucks, but I *did* really want that blanket I saw, so I just grabbed it and stacked some incense on top of it too and tucked em both into my black-knit hoodie and smiled at the cashier as I walked out. Stealing felt real good. I loved stealing shit.

"Look what I got us!" I said to Poe. And I laid the blanket on the ground and stuck some of the incense in the little holes in the cement of the sidewalk and grabbed some matches from Poe's purse thingy and lit em up.

"Yay Greggy this looks so awesome!"

"I was happy I brought some bread home, it made me feel good about myself." Then some kid with a guitar that I'd never seen before sat down next to Poe an I on my Indian blanket, and without saying a word or looking up once, strummed the same note on his guitar for what seemed like an eternity. He kept strumming his damn guitar but only this one damn note. That's it.

Ding ding ding ding ding ding ding…

That was the sound of his annoying fuckin guitar.

"Hey buddy, aren't ya gonna say hi?" But he didn't answer Poe. "Are you just gonna sit here and not say nothin?" This kid hadn't heard one word she'd said. "I like your guitar!" But still no response. Why does Poe love everyone? Maybe she *is* brain dead? Like maybe she has some sorta problem that she can't help? Maybe it's cause her family and all that stuff. Yeah, that whole deal probably fucked her up real good. But then my thinkin was interrupted when the guitar kid finally said:

"Let's go to the beach!"

"How?"

"I've got a car." He said.

THIS KID HAS A FUCKIN CAR? He pointed to an old beat up Oldsmobile parked along the side street and then went back to strumming his guitar again. Ding ding ding ding ding ding ding ding— Then he stopped again.

"Mike." He said.

"What?"

"I'm Mike. Dude! You two should come! Let's go to the beach!"

I remembered the three Mikes from Long Island when I was a kinda normal kid in middle school. Now two more Mikes? FIVE MIKES?! Why is everyone in the world named Mike?

Anyway Car Mike got up and walked to his car without looking back. Poe got up and said "Come on Greggy! Let's Go!!!!" and I was thinkin, wow, now *this* is the start of my beatnik journey. So I wrapped up my Indian blanket and followed after them before they got too far ahead. It felt kinda like they didn't even care if I came or not.

So I got in the backseat, Poe got in the front seat, I don't think Car Mike even remembered what we were doin or where we were drivin but his hand put a key in the ignition and alla sudden we were on our way to Newport Beach, this wealthy rocky beach part of Rhode Island.

We parked the car and went to this rocky cliff by the ocean, and we each found our own rock to sit on and watch the waves. I looked out at the view of the angry ocean crashing it's waves forcefully against the rocky cliffs that I was now, somehow, sitting on, and wondered...

Why is the ocean so mad at me? It felt like it was crashin it's waves into *me*.

Then I wondered if my family was looking for me or if they missed me or where they imagined I might be and if I had made the right move or if I was too crazy or if I was continuing on my trek to the legendary hall of fame. Then I stopped thinkin.

We all tried to fall asleep but we were in the most uncomfortable position ever on these horribly pointy rocks so I probably only slept for about an hour. But the good news is it gave me time to be in the quiet away from Thayer Street. Thayer Street was already startin to get to be a bit much to handle. Just as I was feeling at peace with myself, finally, the water can do that to me… you know, make me calm down and shit… So just as I was calming my nerves, I looked up and Poe and Car Mike were walkin off outa sight holding hands.

Are you goddam kidding me?

I felt horrible. I wanted to rip his head off more than I wanted to rip her head off but then I wanted to burn both their bodies and leave them by some abandoned trash can. I'm leaving this fucking place. Fuck this girl. I knew she was bullshit all along and I don't need her anyway. I had to get outa here.

I did my best to hold in my anger and jealousy and to stop these horrible thoughts, but it didn't take long before I knew if I didn't leave soon, I might fucking explode.

CHAPTER 39

ROVING IDIOT

After a week Poe and I were hardly talkin to each other. I *really* wanted to kill her by then, I mean, she was driving me nuts, everything she did, it drove me nuts, but we still had to make money and eat.

So, we were holdin up this cardboard sign that read: 'NEED MONEY FOR BEER POT AND HOOKERS' and on the back of the cardboard another sign that read 'RAISING MONEY TO KEEP SOBRIETY OFF THE STREETS'. We even found a stray kitten by the payphone and temporarily adopted it and drafted a new sign that read: 'NEED MONEY TO FEED OUR CAT.' And even though I was on the brink of rippin her hippie head off, we cuddled up with the kitten against the brick building with my Indian blanket wrapped around us in fronta our sign and pretended that we needed the money to feed our damn cat… BUT WE HAD NO CAT! So that part was funny and it made me not hate her as much for a moment.

But at about 5PM or so, maybe, I don't really know what time it was, it was later that day, I went into the Brown University Bookstore, it was right across the street from us, and I grabbed *Dharma Bums* by Kerouac and snuck it outa the shop and shoved it in my backpack. That was like the eighth book I had stolen in the last few days, and boy did it feel awesome. I couldn't stop stealing books. I was addicted.

My bag *already* weighed a billion pounds full of stolen books and it had only been a few days into my book-stealing career. It was like, the bigger the book I stole, the better I felt, so *Dharma Bums* was only a mid-sized catch and only kept me feelin good for a small while.

Anyway my backpack was real heavy by then but worth carryin around with me cause every book was stolen with care. Man I loved to steal. Everything I stole became a trophy.

So I got outside of the bookstore still feelin good, it was wearing off already, but I was still a bit high on the rush when I reached into my bag and caressed the book cover over and over again. But it wasn't many more strokes until I felt it and felt it and felt it and fuck, I realized *Dharma Bums* just wasn't good enough. I needed more.

No, relax. Just go to the blanket and beg for change like usual.

So I went back to the blanket and sat down and within one hour I was right back up and in the bookstore shoppin around, lookin for something new. Maybe I should stop stealing so much? Maybe I've got a problem?

Then I saw *Of Mice And Men* by John Steinbeck and *had* to have it, which is weird cause it was only like fifty pages, the smallest book in the world, but for whatever reason, I don't know what it was, I *had* to have it. So I swiped it off the shelf and left the store and *just* as I was about to leave, some dude grabbed me by my hoodie and threw me in a room.

It was this black dude security guard that I think went to Brown cause he looked like a student who was workin for the school maybe, but he looked serious and he asked me all these questions that I couldn't really answer.

"Where do you live?"

"Outside the shop, actually…" I didn't know what else to say.

"What's your address?"

"Umm… Thayer Street?"

"Let me see your ID"

"I don't have an ID, I don't even have a wallet."

"Do you go to school here?"

"No."

"So why are you here?"

"I'm visiting a friend."

"Where does your friend live?"

"She lives with me outside the store, well, tonight I may sleep somewhere else." I kept tellin the truth for some reason. I guess it was the only story I could come up with. But he was through playing the game he thought I was playing:

"Look my man, if you can't prove your identity I'm calling the police."

"No please don't."

Then I think he realized I was like sixteen or whatever, which I was, and said:

"I'm going to need to call your parents."

"You can't do that, they're not even alive." Finally, a good lie.

"Well I need to call someone to verify who you are."

So I gave him Robby Deltorro's phone number cause that was the only number I had memorized. Remember him? Hadn't talked to him in years... Well, luckily, he picked up.

"Hello?"

"Do you know a Greg Cayea?" The man said.

I could hear Robby on the other side of the phone freaking out, asking if I was okay. Hmm... I wonder how Robby is doin anyway?

"I just need to know if you can confirm that you know someone by the name of Greg Cayea."

"OF COURSE I DO! WHY? WHAT IS GOING ON?" He shouted into the phone, I could hear him from where I was sittin.

Then the security guard hung up on Robby and opened up my backpack and looked at all the books. It was stuffed full of stolen books.

"No I swear! I had these when I walked in here! Those are mine!" Which they were, I just stole them all on other days... So the guy grabbed *Of Mice and Men* and took it away from me and he let me off with a warning and I swore I would never steal another book again.

I went back the next day to another bookstore called the College Hill Bookstore or something like that and stole *The Dhammapada,* which is like the bible of Buddhism.

But the point is, when I got back to my hippie-Indian blanket on the day I got caught stealing, there was a new flock of dudes already flooding around Poe, desperate to become her friend, or desperate for a blow job. I wasn't sure what metamorphosis had taken place since

Hidden Lake… maybe she was always like this, but I was beginning to get the picture. She wasn't into me, but she was into every other dude on the face of the earth. I didn't even tell her about what had just happened. Who gives a shit. All these guys are just always tryin to fuck her, fuck her on *my* blanket. Then I would start thinkin about how I was still a goddam virgin, and that made me even more mad. I mean, she complimented even the most talentless of starving artists and invited every bum we met to hang out on *my goddam* blanket.

That's how I met Vincent.

Vincent was this wiry Puerto Rican dude with deep creases all over his dark skin, maybe about twenty-seven or so. He called himself a 'roving poet', but really he was a roving idiot. His poetry was atrocious. It sounded like acid-derived free association mixed with grammatically incorrect prose and *none* of it made *any* sense at all. What made it even worse was the high-pitched frilly voice he performed all his poems in and what made it even worse than *that* was the fact that Poe loved it! LOVED WHAT?! THE SHIT DIDN'T EVEN MAKE SENSE! IT MEANT NOTHING! Here's one right now…

"Love with life and live with love and love to live what life has loved." Silence as he looked down, as if to say 'end scene'. Then he looked up at Poe and was like "Do you like it Poe? Please, oh please just be honest. I beg of you for truth, truth of my work. Poe? Did you like it?"

What a fuckin idiot he was. Like it? WHAT THE HELL DID THAT SHIT EVEN MEAN?!

"Oh it's so beautiful Vincent, read me more! Read more!"

Oh my God. I couldn't sit there much longer, these two fuckin morons. They were perfect for each other. But man did I wanna have sex with her.

Vincent had a buncha tin foil poking outa his pocket. I was starin at it until he looked at me and said:

"They're Pyramids."

"Pyramids?" I didn't know what a Pyramid was. I mean like, I know what the Egyptian Pyramids are… just not these ones in his pocket. He told me that they were:

"The purest of LSD. And I want you to experience the true dimension of compassion."

What a goddam *moron* this guy was. But he ripped two small pieces of paper off of this bigger piece of paper and gave one little square to me and one to Poe.

"Just let it sit there and wait, wait for the wisdom of the universe to infiltrate your mind and free your soul", he told us.

Fuckin nutbag. At least he had drugs. This'll help me figure out where to take my life. So anyway, that was the first time I took acid, and I think it was the first time Poe ever did drugs. But instead of me comin to some wonderful direction of life, what ended up happenin was I dropped more the next day, and the day after that, and the next, and the next. After a week I was eatin acid every fuckin day. So I let Vincent stick around a bit cause he also bought us food.

Then this one night, Poe and I were by Store 24 on my Indian blanket and I had just stolen another book, The Complete Works of William Blake, and my backpack now weighed about twenty-million more pounds with stolen books, and Vincent showed up outa nowhere and sat down like he usually did. Then he looked to Poe while ignoring me and said:

"I have a wonderful surprise for you. I had this feeling, a feeling so strong, a belief that you'd love this so much, I had to come to you at once. This will make you so happy. This is the essence of happiness, just like you, you are happiness. Do you know that Poe? And so I brought for you a gift. I call it, Hippie Crack." And he startin giggling like an idiot before he showed her this tank. It was nitrous oxide I found out later but he called it 'Hippie Crack'.

"OH YAY! Thank you Vincent!" And so they did that without me, I was invited, but I said no. But then when he surprised her *again* with some painkillers the next day, I thought to myself, fuck it. And I asked for one and swallowed lord-knows-what, but it made me droopy and feel better. I'll figure out my life all droopy, I thought. That'll help. *Then* that night he started chopping up a pill of ecstasy right in the middle of Thayer Street on my blanket! This guy was a damn drug addict, I thought… But anyway, we all did *that* too. But that's not the point. The point is Vincent was winning her away from me.

Then *another guy* I had never seen before sat on my blanket.

"JOHN! YAY! HI!!!" Of course Poe knew him. She knew half of New England.

Then this guy, in a *really* raspy New England accent, this white guy, maybe about twenty-eight with dreadlocks and glazed over blue eyes and an everlasting itch, cause he kept scratchin himself all over, in a raspy voice he said:

"How ya doin girly eh? Who's this guy here readin ya some Docta Suess or what eh? How ya doin Vinny Vin Vin, you good?" Then he looked at me and grabbed my shoulder in a buddy-typa way and said, "Hey there guy."

He rubbed my hair, now greasy as ever, I hadn't showered since, well, I can't remember… anyway, he rubbed my hair like he was my dad and said "How ya doin guy eh? This the guy from New York? Eh Poe-diddle?"

"YES YES! THIS IS HIM!" Poe replied eagerly.

OH SHIT, SHE *HAD* TOLD PEOPLE ABOUT ME!

That's why I immediately liked him. He had a good memory.

Then some college lookin student walked by us and asked us all if we knew where he could get some pot.

"How bout acid?" I said.

"Nah, no thanks man, just some grass, if you have it—if not that's okay."

Then I thought, this is my chance to make something of myself! This'll show Poe that I can do shit on my own… So I said:

"Okay, stay here. I'll get you some!"

Then I ran up and down the street asking complete strangers for pot but couldn't find any. So I came back and said "sorry". I had failed.

"Don't even worry about it. Thanks anyway!" And poof, he was gone…

He came back like an hour later and tossed a crumpled up dollar bill on my Indian blanket and said "Here ya go man, thanks for trying earlier."

I opened up the crumpled bill and it was a twenty-dollar bill! FUCK YEAH! I hadn't seen that much money in a long fuckin time, like since

I stole two hundred bucks from my mom… Holy fuck. Now I had like… Twenty-five bucks total! NICE!

Then I thought about the cops again.

Are they lookin all over for me? I mean, they must be, my parents at least. Maybe the cops gave up by now. I wonder if they're impressed that I made it? I wonder how Thea's twat-ass feels now, huh Thea? HOW'S IT FEEL BITCH?! I bet you thought I was *actually* gonna come back you dumb whoreslut! All the kids at Hidden Lake must be impressed as hell. They're *definitely* all talkin about me. Well, I guess I'll find out when I go back to see KC walk in December. I can't wait to see her. She'll be so proud of me that I made it! And if they knew all I had gone through just to get here, I bet even my *parents* would be really proud of me.

I opened up the twenty-dollar bill some more and FUCK!—There was a nug of weed inside it! It was wrapped inside the twenty!! YES!

"Wanna smoke it?" I asked Dreadie John.

But Dreadie John was gone. I didn't even realize it. I was day-dreaming… well, night-dreaming I guess. I always fell into these deep trances every time I started thinkin about shit. But Poe and Vincent were still talkin and they were still reading Vincent's moronic poetry, so I got up and left them on my Indian blanket and walked up Thayer to somewhere else to be alone and think and figure out my life and smoke that pot. I gotta get to Birmingham. I needa call Slutto and tell him I gotta come down there. I wonder how much money I need for that? I should go to the Greyhound station and ask. Maybe Kiki would give me a ride? I still had her number… hmmm… I'll call Slutto then I'll call Kiki. Oh right, I had Slutto's number and a couple other people's numbers on this piece of paper that I jotted down on my runaway blueprint that was still in my bag, along with my mom's empty wallet. Should I throw that away?

Whatever, I'm thinkin too much again. Okay... let's smoke this pot. Well, I didn't have anything to smoke it out of so I walked over to that Dunkin Donuts and asked some of the other homeless kids standin in fronta the door if they wanted to smoke with me.

"You wanna smoke with me? Got some weed."

"Fuck yeah I do." Some dude said to me. Then three others joined behind him and they took me behind some garage with a ton of graffiti all over it and introduced me to some *other* kids that were already back there, doin, well, whatever they were doin, maybe more graffiti? Anyway I went back there and we just hung out and I told them all about Hidden Lake and they asked me how old I was and I paused.

"I'm eighteen."

But I was sixteen. I couldn't actually tell people how old I was, right? I mean, I didn't want anyone to know too much. I couldn't risk it. But they were all fifteen and sixteen and I wanted to be like "YO ME TOO!" and tell them the whole truth but I couldn't, so I didn't. And after the weed was all gone, so were they. So I walked back to my Indian blanket.

When I got back, Vincent said:

"Oh he should come too Poey!"

Poey? Was he really callin her 'Poey'? Fuckin loser...

"Come where?" I asked em.

"Greggy, we're gonna go to a Slip concert, you wanna come?"

Thanks for askin me first you dumb bitch. But I didn't say that. I shoulda, but I didn't, but what I did do was I declined their phony fuckin offer. Then Vincent saw that I was reading *Dharma Bums* by Kerouac for my third time and he said:

"Oh wow!" Stroking the back cover like velvet. "The aura... it's like a dark den of shame and morbid misery. I remember this book."

Then he put it back on my blanket then backed up from the book in an overdramatic stance and said, "You must be careful reading this— it's—powerful."

Oh shut the fuck up you idiot. I swear this guy was more of a moron every sentence he spoke. Anyway, Poe musta felt bad about not inviting me first cause when Vincent said:

"So many books! Is it heavy? Carrying them all around?"

Poe grabbed my stack of books from outa my backpack and said:

"Oh Greggy, you have fun tonight! I'll take care of the books!"

Then they fumbled outa her hands onto the ground, creasing the pages and scraping the covers. Jeez, this chick. I really *am* gonna have to kill her. I was even thinkin about how I might do it. Then she picked them all back up again with an innocent giggle and said:

"Okay Greggy. I'll carry them for ya tonight! You walk around free and have fun!" Then Vincent was like:

"We can put them in my truck!" Right, this homeless poet had a fuckin truck too. What's up with all the homeless dudes having their own cars?

Anyway, it's what happened when they got back the next day that changed everything.

CHAPTER 40

KAHBOOM!

So I waited all night for her that night but she never came back. It was like fuckin noon the next day before she sprang up. And she didn't just stroll on by, she was *running* full speed, running and *laughing* at the end of Thayer Street and she was runnin towards me, but not necessarily *to* me, just in my general direction. I was sitting on that stoop that those two scummy lookin dudes that grabbed Poe on my first night were hangin out at, outside the Tarot Card shop. I guess I was assimilating quite quickly. I graduated the Store 24 dumpster to the stoop of the Tarot Card shop.

Then I saw Vincent. He was sprinting to, well, it actually seemed like he was *chasing* Poe. He def wasn't laughing. In fact, he looked pretty damn livid.

"POE!!!!" I yelled as she whizzed right by me, but she didn't pay attention and took off behind the Store 24 dumpster, which was right across the street from where I was at the stoop, and she slid into this skinny alleyway. I screamed "POE!!" But she was gone. Vincent was fallin behind then he stopped. Yeah, he was absolutely chasing her. I wonder what's goin on?

Well, it was a hot summer sun that day. I was sweatin in the New England humidity and was super uncomfortable, but that's okay, I'm leavin this shithole I had semi-decided. I'm goin down to Birmingham. I'll call Slutto in a sec to let him know that. But first I needed some money anyway. Hmm... Then my mind stopped wanderin and I came back to Poe.

I looked at Vincent and he looked like he was gonna pass out, so that was fun to watch. His dreadlocks were soaked in sweat and he was outa breath and slouched down over his stomach with his hands on his knees trying to catch his air, gasping like he hadn't swallowed oxygen for a week.

"Dude. What the fuck was that?" I asked him.

But he ignored me, another reason I had to get outa here, *ignore me?* Who the fuck did this guy think he was? Whatever, he ignored me and ran into the Brown Bookstore, the bookstore I always stole books from.

So I followed him down the stairs in the bookstore to where there were a few computers, kinda like a mini Internet room. Vincent got in fronta one of the computers and fumbled around a bit and then started slamming the keys on the keyboard like a madman, typing like crazy. I stood still, standing on the stairwell that hovered above him but he didn't even notice I was there. Self-obsessed asshole.

"Dude WHAT HAPPENED?!" I demanded.

He looked up at me straight in the eyes and said:

"POE OWES ME A NEW TRUCK!!"

Then he went back to typing like a goddam crackpot. Not sure what he was typing.

"I'M EMAILING HER PARENTS RIGHT NOW!"

Oh, so I guess he was emailing her parents. Her adopted parents, I wondered? How'd he get their email?—eh whatever.

So I left the bookstore and went back to my stoop and sat down and held up a sign for money, in the heat, dodging the sun as best I could from the bushes that surrounded the stoop and waited. Waited and wait.

Where the fuck is she?

I think it was 4PM, well, it was almost evening, we'll put it like that, and I went back to the Store 24 dumpster and I was lighting some more incense that I had stolen from the Tarot Card shop and... well, just sitting and observing. I was wondering where the hell Poe was, but... I mean, who the fuck cares. This whole thing is ruined, the thing with her and I. So… I guess Slutto and I will just make it work somehow, somewhere.

Which reminds me, I gotta call him!

So I got up and went over to the payphone outside of Store 24 and took out my sheet of paper with all the phone numbers I had collected… people from Hidden Lake, and I took out my calling card… I had very little time left and I was completely outa money except for the seven bucks I had raised that day, and I dialed his mom's number cause his parents are divorced. In fact, his dad had a secretive family behind Slutto's back for like eight years or somethin… he was like a deranged alcoholic or whatever, but anyway, his parents were divorced and they didn't get along one bit… So I called his mom's house.

"Hello?"

"SLUTTO!"

"Graig!!!"

"DUDE! I MADE IT!!!!"

"DUDE!!! ME TEW!! AH WALKED OFF CAMPUS AN JUHST… WHELL, LEFT!!!"

"MAN! I HAD TO SNEAK OUTA THE ECONO LODGE! I GOT HIT BY A CAR! OR MAYBE A TRUCK! MAN I DON'T REMEMBER!"

"Whaight, WHUT?! Got hit bah a CAR?!" He said.

"Whatever man!!! It doesn't matter, I'm here! In Providence! With Poe!"

"Yew found her?!"

"Yeah man! We're doin the whole Kerouac thing! It's AWESOME!"

I dunno why I told him it was awesome, cause, it was awesome, but things with Poe were shitty, but life was free, and I dunno, I guess at the end of the day, anything was awesome compared to Hidden Lake and like I said, it was the most freedom I had ever experienced. So I guess that's why I told him that.

"I'm comin down to see you!!" I told him.

"YES! WHEN? WHERE ARE YEW AGAIN? PROVIDENCE?"

"Yeah man! Providence!"

"What's thayt?!" He said with excitement.

"Some city in Rhode Island!"

He started crackin up. "Man, whut the hell yew doin in Rhode Ahland?!"

"It just happened dude, just happened! I'm comin to you man, can you hide me?

"Of course dude! When yew gettin here???"

"Soon as I get the money! I checked with Greyhound and it's seventy bucks or so! But I'll call you soon as I get on the bus! You gotta come pick me up!"

"I weel man! I gotta car tew!!"

"WHHHAAAA??"

"Yeah man! It's ma mom's car, but ah can drive it an all!"

"DOPE! Okay! I'm comin!"

"I'm here!"

Then I saw Poe.

"Okay, gotta go man, see you soon!"

"Git here safe!"

Then we hung up.

Poe looked haggard... well, a bit more disheveled than usual. She came crawling outa that alleyway she crawled into hours ago. I had no idea she was *still* hiding there! I just wanted my fuckin books back. Then I'm goin down South! I think.

"What the fuck is goin on?" I asked her.

She looked around James Bond style then burst out laughing.

"Where's Vincent?! Is he—Hahahahahahahah—Gone?" She couldn't stop laughing.

"Yeah he sent your parents an email. He said you owe him a new truck. WHAT IS GOIN ON?"

She laughed even harder when I said the word 'truck'. But I wasn't amused, just gimme the fuckin books whore.

"We went to see The Slip—"

"I know you did."

"We drove to Connecticut for the show! Everything is a blur! Umm we were smoking weed and hittin the hippie crack... ya know, laughin gas, and I don't remember the show... But after the show... The truck wouldn't start, it overheated, ya know? So Vincent poured water under the hood and eventually it started workin again so we got back in the truck, but it wasn't right, ya know? So we waited a bit... I lit a candle and put it in a slot where I think a radio belonged but then I drifted off into a sleep. We were all dopey, Oh Greggy! You hafta do it with me!!"

"Do what?"

"Dope dude! It's the best!"

"Like, heroin?"

She laughed then said "Yeah!!! Will you?"

"Where the fuck you get heroin?"

"Well, from Vincent, but that's not the story, ya know? So—"

"YOU SHOT UP HEROIN WITH VINCENT?!"

"Yeah dude, jeez, but listen…"

Man did *that* really set me off. But I listened anyway…

"So I wake up to Vincent screaming 'Get out of the car!!!' I look to see a fire between us! Vincent grabbed the closest bottle of liquid he could find and started throwing it on the fire but he's an idiot cause it was mouthwash! So the fire took over the car! Then we ran to get away from it because it was spreading so quickly! We were probably a car-lengths away when it went BOOM!!! We turned and it was so amazingly beautiful… Wow! This is awesome… Close call! The ambulance, fire truck and everyone else came! Ask him his side of the story though… I just don't want him asking me for money… I wasn't the idiot that poured a bottle of mouthwash on it, ya know."

How in the *world* does anyone respond to *that*? Well, here's how I did…

"MY BOOKS! POE! Where the FUCK are my books?!?!"

"AAAAAHHHHHAHAHAHAHAHAHAHAHAHAHAHAHAH AHAHAHAHHAHAHAHA!" That was Poe laughing harder than she's ever laughed. "OH MY GOD GREGGY I TOTALLY—I TOTALLY FORGOT!!! THEY MUSTA BLEW UP!!"

"YOU BLEW UP MY BOOKS?!?"

"THEY WERE IN THE TRUCK! OH MY GOD HOW FUNNY! HAHAHAH"

And that was the end of my library… and Vincent's truck.

"You're a fuckin idiot Poe."

I grabbed my shit and walked off, and *that's* when my decision to leave her was final. Time to get down south.

CHAPTER 41

CLOWN TOWN

I needed a way to make enough to get down to Birmingham, so when I bumped into Dreadie John, remember the dude with the raspy voice who remembered my name? When I bumped into him on the street and he asked if I wanted to help him sell some dope in Clown

Town, all I said was "Sure." I was gettin desperate, I *had* to get outa there.

"Know why they call it Clown Town guy? Eh?"

"Why?"

And he made a machine gun stance "CAUSE THEY'RE ALWAYS CLOWNIN AROUND GUY! EH? CLOWN TOWN!"

When he asked if I would hold his stash while he sold the dope and explained to me why, cause he had like seven warrants out for his arrest, when he told me he'd pay me in food and weed, I figured that'd help me save my spange money for the bus. So I said yes.

So we went to this horrible section of Providence, a terrible neighborhood where the crack pipes are on display in the gas stations, and a white car pulled up and Dreadie John said, "Wait right here, eh guy?" And he got in. I was terrified lookin around everywhere makin sure I was safe and lookin like mad for that damn car that he had gotten into to come back.

When he pulled back around the corner and got out he took me to some guy that was by a payphone. Dreadie John said a couple things to him and then the junkie looked at me and said:

"WHAT THE FUCK ARE YOU LOOKIN AT MOTHERFUCKER!?"

And he took a step closer to me but then Dreadie John was like:

"Whoa guy, he's with me, he's with me guy, it's okay."

So that was a close call… We did that all day then he took me to this deserted house later that night and we went around to the back and crawled through a window with shards of glass sticking out all over. "Careful guy, eh?" When we got inside the abandoned garage, there were these wooden steps that led to the attic. So we climbed up the raggedy wooden steps but careful to not step on the steps that were broken, cause all the steps were all swollen and some completely broken from water damage and old age. When we got to the top we went through this other small opening to get to the attic. I stood up on the floorboards thinkin they might fall through at any moment. There was insulation and nails stickin out everywhere. I safely put my backpack down makin sure to not get it on any of the trash up there and took out my blanket. I was real tired. I had like ten bucks to my name. AND NO BOOKS... except my journal.

There was another blanket spread over these loose slabs of cardboard, which covered the dusty insulation, splintery wood and rusty nails that were stickin out from all over, and then there was this cruddy paint bucket full of piss right next to me. To make it worse, there were used needles and counterfeit money all around the dirty blanket and slabs of cardboard so I had to be extra careful where I stepped. The one window that the attic had was boarded up, so we lit candles to see. That's when I noticed a girl. She was asleep. I found out her name was Star.

She woke up in the middle of the night while I was tryin to get to sleep with Dreadie John's stanky odor right next to me, and I think she hit the crack pipe and started fussin around with shit, but I can't remember cause I fell asleep and when I opened my eyes she was gone.

Dreadie John was still passed out on the cardboard and wasn't even using the blanket to cover him. It was really early in the morning when I heard him get up... I was so tired I fell back asleep right away, but not before I noticed *how* he woke up. He was scratchin himself all over and told me he had 'dope itch' and that he would be right back.

He left me there alone and came back at about 8AM, or whenever it was, the sun was heatin the attic up is all I know, and he said 'Time to go guy, eh?" And that was it. We did the same shit all over again as we had done yesterday. But one of those days I couldn't find Dreadie John. He had went off somewhere in the evening and I couldn't find him.

So I went to the payphone and called Kiki. She said to come stay with her, but on my way down to South Providence, which mind you is like the projects of Providence, I saw Poe. She looked like she was losing weight and her eyes were a bit lifeless. She was by the dumpster sittin on a milk crate.

"Greggy! Where ya been stayin?"

"With Dreadie John, where you been stayin?"

"Down at Sassafrass!"

"What's that?"

"It's this commune hippie place! I'll take ya there, it's right by Kiki's house!"

"I'm goin there right now."

"To see Kiki?! Oh yay! Let's go!"

So she came with me, I was sorta kinda ignoring her but kinda not and whatever... I mean, she was my weakness, but I wasn't showin the affection I was when I first got there. But at least she showed me how to even get to Kiki's house, cause I mighta got lost in that neighborhood without her, and when we got to the house, Kiki was happy to see us both. She snuck us in her living room window and up to her room and Poe was like:

"Greggy! You and Kiki sleep in the bed and I'll take the floor!"

I was shocked she suggested that. Cause I was on the floor and she and Kiki were in her bed. Kiki didn't say anything, nor did I.

"C'mon Greggy! She won't bite!"

And she hopped outa the bed and got in my spot and nudged me towards Kiki in the bed. I ended up fingering her all night long next to where Poe was and then we fell asleep on each other and then we heard her Aunt.

"WAKE UP!"

And she shoved Poe and I outa her second story window. We jumped from the roof down to her grass and then Poe said she was gonna stay down there for a bit.

"Stay where?"

"Sassafrass dude! You wanna come?"

I walked over there with her and got to this horribly conditioned house. It looked like a crack den, but it wasn't. It was a cult ran by this guy named 'The Grateful Fred' and there were a buncha homeless people painting the porch when we got there. Poe knew all the people in the house, about ten or so of them.

We walked in past the hippie homeless people painting over the cracked paint doorway and Poe said:

"See dude? That's all ya gotta do! Paint an stuff! And you can stay here! Well, I gotta ask The Grateful Fred but he loves me so I'm sure it'll be okay."

But when we walked in I got horrible looks while Poe got 'hellos' and hugs. I asked her how to get back to the bus to get to Thayer and she told me. I got the fuck out and finally made my way back to Thayer.

Jeez. Her life was disgusting.

And so my life went for the next week until I had the money I needed to hop on the bus, but I didn't wanna leave without sayin by to Poe. I just... well, I wanted to say bye. But when I saw her, she was really sick looking. Well, I mean, she had lost a lotta more weight and was wearing tight sparkly jeans and a low-cut shirt. She looked like a whore. She told me she was stripping at a club downtown and I flipped out. She said it was a good thing cause now she could help me out with more money, so she gave me some money, I don't remember how much.

"I'm leaving Poe."

"Wait Greggy, before ya go, here." And she handed me a bag of dope. "Will ya do it with me?" But I took one look at it and threw the bag in her face.

"You're a fuckin mess." I said as I walked away.

I can't believe this girl wants me to do heroin with her. Why does she even *care* if I do it anyway? What the fuck is the big deal if *I* do it? Whatever, I had raised enough money spanging and saved enough by then to get down south.

So I hopped on the trolley that took me downtown and went to the Greyhound station and waited for the next bus to Birmingham, but my mind was all over the place. I mean, not only was this whole fucking thing a mess, not only had she morphed into a completely different person within a matter of weeks, not only was she a junky *stripper*, but she didn't even care that I was leaving. Man, that hurt.

The bus came and I got on.

One-way to Birmingham.

CHAPTER 42

MY LAST DAY AS A VEGETARIAN

Slutto picked me up in his mom's Acura and brought me to his house. His mom took one look at me and told me I couldn't stay. I guess I looked a bit... well, homeless by then. It *had* been over a month or so... But Slutto said:

"Don't worry man, we'll figure this out."

So he took me to one of his friends' houses and asked him if I could stay in his basement... which I did, for a night, until the kid was like man, I gotta go to work and you gotta leave.

So Slutto took me to another one of his friends' houses, but the same shit happened. I couldn't stay. Then he snuck me into his grandma's house and told me she never checked the basement and that I could stay there, but she came home RIGHT as we were breaking into her house to sneak me in.

"Dude, come up to Thayer with me." I told him. "I can't stay here man, and you don't wanna be here! You wanna do this with me! You wanna do the Kerouac thing! I know you do! Grab your guitar and let's do this!"

It didn't take long for him to get on board. So he bought us two one-way tickets to Providence. I assured him that alone, it was tough, but with he and I together, it would be a whole new level of fun. His mom nearly had a heart attack and considered me the devil for comin to her house outa nowhere and takin her son up North. I guess I don't blame her. But anyway, we left, and we had his guitar and a new faith that this would really work.

"You can even come down to Dahlonega with me when KC graduates! I told her I'd be at the Econo Lodge the night before she got out, so we can surprise her together!"

So Slutto got all amped up about it all and we got a ride from one of his friends to the bus station and off we went.

It was September 10th, 2001.

TEN HOURS LATER

We were somewhere in the middle of North Carolina and I was asleep when alla sudden Slutto started shakin me vigorously awake from the cramped Greyhound seat.

"What's going on?"

"DUDE! DUDE!"

"Wha wha?" I said.

"They just bombed th' twin towers er sum shit!"

"What?"

"He just said it! Th' bus drahver! He just said it ah swear he did!"

His accent was all thick all of a sudden. Everyone's accent gets thicker when they rush through their sentences. Interesting.

Anyway, what? I told him:

"Dude... you don't even know what the twin towers are. They're like... the biggest buildings in the world, two of them at least."

Then came the loud speaker. The driver told us another plane had just struck the other tower.

"SEE!? AH TOLD YOU!"

"Oh, shit. This might be... well, real bad." I tried to figure out what was happening but none of it made sense. Were we under attack or something? I had no idea what to make of it. All I knew was the bus pulled off the highway in a town called Fayetteville, North Carolina, and dropped us off at the town's shitty Greyhound Station and there were people walkin around the building holding up signs, but I don't remember what they said. But like twenty people were walkin around this small bus station in the middle of farmland North Carolina holdin up these signs. And we had to get off the bus.

BUT WE ONLY HAD LIKE SEVEN BUCKS!

It was a *huge* inconvenience to our plans.

Slutto and I sat on the ground of the station, waiting for them to let us back on the bus, but the attendant screamed:

"NO SITTING ON THE FLOOR OF THE STATION."

We sat there all night. And I'll tell you, that dude was serious about not sitting on the ground. We slept that night taking turns in this racecar arcade game they had in the corner of the station. It had a more comfy seat than the actual bus station so I'd sleep for an hour, then Slutto, then me, and we did that all night.

The next day Slutto and I went outside and sat on the pavement outside the station right next to the parade of protesters that had formed again and watched them march, still tryina figure out what the hell was goin on. Some guy came over and offered to sell me a ball of hash... but it was horse shit. Literally, horse shit. Like a horse took a shit and he tried to pass it off as hash. So I was like:

"Dude, that looks like horse shit."

Anyway even if it *was* hash… and hash sounded wonderful, we didn't have any fuckin money. Plus, there was nowhere to spange and no scraps of food to pick up off the tables at the cafeteria at the mall like Dreadie John taught me to do…. So, we were fucked. We were desperate for food.

I wonder if Poe is dead?

Right food. We needed food, stay focused Greg.

"Slutto I'm starving."

"Ahright, I got an idea."

And he went to this small cafeteria line where you could buy a couple things of food or whatever, but then he got off line and came back.

"Ah man, sorry dude. Ah thought I could git it."

"Damn man, what're we gonna do for food?"

Then he pulled out TWO huge sandwiched from his shirt!

"JUST KIDDIN! I GOT EM!"

"HOW'D YOU DO THAT?! YES!"

Kid was talented as fuck. I have no idea how he stole those damn sandwiches, but I didn't question it, I ate that shit. Thank God he was there.

So yeah the buses still weren't moving. I wasn't so sure how big of a deal this whole thing was. I couldn't watch the news or anything cause they didn't have a TV at the greyhound station. Even the pay phones wouldn't work! What the fuck was goin on?!

Finally, I called this one kid named Kaz. He was from Lancaster, Pennsylvania and he was another friend from Hidden Lake. I didn't know who else to call and I had his number. I told him where we were and so he gave me the number of this *other* kid from Hidden Lake that lived in Asheville, which is a town in North Carolina. So I called *that* kid, even though I didn't know him, and told him we were desperate and needed a place to go. He told us we were like four hours away and that if we could at least make it to Charlotte, he would pick us up, but it'd be better if we could hitch a ride all the way there to Asheville.

So we tried hitchhiking to Asheville but we ended up going fifteen miles in the wrong direction in the back of some white van with a buncha Mexicans—ANOTHER WHITE VAN! I swear I could teach a course on white fuckin vans.

So once we realized we went in the *wrong* direction, by the time we hitched a ride back to the Greyhound station it was nighttime, but they didn't let any of us lie on the ground again so again, so we had to sleep sitting up in that racecar game.

The next morning we were *really* startin to wonder why the buses were STILL not moving. What the fuck?

Some guy with a beard offered to buy us a pizza at some country pizza joint across the street. All of us in the bus joint were now all talkin about what in the WORLD was goin on. So yeah, that guy took us to the pizza joint, said the meal was on him and we had a nice meal, and a nice chat. Awesome. So Then...

I go up to the Greyhound lady at the desk and said:

"Listen. I'm not jokin here, I got no money, we both got no money, and I *really* need to get to Charlotte or Asheville. Please please please can you get us there?

"Of course honey! We goin west, don't you know? Just ain't goin north!"

And she smiled a nice southern smile.

"It goin to be twenty-seven each."

"Wait, no no, you missed the point, I got no money, but we *both* have tickets to Providence!"

"Well then you gotta wait till the bus leave fo' Providence."

I froze. This *had* to work. There *were* no other options. I didn't have *time* to wait until the buses started goin north again, I was outa money, and outa money now! I needed to get to somewhere that had someone that could help me!

"Please. PLEASE." I begged.

"Sorry sweetie, you gon hafta sit back down."

"And do what? And eat what? I got a friend over in Asheville and he's my only chance! I'M STARVING!" But I mean, Slutto had just stolen us another sandwich, so I wasn't *that* hungry.

But then she got angry. "You fixin to get me angry."

So I walked away and Slutto was already embarrassed cause I was makin a slight bit of a scene in fronta everyone so maybe I just needed to cool down.

We tried to think our way outa the situation but then I got hungry again. So Slutto stole two more sandwiches.

"SLUTTO! HOW'D YOU DO THAT *AGAIN* MAN?!"

"Ah'm gifted dude, Ah'm tellin yew!"

He was right, he *was* gifted. He kept stealin us these turkey sandwiches and I kept takin off the turkey cause I was *still* vegetarian from that time I told Poe I would be vegetarian at Hidden Lake! I was *still* fuckin not eatin meat! I'm a dude of my word, what can I say?

Okay, so I went back over to the Greyhound lady after the sandwich. I had more energy and was in a better mood and I was ready to negotiate.

"Okay, I'm ready to negotiate."

"How old you? Like fo'teen??"

"SIXTEE—EIGHTEEN!"

"Well, usually negotiate mean money, and you ain't got that. So unless you just found some money on the ground, you ain't—"

"Look. I'm sorry. You're right. I am desperate. I have no family and no money. It's just me and Slutto—"

"Slutto? That yo real name?"

"It's Hutto—"

"Right I just call him Slutto, but miss ma'am, I am begging you. I will do anything, I swear, just two tickets anywhere west and I'll leave you alone forever and ever and ever and ever and I'll be your best friend and I'll buy you cake when I get money and, and—"

"Sweetie."

"PLEASE?!!?!?"

And she handed me two tickets to Charlotte! "But that's as far west I can get you."

BOOYAHH!!!!!

"Thank you thank you thank you!"

So we went over to that guy with the beard who bought us pizza to tell him the great news! But he was in an entirely different outfit and had glasses on. And he had no beard! He had shaved his beard? I mean, we knew it was him cause he was wearing the SAME sneakers holding the SAME atlas that he had while we were eating and he pretended to not know us.

THERE WAS ONLY TWENTY OF US AT THE STATION!!!! WE HAD ALL BEEN THERE FOR A TWO DAYS TOGETHER!!!!! IT WAS HIM! WE WERE US! HE PRETENDED HE HAD NEVER SEEN US BEFORE!!! WWWWEEEE JJJUUUSSSTTTTTT HHHAAADDDD PPPIIIZZZZAAA TOOGGEETTTHHHERRR!!!

Maybe he had like multiple personalities or some shit? Or maybe he felt embarrassed to be talkin to us? Maybe he literally didn't remember—no. Impossible. Slutto and I walked outside perplexed and waited for the bus.

FASTWORD TO CHARLOTTE

So we made it to Charlotte and I called my friend! We were SAVED! But my friend never picked up his phone. I guess we weren't really friends, I mean, I barely knew him. And now what made it worse was the Charlotte Greyhound station only had vending machines, so we couldn't even steal food!

We went outside, but the city was real clean and didn't look like we'd be able to spange anywhere close to us, but I said:

"Slutto watch this…"

And I asked this businessman typa white dude for a quarter. He told me to:

"Get a fuckin job."

Hmm. Okay, they're not so friendly around here. Night came and we hadn't eaten. Morning came and we hadn't eaten. Then afternoon came and we hadn't eaten. Finally night came and I felt sick. We both did, but I think I was bitchin about it more than Slutto was. Then this weird thing happened at the bus station, musta all been because of the Twin Towers thing in New York. I actually think I heard some plane flew into the Pentagon too. Honestly, I didn't really care *that* much. I'm sure it'll all blow over. But the head of the station or whatever he was, he asked who was goin North. So we said US! And we ended up in Washington DC by the morning. So that was weird cause he let us ride up there for free since now we were in Charlotte and our Birmingham to Providence tickets were irrelevant… I dunno how it happened or why, but they let us on a bus and we made it as far north as they were driving, which was DC. So that's where we got to. We asked how much longer till we could get to Providence, but they didn't have an answer. Man, at least in Providence I can spange and make money and I know where to steal from. The clock was ticking.

I was really feelin sick. Luckily, I knew someone from Hidden Lake that lived in DC! But I didn't have his number. So I called the numbers I did have until I got his number then I called him and he told me I had to take the subway to some place or whatever and he'd come get us.

We had enough for the subway so walked around lookin for the station we were supposed to get to and along the way I asked people for spare change but no one gave us anything. Actually, Slutto wasn't beggin, it was just me. He kinda just watched me the way I watched Poe for the first day or whatever. So we ended up wandering around until we ended up in a FUCKED UP neighborhood. I asked this thug for some money.

"Yo where'd you get that?"

He was eyeing my beaded necklace Poe stole for me before she became a stripper. The necklace was probably like five bucks to purchase.

"Huh? This? The necklace? It was a gift from my friend in Providence."

"Yeah? Lemme try it on."

"Nah." Dude was gonna rob me right there, I could feel it.

"Why not?" He asked me.

So I tried to divert the conversation:

"You got a dollar? I'm broke and I'm starving."

"Lemme check that necklace homie."

I walked away... fast.

"SLUTTO!"

"WHAT?"

"LET'S GO!"

We ran back to the Greyhound station and sat down on the gummy cement, like there was tar and gum all over the cement, anyway we sat on it right outside the front doors and kept asking strangers for money. I just had to get enough change for a burger for Slutto and a small fry for me from the Burger King they had in the station… Or maybe it was a McDonalds… Whatever, same shit, all I had to do was get enough for the burger and small fry, cause that's all I could eat since I was a vegetarian.

But then I saw this dude. He threw away his tray of food in the trash. On the tray, and now in the trash was a half-eaten Whopper… or maybe Big Mac… I can't remember. Same shit.

I got up.

"Where you goin?" Slutto asked me.

"Fuck it man."

I went to the trash and grabbed the Whopper (or Big Mac) outa the trash. There were some fries left over too. I brought it back to Slutto and we split it. And that was the last day I ever ate vegetarian ever again.

FINALLY… We got to Thayer Street. THREE DAYS LATER. Jeez, these goddam buildings were *really* interfering with my plans. So I immediately went lookin for Dreadie John to introduce him to Slutto.

"I got a place for us to sleep and everything. Wait till you see it, it's awesome." I told him. And I wasn't lying, it really *was* awesome… for me at least. It was FREEDOM. I figured Slutto would like it to…

But when I found Dreadie John and he brought us to the abandoned attic, it was a pretty bad night. What happened is this:

At 5AM, Dreadie John woke up, itching and scratching himself all over, like he always did, and he left his backpack and left us sleeping in the attic to go look for dope, like he always did, cause he always ran out, and anyway Slutto and I were left sleepin on this saliva covered nasty blanket. Well, I had my hippie Indian Blanket too, but we used the saliva one to lay on.

Then we heard footsteps, but there were two sets of feet. Next to the blanket was a plethora of dirty needles and counterfeit money, like always, and then there was my poetry book and all three of our backpacks, me, Slutto and Dreadie John.

"GET UP!"

Oh shit. It was two cops. Slutto looked at me and was like "GIT UP!" and we panicked and gathered our shit but then I realized there was all these empty bags of heroin and fake money everywhere! What the fuck do I do?

"GET THE FUCK UP!" One cop screamed at me again.

I was terrified. I used the saliva blanket to scoop up all the needles and fake money and drug baggies then held it tight against my face and chest, it was disgusting, so that nothing would fall out. Slutto grabbed our backpacks, even Dreadie Johns. Then a third cop shouted from below, damn THREE cops? Then a *third* cop shouted from below:

"GET EM DOWN HERE!"

I made sure there was nothin left on the floor of the attic before Slutto and I went down the splintery steps. I was shaking. All I could think about was gettin sent back to Hidden Lake. Slutto was safe, but I was open game.

We stepped over the cardboard and over to the hole of the attic floor to the broken steps. I was gripping the nasty blanket with all my might while staring at the wooden stairs as I walked down cause of those few steps that woulda snapped if I put any weight on them, and we both got to the bottom and to our surprise, the garage door was open.

Wait a minute... Shit, it wasn't an abandoned garage! It was just shitty garage! The owner was standin right there with the cops!

I froze. Slutto mighta just been mad.

I thought about all of the needles and counterfeit money and drug baggies stashed under the blanket coated with saliva and whatever else was all over it, now brushed up against my face and lips as I held it tighter than ever, and I thought about what would happen if any of the contraband fell to the ground.

Fuck.

"Where's the other guy?" One of the cops asked me.

"What other guy?"

"There's three backpacks. Where is he?"

"Umm... It's just us."

Rolling his eyes, he separated Slutto and I, me with one cop, Slutto with the other, and this one cop asked me:

"Where are you from?"

"New York."

Fuck fuck fuck they are onto me. I'm gonna go back to Hidden Lake. FUCK! I'm

FUCKED.

"And what are you doing here?"

"Ummm... Sleeping?"

[another eye-roll] "How old are you?"

"Uhhhh 18." (I was sixteen)

"And where are your parents?"

"In New York sir."

"Let me see some ID."

"I don't have ID sir. I'm sorry."

[eye roll] "How long have you been living here?"

"I'll never come back I swear."

"Don't you fucking move." The cop instructed me.

He went over to the other two cops that were questioning Slutto. They exchanged a few words with each other then he came back to me.

"I catch you two here again I'm gonna arrest you, both of you. Understand?"

"I promise. Yessir. Thank you."

And we ran the fuck away. Away from the cops.

When we got back to Thayer Street, I gave Slutto some money to go get us some food cause I wasn't feelin well. Then he came back with a sandwich and a Mountain Dew.

"MOUNTAIN DEW?! WATER IS FREE WHY WOULD YOU SPEND MONEY ON MOUNTAIN DEW?!" I shrieked at Slutto.

"Right Graig, why don't we just make money an sayve it, just sayve it an nev'r spend it, nev'r, just hold it! Hold it all day all night."

That was our first fight. I was always scared about spending our money, since we had none of it. But then...

Then I got sick. I had these sharp pains jolting through my stomach. I hadn't eaten a good meal in a few days and our fight subsided.

"Help me Slutto."

"Aright, just… uhh… stay here."

He left me on Thayer Street and came back with two candy bars and picked me up and carried me to one of the Brown University dormitories. He waited outside the door.

"I got yew man, don't worry."

"Whatta we doin?" I could barely talk.

Then a student opened the door and walked out and Slutto grabbed the door before it closed and carried me in and we found the library and he setup three chairs all next to each other. He laid me down and said:

"Aright, don't move. I'll be raight back."

As soon as he left, all the kids in the library got up and left. There was some weird homeless kid in the library, and it was me, and so everyone left.

Slutto came back with three more candy bars. "Here man, eat these. You gotta eat."

I ate the candy bars, recuperated, and that was it. We went back to the street that night. That's when Poe showed up.

"Poe! This is Slutto! Slutto, Poe!"

They didn't know each other cause Poe had left before Slutto and KC's Peer Group had formed. So Slutto looked at Poe and gave me a 'This is the girl?!' kinda look.

Well, she didn't look good.

"Poe. You look… terrible." But that wasn't true, she looked REALLY whorey, which really turned me on, but she looked like a completely different person.

"Greeggggggyyy'youu'r'back!" Her words were all slurred.

"What are you wearing?"

Poe was just like:

"Your friend! Hiiiii! I'm Poe!!"

Slutto looked at her up and down. And then I saw this creepy dude staring at us from across the street. So I was like:

"Poe who is *that?*" Cause he was *really* lookin at us hard, some guy with neck tattoos and shit.

"Oh that's Kevin! He's my helper!"

"Helper?"

"Well he helps get me dates an stuff ya'know?"

"Dates?"

"Yeah Greggy thiz'girl at the club tol'me t'ya know, do it for extra cash an stuff ya know?"

Slutto stood up. "Hey man, I think I'ma go for a walk.

But that was it. Poe was a hooker, Slutto was done with this shit, and I was again, on my own.

CHAPTER 43

I BECAME AN IVY LEAGUE STUDENT

When Slutto went back to Birmingham the next day, I was left alone, and again, had to figure something out. I couldn't just stay at this dumpster in fronta Store 24 forever, at least until December when I had to figure out how to get down to Dahlonega to see KC walk free. It'd be gettin kinda cold real soon, in fact, it already was. I had to figure something out, but for tonight, I just needed somewhere to go, somewhere warm to sleep.

I saw this couple walk by me, some college hippie couple, the perfect couple to spare a dollar or two. So I ambushed them to say "Hi!"

Their names were Bammer and Raquel. They were freshmen at Brown University. I asked if they could gimme a buck or two. They

searched their pockets, pretending to look for change then acted
disappointed when they tragically had nothing to offer me.

"Sorry kid we don't—" then Bammer paused mid-sentence—"On
second thought— you think you could help us find some pot?"

Goddammit everyone always wants pot. There *is* no pot around
here. Just crack.
You want crack? But I didn't say that.

"Umm—yeah! I think—yeah! I can get you some! Stay here!"

"We'll be at that bar, right there." And he pointed to some
restaurant. "Try to hook it up."

Okay, here's my chance to do something on my own, without Poe
or Slutto or anyone. I'll take care of myself.

I darted from corner to corner asking anyone if they knew where to
get some pot. And guess what. I GOT SOME! FOR FREE! Know
from who? THAT DUDE ARI! REMEMBER ARI!? THE DUDE
THAT POE WAS CLIMBING THE TREE WITH ON MY FIRST
NIGHT!? WHEN SHE DISAPPEARED AND I WOKE UP TO
THE SHOCKER DUDE'S TOENAIL IN MY FACE?? I spotted him
on Thayer as I was walkin all around askin for weed and I had only met
him once! He was actually a really nice guy. He was a local that lived at
his parents' house but he hung out with us runaways and homeless
peoples so when I was like I *need* to find some weed, he just gave me a
small nug!!

So I waited anxiously on my Indian blanket until Bammer and
Raquel walked back.

"I GOT SOME!" I said all pumped up.

They were impressed. So was I. I had done my job!

I handed them the nug and he thanked me AND gave me money AND I got to keep all of the money for myself AND not have to divvy it up with Poe or Slutto or anyone else… AND, I wasn't done:

"Let's go smoke it!" I said.

Bammer did *not* seem like he was about to let some kid from the street tag along with him and his girlfriend.

"Uhh—you know what? We're good. But thanks. Here, enjoy."

And he ripped off a little of the nug and put it in my hand. My moment of triumph wore off as they started to walk away. Shit. I need a place to sleep tonight, I thought.

"Wait. Can I crash at your place tonight?" I shouted after them.

Bammer, who was a middle-eastern lookin dude, he looked at Raquel, who was a petite Israeli-lookin girl with dreadlocks, everyone in this town has dreadlocks, I thought, and she looked back at him.

"Please?" I persisted. "I'll sleep on the floor. I'll find you pot whenever you want."

"What's your name?" Bammer asked me. He wanted to know my name. Awesome.

"Greg."

"Listen, Greg."

"Yeah?" I asked Bammer.

"Don't fuck me. Okay? Don't you fuck me."

I think he meant don't steal shit from him. I realized that I was just another bum to them. They didn't know my story, how could they? They had no idea how amazing I really was or where I came from.

I tried to hear what they were whisperin about ahead of me as I trailed behind them but I couldn't hear shit. They were probably asking each other in soft tones what the hell they had gotten themselves into. But I caught up to them and tried to blend in and so they had to stop their secretive discussion.

We got to Bammer's dorm room. It was full of tie-dye tapestries hanging from the wall and ceiling. There was a Persian-style rug on the floor. Maybe he's from Iran? He grabbed a large middle-eastern hookah from his closet from the top shelf and then got some tobacco and then some charcoal thingies and began to prep the hookah. I had never smoked hookah before.

Anyway we sat on his Persian rug and made a circle around the hookah. The door to his room was open and there were freshmen running through the hallways. I noticed he had a word document or whatever software he was usin to write his paper open on his computer. I searched for something to say, to break the ice, to make friends, to be normal.

"Writing a paper?"

He gave a weird smile to Raquel.

"Oh yeah... Philosophy. *Crazy* shit." He said as he inhaled a deep breath of tobacco that clouded his room with a quilt of smoke. But he said it in this weird way, like he was fuckin with me. Why's everyone always fuckin with me?? Whatever, we smoked and smoked and smoked and I started to get horny and I moved a bit closer to Raquel and tried to kiss her and she declined and then somewhere along the night I fell asleep.

The sunlight opened my eyes and Raquel was gone. Bammer was in his bed, and his roommate, who I had never met, was in the other bed across the room. He musta stepped over me on his way in. I remembered how I tried to hook up with Bammer's girlfriend then felt really dumb. I looked at myself... I was sprawled out on the floor using his Persian rug as a blanket. The hookah had been put away. What a moron I was. I let myself out quietly without waking anyone up.

When afternoon rolled around, maybe it was like 2PM or some shit, I mean I didn't have a watch or anything, but it was later in the day, I was hungry... again. I was always hungry.

I rattled my cup for *six* hours, but made practically no money. My allure was wearing off... By the time I gave up for the night, I was ready to somehow get high. So I walked around all the neighborhoods till I found a house that was full of people. Parties were always goin on around there, I mean, it was a college town.

So I walked in past the guy at the door... He wasn't doin such a good job cause I just went around him while he was busy checkin to make sure everyone who went in was allowed to be there, and as it turns out, it was a Brown University frat party.

There were these handmade fountains sproutin spiked punch out all over the house that some smart kid probably figured out how to make in the theatre department or something, and so I poured myself like ten into the plastic cups right next to each fountain until I was drunk and secure.

Oh man, did *that* feel good. I so I drank some more. Free alcohol. I forgot how much I loved this feeling. I was now totally safe. There was nothing to worry about. I stayed near the spiked punch refilling my cup all night when suddenly I heard laughter coming from someone standing behind me.

"Dude! What the *hell* are you doing here?"

I turned around and it was Bammer.

"Dude, you're at a frat party?! That's incredible!" He couldn't stop laughing. At least he wasn't mad about Raquel! He put his arm around my shoulder, drunk as fuck. We hung out the rest of the night and went around telling everyone I was a junior studying economics and then at the end of the night he looked at me, and at his drunkest moment said:

"I like you, but don't ask to stay at my dorm every time we bump into each other.
Okay?"

The next night I was on my Indian blanket wondering if it was too soon to knock on Bammer's door. I again had nowhere to go. I needed some food first though, then I could look for a place to sleep. I wonder if I should go back home? But then I heard College Mike's voice:

"This is my friend Lucy."

I hadn't even seen him walk up to me. But there was College Mike, hovering above my Indian blanket.

"Oh hey man! Hi Lucy!" I said super excitedly, I was still thinkin maybe I should just go back home. But then I looked at Lucy. She was well-dressed, I think, kinda pretty, she had blonde hair with fair skin and blue eyes. She was wearing tight fitted college lookin jeans and had on a pretty plain sweater, but uhh... she was from Brown. And that seemed cool to me. Maybe I should go to college? All I gotta do is get my GED. Hmm... Maybe I could stay here and go to Brown?

"—Hey do you know where we could find some painkillers? I told Lucy you were the person to ask." College Mike asked.

Hmm... They were looking for painkillers. I had no idea where to buy painkillers, but I couldn't let them down. I told College Mike to watch my blanket and brought Lucy with me up the street, stopping at every corner.

Lucy kept giggling and shit, like this was the most fun she'd had since prom. Damn, I missed prom. I wonder who woulda been my date? Whatever, I'll have my own prom. Lucy told me she was a nineteen-year-old English major in her junior year. Hmm… cool, I think. I'm Greg. I'm a sixteen-year-old runaway studying the art of grubbing money off anyone I can find.

"How old are you?" She asked.

"I'm eighteen."

Okay, so that was that. Another lie. Time to move on. We went down the street and I showed off my street knowledge and talked to everyone who remembered my name to prove to her I was special. We found a guy who said he had an 80mg pill of oxycotton for forty bucks. Neither of us had ever taken oxycotton before and wondered if he was ripping us off with that price. He opened the palm of his hand and showed us some pill. It coulda been any pill. Lucy and I stared at his hand, not sure what oxycotton was supposed to look like. Was this worth forty bucks?

"I'll buy it for us", Lucy said.

It was an uncomfortable exchange of money.

"Wait, how do we take it? Swallow it?"

"Crush it up and snort it." The drug-dealer dude told us.

So we did. I think it was fake but we pretended it was kicking in. I offered to bring her to one my favorite spots under the statue at Prospect Park that overlooked the city. She said sure and so off we went.

I thought I knew where the park was, but I didn't, and instead got us lost in some neighborhood. When I finally found the park, we stepped through the soft grove-like grass and hopped the gate that surrounded the statue and hid beneath the stone arches out of sight and looked at the city and smoked a million cigarettes.

Finally I worked up enough balls to kiss her. So we kissed and talked and smoked and then we fell asleep at some point and when Lucy woke me up at like five in the morning, maybe, I wasn't sure what time it really was, but it was late-early, she said to me:

"We should find somewhere a bit more comfortable to sleep, come with me."

Oh no.

I started freakin out. She wants to have sex.

Oh no. She's a college chick. She's probably had ten million sexual experiences.

Shit, I was really nervous, but I didn't show it. I went with her as we hopped back over the fence, ran across the park, down the street, through the neighborhood, onto the main green of Brown University and finally arrived at the front doors of her dorm. I wonder what happened to College Mike or where my blanket was? He definitely still has my blanket. He would never leave it. Would he? Dammit! MY BACKPACK. Oh man, I'm about to lose my virginity. Finally.

FUCK YEAH.

I was horrified. Dammit Greg, focus. This is what bein a Beatnik is all about.

So we walked into her dorm and it was all historical lookin and shit like it was built in the 1800's, which it probably was.

She took me up these wide stairs that made fifty million echoes every step up you took. They were long and wide steps and every step felt like it didn't get you much higher than you were the step before. I almost tripped a billion times but maybe that's cause I was nervous that I was about to either lose my virginity or look like a sixteen-year-old idiot, but those steps… I kept overstepping and I kept almost tripping, like I said, I was nervous, and then we got to the second floor.

We stopped in front of a door and she stuck a key inside and we walked in and it was a small chick-lookin-dorm room with dull shades of girly colors all over and a small bed and a small tube computer and a telephone and a closet and that's pretty much it.

The bathrooms were in the hall. She leaned in to give me a slow kiss as soon as we walked in her door but I didn't make any moves other than kiss her back. I didn't even move her closer to the bed, but she grabbed my hand and hopped on the bed and waited for me to join her.

I was so nervous, jeez. I couldn't concentrate.

She took off her shirt and she was in her bra. I remembered Second Base Night back in middle school and frantically started fuckin with the back of her bra and probably almost ripped it but it finally got off and now it was the real deal.

I was supposed to take off my pants, but I didn't. I was too scared. I wasn't hard. I was so scared. Fuck. She started tuggin at my baggy jeans button to undo em and take em off and she did. She took em off. I was in my boxers. I was soft and not hard and not ready for sex but I really wanted to fuck the shit outa her but I was so nervous about not doin it right. Goddammit! This was as close as I had ever been and my pulse was pounding outa my neck and my heart was about to pop.

"Are you a virgin?"

OH MY GOD! I CAN'T BELIEVE SHE ASKED ME THAT!

GET OUT!! GET OUT!!!

RETREAT!

But what I said was, "Nah", and I kept kissing her hoping to God everything would work out. But it didn't.

When I pulled my dick out it was worthless. It was the most embarrassing shit ever. She asked if a blow job would help, so she blew me, it was my first blow job...

NICE!

So that made me hard, and I came, and that made everything all right and then we relaxed, but I could tell she was really upset we didn't have sex. Man, how do I bounce back from *that?*

If I could just keep makin sure she blew me and keep cummin before we started havin sex, then I'd have an excuse to not have sex and never look like a moron again. So that's what I gotta do. Wait, what the fuck am I talkin about? Of course that's not what I'll do, I'll fuck the everluvvin shit outa her! But if I don't:

Blow Job.

That's my exit strategy.

Man, how long can I uphold all this? Maybe I should just come clean. I wanted to be honest for once in my life, but it felt like it was too late.

Whatever, just make it till tomorrow, then we'll see what happens. Maybe the lies will subside. Just go to bed Greg, too much thinking. All this will be gone tomorrow.

But they weren't. The lies only got more confusing.

CHAPTER 44

STAY WITH ME JUST ONE MORE NIGHT

    I opened my eyes and Lucy was lookin right at me all googily-eyed.

That made me feel uncomfortable cause I wasn't used to that kinda shit.

So I was like:

"What?"

"Stay just one more night", Lucy said to me.

One more night? It's only the morning. Why she already talkin about tonight? I mean, I *did* enjoy the time we were together, but it was all mounting anxiety. A mountain of pressure every moment that swung by. Stay another night?

But so yeah, that's what I did. I stayed with her in her dorm-room one more night and pretended to fall asleep so we wouldn't have to have sex. But then I stayed another night, cause it was gettin cold outside and I had nowhere to go. And then after that night, I stayed another, and another, and pretty soon I had a girlfriend. A girlfriend who thought I was an eighteen-year-old world traveler just making a pit stop in Providence. And a girlfriend that I *still* had not had sex with.

I walked into her room this one day, cause by now she had made a key to her room for me and had given me her cafeteria card so I could eat one meal a day in the Brown cafeteria for free, so yeah, anyway, I walked into her room and there was this brand new condom in mint condition packaging lying right next to her bed, waiting to be opened.

It was like 10PM at night... and I know it was 10PM at night cause I finally had a clock to look at. She didn't say anything about it, the condom, she was layin there on her bed in silence and the condom was just there. It was real awkward. The fuckin condom... it was just sittin right next to her bed by the lamp. It was the only thing on her nightstand... except for the fuckin lamp. But I pretended to not see it, like it wasn't even there and said:

"Let's go on an adventure!" And I grabbed her hand and rushed her into the hall and said, "Let's go find Mike! Where's his dorm?"

"Wait, you wanna leave? Can't we just lay down next to each other?"

But I didn't wanna do that, it may lead to more questions... So I just wanted to go on an adventure and avoid it all. So I said, "But, I'm not tired yet." And finally she was like, aright... whatever, and she came with me.

So we went on a hike over to Mike's dorm room, I'd never been there, I also made sure to not call him 'College Mike' while I was with her cause that might blow my cover, and when we knocked on his dorm room door, he was listening to this weird music that kinda sounded like it was from South America or some shit. Or maybe it was Gypsy music or whatever. I dunno but he looked ready to do somethin other than what he was doin right then so he joined us happily and then I felt safe. Safe from the embarrassment of fuckin up sex again. Maybe there's somethin wrong with me? Don't think like that. I kept thinkin too much.

So we went to this old, classic-lookin wooden room on the university campus that had a piano and so we closed the doors and it was real echoey. Everything I said bounced against the mahogany shelving units that were empty and slapped me right back in the face. It was like the room was haunted. It was pretty cool actually, I felt like a college kid again, the college kid that I never was. Maybe I was actually a college kid after all? Wait, what the fuck am I talkin about? I'm a high school dropout.

Anyway, we hung out there and College Mike, I mean Mike, Mike brought the music he was listenin to in his room and we put it on some stereo system that was already in the room. It was an artist named Manu

Chao and it was the first time I'd ever heard of Manu Chao, I mean, I was kinda locked up away from life for the last few years so I didn't know any of the new movies or musicians or video game console thingies and what not, so I felt like I had to play catchup… or maybe I didn't wanna play catchup, maybe that's what made me so unique? The fact that I was in my own little world. But this guy, Manu Chao, he sang in English and Spanish and French and it was awesome. That's when I decided I should learn three other languages. I could probably do that here, at Brown, I just gotta get in. Hmm… I'll print out an application later on Lucy's computer. But then I gotta dodge sex again, or maybe just go for it? Jeez this is too much to think about. The weight was getting heavier.

Anyway, Manu Chao and Eminem became my favorite musicians and I listened to them incessantly and eventually it was so late that we *had* to go back to Lucy's room. But luckily, it was *so* late that she didn't question why I just phony-passed out as soon as we got in the room.

So yeah, another night passed where we didn't have sex. *Every* night I had to come up with an excuse and had to avoid the subject of sex, terrified the same thing would happen again. It got to be all weird and I felt like such a loser. Oh no. A *loser?* No, those days are far over. Maybe I should leave and just go back home? But what if they send me back to Hidden Lake? What in the fuck are my parents doin anyway? They can't *still* be lookin for me… But where the fuck would I go *then?* What the fuck would I even do there even if they did let me stay? Live with them? In Long Island? Yeah right. Ugh… too much thinkin. Fuck. It's gonna get cold out soon and I still had months before December came when I'd have to go to Georgia to see KC walk free, not sure how I'll even get down there… but I made a promise and a promise I'll keep. At least I got *that* excuse for December, which by the way, I had told Lucy about a million times. I told her in December I'd have to go to Georgia. But I said KC was graduating high school and just left it at that. But I can't stay here till winter, I thought. Man, maybe I *should* just go home, at least till then. It's only twenty-seven bucks to get to Hempstead, Long Island.

"Can you do me a favor?" Lucy asked me.

Thank God, maybe I can leave the room now. "What's up?"

And she handed me money. "Will you go and grab us cigarettes?"

Oh fuck. I was only sixteen. She thought I was eighteen. Man… this is gonna be a project. "Sure!" I said and I booked it outa the room and *ran* to Thayer Street cause I knew it might take me some time to figure out how to get her cigarettes.

So I got down there and I asked every single person I saw to buy me cigarettes. No one said yes. I mean shit, I was only a kid.

I came back an hour later with smokes.

"Where the hell were you?!" Lucy asked all flustered as I threw her the pack on the bed, not even able to tell her how fuckin hard it just was to get her the goddam cigarettes.

"Oh… uhh, you know, I got caught up in a game of hacky-sack. You know how it goes." You know how it goes? Did I really just say that? What a dumb thing to say. That's not how I talk. Uy… Whatever. Move on man, it's in the past.

And then, *another* night of non-sex. It was completely obvious by this point. Lucy woke me up the next morning shaking me.

"Do you have an STD?"

"What?"

"Is that why you won't have sex with me?!"

And she got all frantic and I had to calm her down and say something.

"No, it's not that… it's something else." But that's all I said, cause that 'something else' was me being a pussy, but I didn't know what else to say. Plus, by now, I wasn't even sexually attracted to her anymore, so it was all really gettin a bit too much to handle.

We argued for about an hour. She kept demanding for me to tell her what it was, and I kept not knowing what in the hell to say so I just kept saying, "No, I don't wanna talk about it." That only made shit more confusing. Finally, the fight was over and all was back to normal… I guess. Isn't normal just a setting on a dryer?

Lucy looked at me and with revitalized eyes, she said, "Wanna come to class with me?"

YES! WHAT A GREAT IDEA! I could see if I liked the school before I applied. That might actually make my parents proud of me if I got into Brown. Not that I cared about what they thought of me, but it would be nice, I guess, if they were proud of me and all. I probably need to get my GED and all that beforehand though, before I apply. Maybe I should look into that? I could probably steal a study guide or whatever from the bookstore.

So anyway, we walked over to the building that her class was in that morning and the class was called 'Christianity With Late Antiquity'. I wasn't quite sure what that even meant. Maybe it was some bible class? Whatever, who cares… I'm goin to class, that's what matters. The only thing was, when we got there, we were twenty minutes late and everyone turned their heads and looked at me up and down as if to say, 'Isn't that the homeless kid from Thayer Street?' Cause by then I was pretty recognizable with my long black wavy hair and tie-dye shirt and eyebrow ring. Oh yeah, Lucy got me an eyebrow ring and the tie-dye shirt I wore, well, I stole it obviously.

So anyway, we walked in and everyone stared at me like I was death and to make matters worse, there were no more seats when we walked in and it was a really small class, about twenty kids or so, actually wait—*is* that a small class? I dunno, I never been to a class. But everyone was sittin in a circle and starin at me and I had to sit on the floor with Lucy next to the professor cause there were no seats, and the professor looked at me as if to say, 'What in the *fuck* are you doin?' Well, it was real uncomfortable to say the least. I stared at the clock above the professor the whole class sweating like a sweaty dude until the clock struck over. Maybe this isn't the right school for me?

Then my birthday came and everything fell apart.

It was September 29th 2001, and I was turning seventeen, but I would be celebrating my nineteenth birthday with Lucy and College Mike, I mean Mike, and these two other Ivy League kids I didn't really know too well.

Lucy surprised me with a huge ice cream cake with nineteen candles on it and one for good luck. We ate the cake on Thayer Street cause, well, that was my home and Lucy wanted me to feel at home I guess. I dunno, but that's where we all were. You shoulda seen Adam and this other chick he was dating, Adam was one of the other two kids that

Lucy brought with her, you know, the Ivy League friends of hers, anyway, you shoulda seen them sitting on the cement of the sidewalk brushing off the dirt off their pants and shit and lookin around to make sure none of their other college friends walked by them. They were so nervous and embarrassed to be seen with me and it was kinda funny… I think.

Then the celebration was over and the pretty couple left and then it was just College Mike, I mean Mike, and me and Lucy. Mike left and Lucy invited me to see her friend Calisse perform in Arthur Miller's *The Crucible* at the Brown Theatre Department. I really didn't wanna go and I really wanted a slice of pizza so I was like:

"Can we go get a slice of pizza before the show?"

So we stopped at the cafeteria on our way there. Here's where another layer of chaos was added to the cake.

So Lucy went to get a salad and a slice of pizza for me and I waited at a table while she was in line when alla sudden I heard a loud familiar voice.

"CAYEA?"

I turned around.

OH MY GOD. It was *Ben Parker.* BEN PARKER?! I looked around, as if I could run somewhere fast. But there was no hiding. I bet you're wondering who the fuck Ben Parker is… Well, Ben had been a senior when I was a freshman at Roslyn before I got sent away. He knew Gavin Wick and was the older brother of some other kid in my grade and basically, this would ruin it all. Lucy was gonna find out I was a fraud. My life was over. Or maybe it would get word back home that I was fuckin awesome? I couldn't decide. Tough choice, but I freaked out and realized that NO WAY could I have this guy let Lucy find out I was sixteen—I mean seventeen. Seventeen, I'm seventeen. Jeez, all these lies are confusing.

"CAYEA?!"

"Heeyyyyy, Ben!"

And he looked around.

"What the *hell* are you doing here? Where you been? What happened to you?" His look was priceless.

"Uhh, well it's a long story."

He stared at me all weird-like then asked "Well, how ya been?"

"Sorry, umm— just keep it down for a second. I uh— I met a girl, she goes to Brown and thinks I'm nineteen. So—if you ever see us together, she's right there", and I pointed her out with my chin, "can you just pretend I'm nineteen? She's about to come back, so yeah, just uhhh… say I'm nineteen. Cool?"

"What? You met a girl? That goes here? Wait, do you live here now? I'm confused. Are you not going back to Roslyn for high school?"

"Yeah, I know, this is all weird, I'll tell you about it later. Just uhh— Everything's good. How are you?"

Then Lucy joined us, so I switched tempos immediately.

"This is my girlfriend Lucy, Lucy this is Ben."

They looked at each other.

"Hi!"

"Hi!."

Good, they're friends, okay, "Yo Ben, gotta go man! Good to see you!"

And I rushed us outa the cafeteria. This was gettin to be too much. I needed some time to think. Maybe I *should* go home.

Fuck it.

"Okay! Let's go see Calisse's show!"

So we went to see *The Crucible* by Arthur Miller. When the show ended, we had to walk down Thayer to get back to her dormitory. I was tryin to think of a way outa goin back with her.

My heart was pounding as we walked down Thayer Street back to her dorm room. Then I got to thinkin, I miss Thayer. I was free on Thayer. Now I feel kinda trapped—and then I saw her.

It was Poe! But she uhh… she didn't look so good.

"POE!!!"

"You *know* her?" Lucy asked in disgust.

"Yeah she's my, umm… friend! I met her at, I mean on the street, you should meet her!"

Poe ran over when she saw me and gave me a big hug without acknowledging Lucy. She looked paler and skinnier than ever. The whole situation made Lucy pretty mad. But it made me really happy. I was right back at Hidden Lake. Finally something familiar. I could see our VW bus we had drawn. I could see our future that never panned out, but it wasn't too late. I could save her. She needed me and I needed her. So when she said:

"Greggy! Can I please stay with ya'll tonight? It's real cold out."

It made my heart sink. Lucy was speechless. She walked away pissed the fuck off, Lucy did. I stayed with Poe for a moment talking secretively. I told her the whole deal, what had happened, but she could barely stand up. My head hurt just lookin at her. She looked terrible, but hot. She looked like the hottest sluttiest lookin girl the world had ever produced. I missed her so bad, but the old her that is.

Man, what do I do? This FUCKIN girl! I couldn't turn my back on her. It *was* gettin cold out and she *had* given me places to sleep when I needed them… What should I do? I mapped out to Poe where Lucy lived and told her to meet me in front of the dorm at midnight.

I lied to Lucy, but she was no idiot, and knew what I was doing. The minute I tried to leave her dorm room later that night I was bombarded with a series of questions

"Where you going?"

"Just, downstairs."

"To let that girl in?"

"Just for the night, I promise."

"Don't you dare bring her to my room."

But I left as Lucy was still talkin. I had to. Poe was waiting outside the front door, freezing.

So I let her in and showed her to the lounge area of Lucy's dorm and said:

"You have to sleep in here."

Then I walked away.

"No Greggy! Stay with me please!"

"I can't Poe."

"Stop."

"No."

"Please? Just for ten minutes? PLEASE?"

But I didn't do it. "I can't Poe." And I walked back upstairs to Lucy, but when I got to her dorm room, she was already sleeping. I crawled in her bed next to her and put my arm around her and she smiled in her sleep like she always did. I loved that. Maybe I *do* like this girl? But I couldn't get Poe outa my mind and the thought of her so desperate and alone kept me up.

Halfway through the night, I snuck back downstairs to see if she was still there. I opened the door to the lounge I had snuck her into and at first glance, didn't see her. But then the door closed behind me and there she was. Curled up behind the door to stay completely out of sight. Smart girl. I sat down next to her and held her in my arms while she slept.

When I got back to Lucy's room it was nearly six in the morning, she was already awake.

"Where have you been? With her?"

"I was just making sure she was okay."

"Are you sleeping with her?"

"What? No no! We are just friends! Always have been. I swear. Can you try to be nice to her? She has nowhere to go."

"I don't like it."

And she left for class fuming with me.

So I took Poe to the Brown cafeteria and snuck her in using Lucy's meal card to feed her. Everyone looked at us as if security would surely ask us to leave at any moment, especially her. She looked like a hooker. Cause she *was* a hooker. Then I heard:

"Greg?"

You're fuckin kidding me. It was Ben fucking Parker! *AGAIN!*

"Hey—man!" I said all fake-like.

"This is becoming a regular occurrence, isn't it?"

"Weird, huh? This is my friend Poe."

"Hi! I'm Poe!"

"Nice to meet you."

Jesus Fucking… aright, this has to end. Get me the fuck outa here.

"Poe, come here for a sec—be back Ben!" And I rushed outa the conversation and we went back to Thayer Street, back to home, well, as much of a home as I had. I felt like more shit than ever before. Lucy was still in class, but I knew something had to happen soon, I just needed some time to figure it out before I went back to her dorm that evening. I couldn't do another night like this. I needed to talk to someone, but Poe was useless. Besides, she disappeared after I gave her that food. In fact, I never saw her ever again. Well, not for a while at least, and the next time we saw each other was under very different circumstances. But I'll get to that later as well…

So I called the one person I had left, I called Kiki.

"Kiki please, can you come to Thayer Street?"

"You come here."

"I can't I gotta be back to Brown in like a couple hours. I don't have time."

"You have to be where?"

"It's a long story. Please can you come see me?"

So she got off the phone and it was about an hour before she popped up on Thayer. I saw her before she saw me. She was with her boyfriend by the Dunkin Donuts. Right, she had a boyfriend by now, so she made it clear that we had to be separate, or more separate than before I guess. Whatever, I actually liked her boyfriend a lot. His name was Jeff. I think he knew we used to hook up, but he never made a fuss of it. He was just some high school kid from Providence… like a normal kid. Like the normal kid I never became.

When I saw Kiki I said to her with a strong face:

"I'm leaving. I have to leave here… and I uhh, I just wanted to tell you that."

She looked sad. "To where?"

"Well, I don't know. But I just wanted to tell you that."

She stared at me like I was the devil and then just finally said:

"Okay… Well, bye."

And she walked away. What a waste of her time she musta thought *that* was. Man, everything is gettin all twisted up. And I told her I was leaving! Why'd I say that? Where the hell was I gonna go? But I mean I had nothing left here on Thayer, why would I stay? Poe was all strung out and MIA, Slutto was back in Birmingham, I got word Dreadie John was bumming around Bloomington, Indiana by the college over there, Lucy had too many questions… There was Ben Parker and the cold weather and Bammer and Raquel and the cops. Nothing I said to Lucy made sense anymore and I mean, like I said, life was getting more and more complicated by the millisecond. She was onto me. I could feel it. I was a fraud. My anxiety was mounting. Every night I was there she asked me questions I couldn't answer, so I made up more lies. I was panicking every day and every night and the only time I calmed down was when she went to class in the mornings and I knew I had the day to decompress in her room, alone.

Lord knows where Poe was, I thought about her often. It was too cold outside to even leave Lucy's room within a few weeks, but I knew I was using her and nothing coulda felt worse. I had to leave her damn

room. My heart was submerging with pain and get this: WE STILL
HADN'T HAD SEX. But, I made it. I made it to winter till KC's
graduation. I stayed with Lucy for another two months. Can you
believe that? Another two months of all that bullshit. But then I stood
up one night.

It was December 13th and after months and months of lies and fear
and chaos and fraud and theft and her buying me shit and me using her
then feeling like a scummy trash bag fuckrag... I stood up from her bed
before another night of non-sex and she said:

"Where are you going?"

"I have to go to Georgia. Remember? I told you. You knew this."

"Now? You're just going to Georgia right now?"

"Uhh, yeah."

She just looked at me like she knew where this was going and said:

"You're coming back, aren't you?"

"Well—I mean, I told you I had to go see my friend KC and I'll be
back, just, I don't know when."

But my face said it all. I grabbed my backpack and blanket from off
her floor. Memories of us parading through campus on painkillers
having a blast flooded my eyes. I heard her cry as I quietly shut her door
behind me and walked down the stairwell. I had to close the door on
Thayer Street and move on to somewhere else, and so I did.

And I never came back.

Now I just had to find a way down to Georgia in the middle of the
winter without a bed to sleep nor roof to lay under. This was gonna be
hard.

CHAPTER 45

OUT OF IDEAS

I stood next to the payphone by Store 24 freezing my fucking ass off. Nobody was on the street, nobody but me. I took out my paper of contacts. I called Kaz, that one dude I called when I was stuck at the Greyhound station in Fayetteville North Carolina on September 11th, which *man*, what a big deal *that* turned out to be! Right? And I just thought it was some airport problem… Guess not. Anyway, it wasn't a huge factor in my life at the moment, but I *did* use it as an excuse to call my parents and make sure they were okay when I was in Winston-Salem on my way to Providence with Slutto at the Greyhound Station. I never told you that, but I'm telling you now. I called them cause I figured it would be safe if I called before I boarded another bus. And I missed them.

RING RING

"Hello?"

"Mom?"

"GREG?! WHERE ARE YOU!?"

"Is everyone okay?" I was really nervous when I called.

"Yes. We are all safe. Where are you?"

"I'm okay. I just wanted to make sure you were all okay."

"I understand why you left." My mom said to me in a surprising moment of communication.

I teared up.

"I'm in North Carolina. I have to go. I'm—"

But I hung up. I couldn't hear her voice for too much longer. It was makin me cry.

But I just wanted to tell you about that real quick, at the moment, all I got on my mind is how I gotta figure out a way to somehow get to Georgia, and I certainly don't have time to spange up enough cash for a bus ticket to Atlanta, I'll freeze... So like I said, I called Kaz.

"Hey man! It's Cayea!"

"Heyyy Gregory! Great to hear from you man! How'd everything work out with Ram?"

"He never picked up." Remember that kid who told me he would pick me up if I made it to Charlotte but then never picked up his phone? Yeah, that was Ram.

"Oh, bummer man!" Kaz said.

I was shivering so bad.

"Is the wind blowing or something?" He asked me.

"Yeah man, it's a bit cold here right now. I'm in Providence. Rhode Island. I decided to come back here to be on the road with Poe."

"Ohhhhh right! How is that girl?"

"Oh, well… uhh, good! She's good!"

"So guess where I'm going tomorrow…" Kaz said as he slightly cut me off, which is fine cause I didn't really have much to say other than to beg for help.

"Down to Atlanta?" I said… Wishful thinking I suppose… But then he said:

"Close! Hidden Lake! Going to see Peer Group 36 walk free."

My heart stopped.

"Wait, are you serious?"

"Yeah man, why? You want to come? We're driving! Me and my friend over here. We might stop by North Carolina too on the way down. Where'd you say you were living these days again? Rhode Island?"

"YES! I WANNA COME! Yes, I want to see KC walk, she's in 37!"

"Right on, right on! Well, if you can figure out a way to get down to Lancaster by tomorrow, you're more than welcome to join! Might be fun!"

"I'll be there."

Click.

Oh my God. This was perfect. This was so good. Yes. Okay, calm down. Think this out. New goal Greg, you've got a new goal: Get to Lancaster, Pennsylvania. THAT'S SO MUCH EASIER THAN

GEORGIA! You can do this. Right, I can do this. But how? Well I gotta find out how much a ticket costs, maybe it's not that much?

So I called the Greyhound 800 number and pressed a buncha buttons with my cold fingertips until I got to what price it would be to leave from Providence and arrive in Lancaster. It was only like thirty bucks or something, I can't remember the exact price, but the wind was rubbing my cheeks raw. I was so damn cold. Fuck. Okay, okay, concentrate. So I need thirty bucks within like three hours. If I want to get there by tomorrow at a reasonable time, I gotta move quick. Okay, thirty bucks, thirty bucks.

Well, I had only perfected two tactics: Begging and stealing, so I shivered until I could shiver no more and stood out on that street for about two hours begging for change... I didn't even have a sign. Good news about me being freezing is everyone felt bad for me, bad news is nobody gave me shit.

Then the craziest thing happened.

This black couple that was also homeless but they weren't really homeless cause they owned a home, but they both spanged every day for a living, they saw me by the phone. The man came up to me and the woman went into Store 24 for groceries I guess. We were all friends. All of us homeless people... even though they weren't really homeless. What's even crazier is they each made about a hundred bucks a day, two-hundred between the two of them spare changing on the street! And they were like sixty! But they had way more practice than I did. I'll get there one day. Anyway, the man was like:

"Colder the days the closer we stays!"

He always spoke in these rhymes.

"You not workin tonight?" I asked him.

"Not today young man. I think you oughta take the day off for yourself! It's cold out here!"

"I don't have anywhere to go and anyhow I'm trying to get to my friend. I got a friend in Lancaster who's gonna let me ride with him down to Georgia cause I gotta go there, to Georgia, but the bus is thirty bucks to get to Lancaster and it leaves tomorrow morning and if I don't make it I'ma miss my ride down south… I don't know. I'm stressed out. I'm tryin to get as much as I can."

"Lancaster? What's that?"

"It's in Pennsylvania."

"Thirty dollas huh?"

"Thirty bucks. I was staying with this girl and she was buying my food and, I don't know, it's a long story… but now I got nothing. Thirty bucks I need. Well, that's just for the ticket I suppose. I needa eat too. I'm hungry. Fuck it's cold."

"All these months and you hadn't saved one dime? One penny at a time for us, you should know that by now!"

"Yeah I fucked up."

Then he took out a hundred-dollar bill.

"Here."

"Wait, what?"

"I'll make this back tomorrow, you take it. Go on to Transylvania."

"Pennsylvania."

"I know boy, don't you know when a joke is tappin ya forehead?"

I had no idea what to say. Life had never been this nice to me. He was the nicest man I ever met. He and that truck driver down in Louisiana when I ran away from New Beginnings. Then he said:

"Need a place to sleep tonight?"

So not only did the homeless man give me a hundred-dollar bill, but he and his wife took me over to their house, fed me dinner and let me sleep on their couch before they bid me farewell the next morning.

I guess sometimes when you fall off your path the road changes the direction you're walkin down. So I suppose that's what happened to me, cause now I was ready to go, ready to finally move on. The universe had taken care of me.

So I boarded the bus in the morning and got to Lancaster the next evening at 5PM, and boy was this about to be another adventure…

CHAPTER 46

DOWN TO GEORGIA WE GO

It wasn't a happy car ride. Kaz and his friend, they mighta been gay together, I don't know, but they were fighting the *entire* time we were in the hundred-dollar car we drove down in. The car fuckin *sucked*. I'd rather be riding in Car Mike's car. But anyway, when I got off the bus at the Lancaster station, they were already arguing about how long they'd had to wait for me to get there and how we'd be late now. Late for what?

Whatever, we did a straight shot down to Georgia but we got there a day too early, so much for being late... And so we didn't know what to do with our extra time. Hmmm... So I said:

"Isn't today the off-campus AA meeting?" I asked Kaz, cause the other guy, his gay lover maybe, he never went to Hidden Lake. He was just pissy and bitter and shit.

"Oh right! Yes! It is! Should we go?"

"Oh man, how funny would *that* be. YES. LET'S DEFINITELY GO!"

So we showed up and guess what? KC WAS THERE! Damn, the second I saw her I forgot how pretty she was, anyway, I told her, "SEE?? I PROMISED YOU I'D BE HERE AND HERE I AM! AREN'T YOU SURPRISED?"

"Of course not! I knew you'd be here!" And we hugged it out. Then I started buggin like mad right as we sat down at the AA table and right before the meeting was about to start.

"Okay listen KC, I'm freakin out. I got nowhere to go", I tried to keep my voice down, but I was frantic, "I was with Poe but then she turned into a hooker—"

"Wait, what? Who's Poe? Oh right, oh right, that girl."

That girl? Had she forgotten who Poe was? Or maybe she just wasn't thinkin about her as much as I was? I mean, I know she'd never met her, but I *did* talk about her all the time. Was she jealous? I didn't get it. So I just continued:

"—It's a long story, but she's got some drug-dealer pimp now and I got no one to stay with and it's cold and I don't know, I had to leave the other girl at Brown—"

"Who did? You? Wait, what other girl at Brown, Poe?"

"No no, it's, well, it's a long story."

But then the AA meeting started. The guard that was guarding the Hidden Lake kids at the AA meeting didn't really know what to do, and actually, I don't think he really cared so much that Kaz and I and the other kid had shown up. It seemed like he was just lettin us all talk, I don't know. It was so weird being back there. Back in Dahlonega. Back with KC, especially with the other kids that *weren't* leaving the next day, the kids that were still trapped, it was *really* weird bein around them cause I was free, and I don't know… They weren't. But I was so happy that I was FREE! FUCK THEM! But I did feel real sorry for everyone.

So I gave all the kids that were there cigarettes and Kaz had this pre-paid phone that we also gave to everyone to use to call their friends. One by one, everyone got up to go to the bathroom and made a phone call, the only phone call they'd ever actually had since they had been there… which felt great that we were giving them that opportunity. I wish someone had done that for me. And the guard didn't say shit. I mean, what could he do? Not like I was breakin the law or anything.

So later that night, after we bid everyone farewell and I told KC I'd see her tomorrow, we got a room at The Econo Lodge… well, Kaz did, and we waited till the next night, the night before Peer Groups 36, 37 and 38 graduated, the night that everyone was allowed off campus to celebrate… the night that I almost died.

So here's what happened.

We decided to drive up the mountain to see the sunrise at like 5:30AM and Kaz was driving up some Appalachian mountain road while our friend Jack, who was also my roommate for a bit at Hidden Lake, he was graduating with KC cause he was in Peer Group 35, he was in the passenger seat and KC and I and Slutto were in the back. Yup, Slutto showed up too! He drove his mom's car from Birmingham!

So we were all together in the backseat and the sun was coming up after a long night and we were all a bit high and it was sleeting outside and cold and the mountain road was slippery and I was tryin to explain everything that had happened to me to KC, but it was hard…

"—She's the girl I was with in Rhode Island, Poe, but now it's cold out and I was seein this girl at Brown and was hangin out at frat parties and stuff but she thought I was nineteen and shit just got too real and she fell in love with me and so I just left her and all my stuff is there." Oh right, I had collected numerous items as life as a teenage homeless runaway, and they were all still in Lucy's closet.

I was outa breath tellin the story cause there was so much to tell and I knew that the story didn't really add up, even to me it didn't add up and it especially didn't add up to KC.

"Wait, Poe goes to Brown?" Man was she confused…

"No no, the college girl, Lucy, she goes to Brown. It's a college. It's an Ivy League school."

"So you have a girlfriend?" She looked befuddled as fuck.

"Nah, I mean, I did, but we broke up."

"Did you have sex with her?" I thought long and hard. The lies HAD to stop. But if I told her no, then what? I just had a girlfriend and didn't have sex with her? I couldn't tell her that. That'd be fuckin ridiculous. So I did what I did best.

"Yeah of course we had sex, I mean, I was livin with her." Then I changed subjects, another skill of mine, "I REALLY need a place to live KC."

"Did you have sex with Poe?"

"No. Never."

"Why are you lying?"

For ONCE, I was tellin the truth. I couldn't *believe* she thought I was *lying*. Why would I *ever* lie about that!?

"NO I AM NOT LYING!"

"Jeez okay, calm down."

"Please. Can I stay with you? Just for a bit and then I'll leave. Please. I have nowhere to go." I begged her.

"You were there too?" She asked Slutto.

"For a bit, yeah!" He said. "Shit was too crazy for ma ass. Went back down to Birmingham after laighk a week."

"Yeah he did, but it was fun, he brought his guitar and he played music while I sang and we made money! It was fun, right Slutto?"

Slutto thought for a moment… "Well, yeah, some of it was ah guess."

"So can I stay with you please????" I begged KC again.

She told me I could stay with her at her apartment in Worcester, which is a city by Boston in Massachusetts, also where she was doin this weird internship thingy at a pottery studio, and she told me till I found somewhere to go that it shouldn't be a problem. The only problem was she wouldn't be there for another month.

"KAZ SLOW DOWN DUDE!" Slutto screamed.

But I was lost in thought tryin to figure out where the fuck I would go for the month of January. Jeez. ONE MONTH?!

"KAZ!!" Slutto screamed.

"WHAT?! JEEZ CALM YOUR HORSES!" Kaz responded.

"Yo this shit is FUN!" Jack, the big dude in the front seat said.

By the way, Kaz's friend, or gay lover, he was back at the hotel sleeping. Thank God. Anyway, KC looked like she was rethinking everything she had just promised me already. I looked pretty damn homeless by then and I wasn't so cute and cuddly anymore. I was just kinda… well, beat-lookin. Maybe she didn't wanna help me?

Enough mind chatter Greg.

"YO LET'S SMOKE A BLUNT WHEN WE GET BACK!" Jack screamed over Guns N' Roses. Yeah, "November Rain" was on the radio and Slash was about to break into his second guitar solo when suddenly…

SSCCCRRREEEEECCCHHHHHHHHH—

Kaz tried to break, but the car swerved and drove off the cliff.

CHAPTER 47

AM I DEAD OR ALIVE?

The car was swaying in the wind as we all sat still as hell. We hadn't fallen yet. Down the cliff was a million-foot drop. It would for sure kill us all. The front right tire was completely off the ground. Any gust of wind could send us spiraling to our death.

That's when Slutto came to the rescue.

"GET THE FUCK OUT!" Slutto screamed.

He reached over me, cause I was in the middle seat, and reached over KC and unlocked the door and yanked the handle and pushed the door open.

"GET THE FUCK OUT! GO! WE'RE GONNA DIE!!!"

And so KC got out. I got out. Slutto got out. Kaz got out. Jack got out. We were in shock. The car was tilting off the ground. Then a miracle happened.

A pickup truck drove by. We hadn't seen more than two cars the whole drive up... it was like, we were the only car in the world.

The driver got outa his car and took one look at our situation and grabbed a hook from the front of his truck and tied it to Kaz's beater and pulled the car to life. I couldn't believe it. No one died and the car was now back safely on the ground.

Holy shit.

Nobody died. It was a miracle. Well, nobody died that night.

Rest in Peace Jack.

He died of a drug overdose not too long afterwards.

Sorry for that... but anyway, when word of our car accident traveled back to Hidden Lake, no Peer Group was ever allowed to go off campus ever again the night before graduation, all cause of us. It made me feel kinda special actually.

But that was that. So I had about fifty bucks to my name still from the homeless slash non-homeless black couple that had given me that hundred-dollar bill, and I was back in the car with Kaz and his gay lover, unless they weren't gay lovers, the next day. I didn't know what to do or where to go, so I hoped the road trip would eat away some time for a bit.

We stopped off in North Carolina like Kaz had said and we went to this trailer that the old English teacher at Hidden Lake lived at. He and Kaz were friends cause they were both hippies that loved fine literature... but so was I... hmmm, I wonder why he liked Kaz more?

Anyway, this teacher left Hidden Lake when he learned about the abuse and what the school was really like and what was really goin on, but now he and his wife and kids were dirt poor living outa this trailer on this mountaintop near Cherokee, North Carolina on a mountain that only had a few other trailers on it. So we were on top of that mountaintop in their trailer as I tried to figure out my next move… Where to go before KC's apartment in Massachusetts was ready. I had an idea. So I asked to use the phone.

"Is it long distance?" Teacher dude asked me while he and Kaz were in the kitchen part of the trailer smoking tobacco out of a pipe.

"Uhhh, no, it's fine." I said. "It's local." But that was a lie. I mean, who did I know that lived on this damn mountaintop?

He looked at me funny, but I dialed the number anyway before I had second thoughts.

RING RING.

"Hello?"

"Kiki! You answered! You never answer!"

"Who is this?"

But she knew who the fuck it was. "It's me. You know it's me."

"What do you want? You can't just keep showing back up in my life and leaving."

"I'd really like to see you. Can I please see you?"

"I have a boyfriend."

"Still?"

"Well, no."

"You guys broke up?"

"I don't know."

"Can I come over?"

"Now?"

"Well, I'm in North Carolina—"

"—Goodbye Greg"

"WAIT! WAIT! BUT I WAS GONNA SAY THAT I'M COMING BACK!"

"You can't keep doing this to me."

"Just please, when I get back, in a day or so, can I please come see you?"

She paused before saying, "I guess. Call me when you're here. We'll see."

And so I had Kaz drop me off in Trenton New Jersey on our way back up. By the way, eight years later, when I was like twenty-five or so living in New York City, I got a call from that teacher asking for the ten dollars that I had run up his bill. Apparently he was still pissed off about that long distance call I made, so I wrote him back on Facebook, cause by then Facebook had just been invented, and I got his address and mailed him a check for twenty bucks. I mean, by then I was making a quarter-million dollars a year, but I'll get to that a bit later on... For now, just know that I paid him back for that phone call and was let out in Trenton New Jersey after that trip and I got on a train to Penn Station then walked from 34th street up to 42nd street over to Port Authority in Manhattan and bought *another* Greyhound ticket up to Providence.

And off I went.

This time, when I called Kiki and told her I was coming over, I figured out how to get there on my own. No help from Poe or anyone.

This time, walkin through South Providence at night didn't scare me one bit.

When I got to Kiki's house, it was late enough so that her Aunt and Uncle were already asleep, so she snuck me in through the front door, an amenity for sure, and up she smuggled me to her room.

She told me all about how she and Poe met in Switzerland. As it turns out, when Poe was pulled from Hidden Lake by her adopted parents when I was in Utah, it was a pure coincidence. She just happened to get pulled while I was away, and then they sent her to Switzerland to this all-girls specialty school where she met Kiki. But then she and Kiki ran away and took a flight back to America. Kiki told Poe that she could stay with her at her Aunt's house, I don't know where Kiki's parents were, I never asked, but anyway, I guess Poe musta done something that *really* fucked all that up cause Kiki didn't even wanna talk about it.

So she and I stayed up all night and we made out and read poetry to each other and it was amazing, but the next morning it was just like every other morning with Kiki... I had to crawl out her two-story bedroom window at 5AM and find something else to do while she went to school and her Aunt went to work... So, I went to the only place I knew where to go:

Thayer Street.

CHAPTER 48

THE LAST DANCE

I just had to last three more weeks or so before I could head over to Worcester. So what I did was I found some obscure dorm that was really buried deep down in the Brown University campus and I waited for some kid to walk out of the front door and I went in after him.

First thing I did was I walked up the stairs and down the hall and found a bathroom, cause the bathrooms were in the hallways. So I ducked in there real quick and grabbed some toothbrush that was in the mirror thingy and some toothpaste on the sink and brushed my teeth. Then I turned on the hot water till I got it nice and warm and showered up. There was one of those fluffy shower puff ball thingies in the shower so I soaped myself up with some kid's Herbal Essence and used some expensive lookin shampoo and cleaned up my kiddie-like beard and then toweled off. I put the same clothes back on but at least now I was fresh. And warm.

So I went downstairs and found the TV room, all the dorms had a TV room. I found the TV room and nobody was in there so I closed the door and locked it shut. I lay down on the couch and watched movies till very late at night, until the very last second that Dunkin Donuts was open… cause I got real hungry and I didn't wanna leave. So what I did was I left the doors locked and climbed out the window and went and got a few donuts before they closed and came back to the TV room and crawled through the window.

The next morning I woke up to some students tuggin at the door, tryin to get in, but I had locked it nice and tight so eventually they went away. I stayed in that room again that night and realized it was New Years! Oh shit! Happy New Year's me! It was finally 2002. Jeez, that year took forever. Especially with those planes and Hidden Lake and Thayer AND Utah… man, a lot happened that year.

Anyway, once a week Dunkin Donuts and Store 24 got rid of their stale sandwiches and donuts, so I'd show up before any of the other homeless people to get the sandwiches and donuts. Dunkin Donuts used to give em to me in a trash bag. There were hundreds of leftover donuts it felt like… well, maybe less than a hundred, but there were a lotta donuts… too much for me to eat on my own, so I went up and down the road givin them all out to the other homeless people and then I went back to my TV lounge, but on my there I bumped into this street kid I knew named Shroomy.

"FUCK YOU DUDE!" He said to me all agro and shit.

"What for?"

"Your dumb bitch friend just pulled a gun on me!" He said then walked away.

"Who Poe?! A gun?" But he was already gone.

Hmmm… I wonder if that was true. Where the hell was Poe anyway, glad she was still alive at least. I had started thinkin of her in such distant terms that she barely existed in my head anymore. But there was one night when I saw her.

I told you that I never saw her ever again, well, not for a long while at least, and when I did see her again it was under very different circumstances, but I forgot to mention this other time I saw her. Just now. This isn't the very different circumstances I was talkin to you about.

It was a regular freezing night on Thayer and I was staying in that TV room still, but during the day I stayed out on the street for as long as I could, but it had been a couple weeks or so that I was stayin in that TV room and still hadn't gotten kicked out, which is awesome. I also got to watch all these movies and shit while I slept on this really comfy couch. It was dope. Anyway, it was a normal night when I *did* see Poe, but I only really saw her from a distance.

I was hangin out on the stoop askin for money, holding a sign out that said 'DIRTY JOKES FOR ONE DOLLAR' but I didn't have any jokes so it was always real awkward when someone actually gave me a dollar. Usually they gave like a few quarters and so I didn't have to tell the joke, but sometimes I had to do the joke and it was really bad.

Poe was across the street with some skinny guy with stringy hair and a face tattoo down his lower cheek, and I don't think she saw me so I wasn't even gonna say anything. But, she looked over and saw me and so did the guy with face tattoos and he just stared at me but didn't move and she came over. But when she got closer, I could see that she was skinnier than ever and stumbling over her feet as she walked and told me this story:

"Hiiii Greggyy, 'M bettr'now." Her words stumbled over one another.

Better from what? Being a whore? But I didn't really say that. She told me this weird story.

"I've been staying in an abandoned house on Penn Street with Kris."

"Who's Kris? Did you pull a gun out on Shroomy?"

And she started laughing. "Did he say that?"

"Yeah he did." I didn't think any of this was funny. Jeez, what a mess she was... but she didn't even answer me. She just kept talkin, so I listened... kinda. I let her talk is a better way to put it.

"I wasn't, ya know, wasn't feeling well. I was in so much pain I couldn't even climb through the window. Kris came down and fixed me a shot of dope but I was still in pain and he knew there must be something seriously wrong with me because dope is the cure for everything, ya know? So he took me to the hospital and they put an IV in me and gave me a shot of morphine. They said that if I hadn'ta reached the hospital when I did I would have died. I had a kidney infection. I had to stay there for a couple of days before they would release me, so Kris came by each day and put my dope directly in my IV for me."

I had no clue where to—I mean, I had nothin to say or do. I was just... stumped. Just go the fuck away. One week she needs my help then disappears after I give it to her, the next she's tellin me this and doesn't even realize I was gone for... well, a week or whatever. I don't know I just wanted to go back to the TV room to be honest.

"You don't look good Poe."

"Don't worry, I got another job, ya know? At this club downtown and I'll be able to help us out with more money now." But she never gave me any money...

"Poe you're a hooker."

"STOP! I AM NOT!"

"So what are you?"

"I just do the dates dude to help out on the side you know?"

But it doesn't matter, cause a week later she got fired from the club for shooting up in the back while she was supposed to be on stage, so all she had were her 'dates'... and then Kris, her pimp I guess, he went on vacation for a day and asked her to man the phones, and she stole all the 'dates', did em all herself, then ran off with the money and THAT was the last time I ever saw her again...

Until we met under those very different circumstances. Anyway, the point is when I got to Worcester, KC was waiting for me at the bus stop with her roommate Becky, Thayer Street became a foggy memory and a new street took its place.

High Drive.

CHAPTER 49

HIGH DRIVE

So our address was 2 High Drive, Worcester, Massachusetts. It was me and KC and Becky and this other girl named Jill that I'll tell you about in a bit. But before all that, when I got in the car at the bus station after I got off the bus from Providence, I noticed how fuckin hot KC was now that she wasn't in that dumb Hidden Lake uniform. Man, I hope I don't blow this. She was wearing this hemp choker necklace and whatever, KC was… but point is she was happy to see me and to show me off to Becky but she wasn't half as happy to see me as Becky was.

Becky was ecstatic. She was also wearing hemp, but a hemp head-wrap and this knit-sweater with patchy jeans, but not cause the pants needed patches, but cause the patches made the pants look cool, at least she thought they did. Actually, I thought they did too. She was pretty cool-lookin, Becky was. But they probably didn't have one hole in em though, Becky's pants that is... amateur.

Anyway, when I got in Becky's car, she was more excited to meet me than KC was to see me, at least that's what it felt like. Becky told me all about how cool Worcester was and how we were gonna have the best time and all this shit.

So we pulled up to some triple decker house and walked inside and that's when I met the other girl that KC and Becky (and now me I guess) lived with. Her name was Jill.

Jill was not cool with this.

When I opened the fridge the next day all her food had a slice of masking tape on it labeled 'Jill'. I guess she thought I was gonna munch on all her food, which I probably woulda, I mean, I *was* homeless.

Becky showed me to her room. I walked in and there was one bed that she and KC both slept in. She said "You can sleep with us!"

Oh man. That sounded great! So later that night I got between both of them and tried to sleep, nervous as hell, but horny, and KC was kinda touchin me, but maybe that's cause we all had a bit to drink. So I leaned into her and kissed her, but that's cause I had beer courage. But the thing is, Becky was still awake while this was happenin and she mighta got jealous or whatever cause the next night she asked how long I would be stayin for.

Then she said I needed to find a new place to sleep, that I couldn't just sleep in bed with both of them. So KC and I setup a bed in the living room on a futon and instead of KC sleepin in her room, she joined me that night, which made Becky even more angry.

Oh no. I hadn't had anything to drink or any pills to take and now I'm in bed with KC. Fuck. What if she wants to have sex? I started gettin nervous, but then I got un-nervous. I knew she was a virgin too and there was something about her butt that just simmered my nerves. She had this butt that, man, it was one great butt. I squeezed it over and over again until:

Oh no.

She started slidin her pajama pants off. But I guess that's okay cause she was wearin this blue thong and it made me go crazy in my head. A *blue thong*. I'd never seen shit like that before. She musta been like, a freak. I started gettin real worked up.

Then I couldn't help myself and I kissed her, but it wasn't a soft kiss, it was an aggressive I'ma pound you to the ground kiss. So then I held myself back even though I didn't want to cause I didn't want anything that might lead to sex. So I tried to take it slow and just acted like kissin her was enough for me.

I tickled her back and she started moaning. Oh man. Oh man. Oh man. I flipped her over and pushed my lips against hers, hard, with force, passion. I couldn't control myself. She smiled and that made me even more sexually frustrated. Fuck I needed more than this. I wrestled her in the bed cause I just wanted to pin her down and take her and it seemed like that's what she wanted to and so we wrestled until we got all tangled up into a love-fuck pretzel and we were kissing each other furiously.

I wasn't even really that nervous, just pissed off. I wanted more. I needed to be inside her bad.

I was still wearin my tee shirt cause if I took it off that meant I wanted sex, and I was still in kinda a safe zone for now, like I could still back down and come up with some excuse right then if I had to, but I took it off anyway. I had to. Then I grabbed her shirt and nearly ripped it off her back. Then I saw her matching blue bra. Oh man. What a fucking slut. I loved it. She musta planned this out.

I grabbed the bra and without undoin the buckle thingy in the back, I lifted up the bra cups and started kissin her nipples all over. I couldn't control myself. Then I noticed she had taken her bra off for me. She was almost naked. I still had my jeans on, and belt. The belt was the worst. The belt really put a damper on things. I had to just take it off, I'll leave my jeans on, but the belt has to go. I took the belt off and I was so hard I thought I might cum right then.

But then she undid the button to my jeans and she unzipped my zipper and without takin my jeans off started rubbing me all over. So I just took my jeans off for her, I had to, I couldn't control myself. Then I took my boxers off, fuck it, right?

I got on top of her cause I wanted to keep her still but she let me keep her still and that was hot enough to make me fuming mad. I grabbed her thong and nearly snapped it off her ass, but she didn't even stop me. GODDAMMIT WOMAN!

Her thong was soaked. I had to get rid of it, but I didn't have the patience so I just pushed it over to the side and I grabbed my dick and put it between her thighs against her warm thong that was dripping wet. She moaned and I got angry so I pushed into her. I pushed harder and she said "ouch" and I said "are you okay?" and she nodded and so I said "Do you want me to stop?" But it was too late, she was rolling her eyes in the back of her head and I was going into her as deep as I could and we were rough fucking like animals.

I pulled out again and pushed into her even harder and harder and harder you fuckin bitch take this motherfuckin shit you GODDAM BITCH FUCK ME COCK YOU WHORE YOU DUMB BITCH FUCK ME FUCK FUCK FUCKKKKKKKKKKKKKKKK "I'M GONNA CUM!!!!!!" And I pulled my dick out quickly but she immediately put her mouth over it and swallowed it all.

All my frustration.

All those years of sexual anger, gone. In her mouth. She kissed me and laid down and that's when alla sudden I thought to myself:

I DID IT!

I'M NOT A VIRGIN ANYMORE!!!

BUT… that's when *she* said:

"I wish I woulda been your first." Then she looked at me and said, "You were my first." And then she went to sleep thinkin I hadn't lost my virginity to her, cause I told her I slept with Lucy, which I never did, and KC went to bed thinkin she was number two… Now I had to pretend that I hadn't just lost my virginity to her and that she wasn't the girl I lost it to.

Another secret, another lie.

But from that day forward, she and I fucked all over that goddam apartment like three times a day. I was on a high and I finally had a partner in crime:

KC.

Then I got myself into one very twisted situation.

CHAPTER 50

ONE VERY TWISTED SITUATION

Remember I told you that when I saw Poe again it was under very different circumstances? Well, I called Kiki a few days later to let her know where I was and guess who was over her house?

Poe.

"Wudjya ask KC if I cud c'm'over? Ya know, just for a few nights? I got in some trouble over here but it's not bad ya know? Just gotta get outa town for a bit ya know? Can I come?"

Oh man.

"Is everything okay?"

"Yah dude, it's just Kris an stuff, ya know?"

No, I didn't know. I never knew. Not with her at least... I didn't know what to do, but I did know what 'trouble' meant, especially when it came outa her mouth. It meant someone was tryin to kill her. So I thought long and hard.

"Okay but look, really you can only stay for a night, okay?"

"Yayy Greggy I can't wait ta see ya!"

I hadn't even asked KC is this was cool, not to mention Jill was ACHING for a reason to throw me out and Becky had alienated herself from KC and I too... it was really just us two squatting at these two girls' apartment, at least that's how it felt. I guess I was the only one not payin rent.

Well I told you before that KC and Poe didn't know each other so when I told KC that Poe was comin over she flipped the fuck out. I assured her it was JUST for one night. Again, she asked if Poe and I had ever hooked up. I said never. Which was the truth. She told me ONE night, that's all Poe could stay for.

ONE NIGHT.

Poe got into town and called from the Greyhound. By now, after KC told Becky about Poe... Becky *really* hated us, KC and I, but she still drove us with contempt to get Poe cause she was the only one with a car.

And when we picked up Poe, *man* did she not look good. She had on these tighter than life black pants and this cut-off shirt with no bra and her eyes were sunken in and jeez, she *really* looked like a hooker. KC was NOT happy about this.

THEN… halfway on the way home from the Greyhound, in some shitass neighborhood, Poe told Becky to:

"STOP THE CAR! QUICK!"

Becky came to a screeching halt and turned around like the car mighta been on fire, but it wasn't. Poe unlocked the door and ran outa the car and over to a gas station and started talkin to some random dude.

"The fuck is she doing?" Becky asked as she and I and KC peered through the car window to see what the hell she was doin.

Then Poe left that dude she was talkin to and went over to the bus stop that was right there and waited. We were all in the car waitin for her while all this was happenin and we were like in the middle of the street while traffic was honkin at us.

"Hold on, sorry, I'll get her" and I ran outa the car over to her. "POE! WHAT THE FUCK ARE YOU DOING?!" I'ma kill this fuckin bitch right now, she'll be gone forever.

"I just gotta do this thingy real quick Greggy okay?" She was alla sudden really stressed out. "Just tell em to wait."

"I can't Poe. You can't bring any dope in the house okay?"

"It's not dope Greggy."

"Then what is it? Why are you standin out here at the fuckin bus stop?"

"I just gotta make some quick cash ya know?"

My face froze. "Are you kidding?" And I walked away.

"Wait! Greggy! Okay, okay" and she followed me back in the car.

An hour later the whole apartment was in silence. Everyone was angry: Poe at the world, me at Poe, KC at me, Becky at KC, Jill at everyone in life. Everyone hated each other.

The next day, Becky left for work, Jill wasn't home and KC was on her way to that weird internship at the goddam pottery studio that her dad setup for her. It was her first day and she was nervous and still angry and she *really* didn't wanna leave me and Poe alone together, but I mean, she didn't get it. Poe and I... we'd been livin like this for however long. So I assured her everything was okay. So she finally left.

And while I was lying on the couch listening to all of Poe's craziness, nobody was home but us, I couldn't help to think how different she looked now than what she used to look like at Hidden Lake, and even when I first got to Thayer. I mean, her long knotty hair was now short, straightened, bleached and dyed red. From full-figured, not fat, but just, you know, normal, to skinny as all hell. Hippie dress to tight halter top with no bra. Smiley face to sunken-in desperation. No makeup to sparkly makeup. She was like a cross between Sharon Stone in Casino and Jenny from Forest Gump. But the truth is, she looked hotter than she had ever looked before, to me at least. Maybe it was just cause I had just lost my virginity and now I was always horny. Or maybe I just loved how trashy she looked, I dunno.

But then Poe walked over to me and said "Hi Greggy" as she got on top of me.

Wait... what? What is happening right now? I thought.

"You gotta get off me Poe." But I didn't really mean that. Beneath my words were PLEASE STAY ON TOP OF ME. I felt like I was doing the wrong thing. I had just gotten a girlfriend. I loved KC, but she would understand. I mean, if she knew how long I had waited to just FEEL Poe against me like this, she would get it. God would forgive me. This was okay. I was so scared.

"Poe you gotta get off." I said again, as if I meant it… but I didn't.

"Why Greggy? Don't you wanna fuck me?"

She could feel me hard against her. Oh no, my cover was blown. Damn I just wanted her all over me. I don't know why but I liked how much of a whore she seemed to me. I felt fucked up in the head. Then I thought of KC. I had to not cheat on her. Fuck.

I said "Please stop" in this fake ass voice again.

"Fine" and she got off me on the couch and I was terrified she wouldn't come back. I was JUST kiddin POE! COME STRADDLE ME MOREE!!!!!! But I didn't say that.

She went over to her now non-hippie lookin purse, her hooker-lookin purse, and took out this little dress that she NEVER woulda worn when I first met her. She took off her shirt in fronta me. All these months on the street with her and she NEVER took off her clothes in front of me. Even though she was stripping for the entire city, *now* she wants to get naked? You stupid bitch. But her tits were perfect.

I couldn't even think. She put the dress on over her shoulders and snug it up tight around her curves. Here nipples were pokin through the dress. Her eyes never left my face as she took her pants off. I couldn't feel my conscience. I couldn't feel my values. My life was warped. My heart was full. My dick was imploding. She smiled and reached her hands up into her short dress hugging her thighs and slipped off her thong and left it on the floor where she was standing and walked back over to me.

I was paralyzed.

"What's wrong Greggy" and she got back on top of me. "Don't you like this?" And she let her dress lift up so that her pussy was right in fronta my face, staring right at me. Oh man. She leaned in and kissed me all over my neck.

She unzipped my jeans and I let her warm breath blow into my ear as she pulled them off all the way. I didn't stop her once. She moved her lips from my ear to my lips to my neck and licked my nipples as she let her long hooker nails lightly scratch my stomach before she held my dick in the palm of her hands. She moved her lips from my nipples to my stomach and down to my thighs before her warm tongue slid down the side of my dick. She picked her head up and smiled at me like she had won.

Then she started talkin all dirty

"I'm on my period Greggy. You want my blood all over your cock?" As she spread her lips perfectly around my pulsating dick. I didn't even think of a condom. I was in a trance. Her bein on her period made me even hornier. I don't know why, it just did. She lowered herself on me then slowly lifted back up then back down on me again.

"Cum deep in me Greggy, cum inside my pussy. Fuck me Greggy."

I couldn't move my arms or say anything. I was in sexual prison.

"Don't you like my blood all over your hard cock?"

Is this what she said to all the guys? Am I special? What's going on? This was the moment I had been waiting for my entire life.

"Cum in me Greggy. Cum."

I felt a surge of explosiveness move from the gut of my stomach to my pelvis to the bottom of my cock.

"Cum in me Greggy. Fuck me" she said between her grinding teeth. Her eyes demonically possessing me as she ground into me harder and harder. I felt the cum rise to the top of my cock.

Harder and harder and harder and-

BLAST. DEEP INSIDE HER. All my cum from years of wanting her rushed through my body and into her pussy as she smiled and laughed while I came. After I was done she didn't pull me out of her. She left my cock get soft inside of her before she got off me.

Then what I had just did rushed to my conscience. I had cheated. FUCK. Another goddam lie, another secret another—FUCK! Everything special I had JUST started with KC was now ruined cause of POE. Another piece of my life I had just ruined for Poe, again, another piece of my sanity, gone. A wave of guilt crashed into me and I panicked.

How was I gonna keep *this* a secret? No more secrets. I couldn't take it anymore. What if KC and I get married? Now I got this big fuckin lie I gotta keep forever? I was already thinkin that KC and I might get married. What a crazy person I am. I was so remorseful I lied and confessed at the same time. The next morning I told KC that I had not been truthful with her, that Poe and I *did* have sex… but back in Providence. That was my way of gettin it off my chest without having to say anything about what had happened yesterday.

Well, KC flipped out and made Poe leave, but Poe was ready to leave anyway… of course she was. She was dope sick and withdrawing and needed more heroin and I was already a distant memory in her mind, so it seemed.

Becky and Jill were sick of my shit and now that KC was ALSO sick of my shit, I suppose it seemed like the right time to kick me out. So Becky demanded that I leave. She called management and they threatened to call the cops on me if they ever saw me again.

But after a million 'I'm sorries' and a billion apologies, KC slowly started to forgive me.

"It's not like I cheated on you KC!" I said to her. Oh man, what a liar I was.

But little by little KC began to forgive me a tiny bit and by that evening, after they threatened to call the cops on me, she and I were already back in love and she had forgiven me. I promised her I would never lie to her again, and I promised myself I would *never* cheat on her *ever* again. What a terrible feeling.

So the next morning I asked her the BIG question:

"Do you wanna go to Miami?"

She smiled at me and said:

"Yeah. Let's leave and never come back."

I had NO idea how the FUCK we were gonna get to Miami, but I knew we needed a fresh start.

I never heard from Poe ever again, not for years and years at least, I'll have to tell you about that some other time, and I never heard from Becky ever again and KC and I… well, we lived together for the next five years until an explosive New Year's Eve in 2006.

It all started when KC and I moved down to Little Haiti, an extremely fucked up part of Miami.

I was seventeen-years-old.

TO BE CONTINUED...

THE DRIFTER CHRONICLES: VOLUME TWO

Coming soon…

SHORT STORIES CAN BE FOUND ON MY BLOG:

WWW.SCRAMBLEDGREGS.COM

Made in United States
North Haven, CT
22 June 2023

38106386R00241